# Meaning and Method in the Social Sciences

# Meaning and Method in the Social Sciences

## *A Case for Methodological Pluralism*

PAUL A. ROTH

*Cornell University Press*

ITHACA AND LONDON

First published 1987 by Cornell University Press.

International Standard Book Number 0-8014-1941-7
Library of Congress Catalog Card Number 87-47718
Printed in the United States of America
*Librarians: Library of Congress cataloging information appears on the last page of the book.*

*The paper in this book is acid-free and meets the guidelines for permanence and durability of the Committee on Production Guidelines for Book Longevity of the Council on Library Resources.*

In memoriam

Professor Louis O. Mink

# Contents

# Preface

My central claim is that the plethora of explanatory strategies for the study of human behavior is no accidental feature of our epistemic situation. I offer an account of why a multitude of such theories is to be expected and why this situation is not to be regretted. I am not the first to endorse a pluralist approach to the interpretation of human behavior; my contribution is the argument I have charted to that conclusion.

This book is intimately linked both to the earliest and to the latest phases of my intellectual life: the earliest because the concerns motivating it were inculcated in me while an undergraduate in a remarkable program—the College of Social Studies at Wesleyan University; the latest because it was written during a respite from my teaching obligations at the University of Missouri–St. Louis.

Professor Louis O. Mink inspired and supported me both early and late in my study of the topics to which this book is addressed. He is a presence now only in memory, but he is very much a presence for me still.

When one is working on a manuscript, the generosity of sharp-minded friends is frequently put to the test. I owe very special thanks in this regard to Roger Gibson, Jr., for his critical reading of and extensive comments on an earlier draft of this manuscript. I have been aided, as well, by the efforts of John Barker, Lawrence H. Davis, Eugene Meehan, and Bonnie Paller on one or another parts of this book. I also acknowledge a debt of gratitude for financial support from two institutions: the National Endowment for the Humanities for a fellowship in

1983–1984 and the University of Missouri–St. Louis for Summer Research grants in 1982 and 1985.

Portions of this manuscript have previously appeared in print. Chapter 5 is a slightly modified version of a paper by the same title which originally appeared in *Metaphilosophy* 15 (July/October 1984): 225–238; Chapter 6 is a revised version of a piece that first appeared as "Pseudo-Problems in Social Science," *Philosophy of the Social Sciences* 16 (March 1986): 59–82; Chapter 9 is a modified version of an article originally published in *Archives Européennes de Sociologie* 26 (1985): 142–157. I thank these journals for permission to use this material.

PAUL A. ROTH

*St. Louis, Missouri*

# Meaning and Method in the Social Sciences

It would be absurd to pretend that people ought to live as if nothing whatever had been known in the world before they came into it; as if experience had as yet done nothing toward showing that one mode of existence, or of conduct, is preferable to another. Nobody denies that people should be so taught and trained in youth as to know and benefit by the ascertained results of human experience. But it is the privilege and proper condition of a human being, arrived at the maturity of his faculties, to use and interpret experience in his own way.

John Stuart Mill, *On Liberty*

INTRODUCTION

# The *Rationalitätstreit*

The positivist epistemologist asked what general methodological principles are characteristic of good scientific practice and took the answer to represent the universal canons of rationality. The chief epistemological task was to distill the essence of scientific method and to justify confidence in it. One aspect of the positivist epistemological program was the "unity-of-method" thesis. This tenet asserts that there is, in principle, no methodological distinction to be made between the natural sciences and the social sciences. Consequently, explanation in the social sciences was expected to conform to whatever general account of explanation was held to be characteristic of the natural sciences, for example, the covering-law model.

The unity-of-method thesis is still very much with us, but the notion of scientific rationality which motivated acceptance of the thesis has not been sustained. One of the chief glories of positivism, surely, was that it offered a cogent account of rationality. But, of course, the history of epistemology in the last half of this century consists of the development of a host of critiques of the key assumptions of this account, assumptions that the positivists wrongly took to be unproblematic. The general collapse of positivism leaves uncertain just how the notions of rationality and rational justification are to be explicated and understood. Yet, and this is the central point, although the philosophical community concurs in the rejection of positivism, there has arisen no corresponding consensus concerning the replacement of that conception of rationality propagated by the Vienna Circle.

It has now become a commonplace among writers in the philosophy of social science (although not one limited to this group) to speak of a "post-empiricist" philosophy of science.[1] By this is generally meant the view that the account of objectivity and explanation developed by the logical positivists is to be rejected as philosophically passé. The philosophical lessons learned from Willard Van Orman Quine and Ludwig Wittgenstein (among others) and the historical lessons learned from Thomas Kuhn and N. R. Hanson (among others) leaves us without the panoply of distinctions (analytic-synthetic, observational-theoretical) required for rendering scientific method paradigmatic of rational inquiry.

One task confronting a "post-empiricist" epistemology is that of reforming the shattered consensus regarding the canons of rationality. In the post-positivist vacuum, a dispute has developed in the philosophy of social science which I refer to as the *Rationalitätstreit*.[2] This "dispute about rationality" also draws arguments and inspiration from the critics of positivism.[3] The substance of the dispute concerns which set or sets of canons of justification qualify as rational.

The sides in the dispute are determined by how each party responds to the demise of the positivists' project. One side wants to redo that project; the other side wants to *undo* the unity-of-method thesis. Those who would redo the project seek a single set of justificatory canons; the hope is that philosophers of science will specify these. Those who would undo the original program maintain that the unity-of-method

[1]Characteristic works in this area include the following: Richard Bernstein, *Beyond Objectivism and Relativism* (Philadelphia: University of Pennsylvania Press, 1983), and *The Restructuring of Social and Political Theory* (Philadelphia: University of Pennsylvania Press, 1978); David Thomas, *Naturalism and Social Science: A Post-Empiricist Philosophy of Social Science* (Cambridge: Cambridge University Press, 1979); and Andrew Tudor, *Beyond Empiricism: Philosophy of Science in Sociology* (London: Routledge & Kegan Paul, 1982).

[2]The term *Rationalitätstreit* is my own. By it I intend to connote a relation to the methodological dispute that was so prominent at an earlier time. For a nice historical overview of the *Methodenstreit* and some of its contemporary manifestations, see David Frisby, "Introduction to the English Translation," in *The Positivist Dispute in German Sociology*, ed. T. W. Adorno et al., trans. G. Adey and D. Frisby (New York: Harper Torchbooks, 1976).

[3]The opening shot in this controversy is surely Peter Winch's now classic monograph *The Idea of a Social Science* (London: Routledge & Kegan Paul, 1958). The controversy is developed and perpetuated through a great many books and articles; interested readers should consult B. Wilson, ed., *Rationality* (London: Basil Blackwell, 1970), and M. Hollis and S. Lukes, eds., *Rationality and Relativism* (Cambridge, Mass.: M.I.T. Press, 1982), for many of the central articles in this debate.

thesis fails because, for one reason or another, there can be no *science* of society. The redoers view the term "rational" as denoting forms of reasoning which are independent of the vagaries of cultural practices; the undoers take the term "rational" as an honorific label bestowed by people upon their favored fashion of reasoning.

The *Rationalitätstreit*, as it has developed in the context of the philosophy of social science, vacillates between these two poles. One central faction (the redoers) advocates social *science*. Here the emphasis falls on explanations of behavior which allow predictions concerning future behavior. The concern of such theories is to construct an account of social organization on the model of the account that physics provides for the natural sciences. On this view, references to goals and purposes and to the mental states of humans are tolerated only insofar as they may abet the ability of a theory to make predictions. This attitude toward the study of human behavior—which finds its exemplars in the work of B. F. Skinner, of sociobiologists, and of economic and functional determinists of various political stripes—presumes that there is a well-enough-defined notion of scientific method and that social science is a type of rational inquiry insofar as it conforms to this method (some of the history and the assumptions of this view are discussed in Chapter 5).

Opposition to the vision of social science sketched above comes from those (the undoers) who argue that the understanding of human social behavior is a matter of making explicit or reconstructing certain rules that members of a society share. It is these (implicitly or explicitly known) rules that allow people to comprehend one another's behavior. The explanation of social behavior, on this view, is *not* a matter of noting lawlike relations. A further assumption often made by thinkers holding this position is that other cultures do not share very many of the investigator's beliefs, including his or her beliefs regarding how beliefs are properly warranted, that is, what it is to be rational.

Part of this conception of social science is a view that I dub "meaning realism." A meaning realist is anyone who, contra Quine and Wittgenstein, believes that some intentional or subjective set of beliefs (and not social and behavioral conditions) determines the significance or meaning of an utterance. In methodological terms, the purpose or goal of social scientific investigation is taken to be the recapturing or reexpressing of what those persons under study "have in mind."

Critical to evaluating meaning realism and the larger view of which it is a part is Quine's thesis of the indeterminacy of translation, which is the claim that there is "no fact of the matter" to translation—no objective basis that uniquely settles questions concerning what a given utterance means. One implication of this thesis of translational indeterminacy is that any explanation framed in intentional terms—expressions referring to mental states or attitudes—is neither objective nor scientific. Hence questions about meaning cannot be subject to full rational adjudication. (The notion of meaning, as I use it throughout, involves, at least, questions of the synonymy of terms and their intensions.) Since it is just such explanations that some social scientists have claimed as their own, I have sought in the chapters that follow both to assess the arguments for this Quinean claim and to plumb its implications for certain standing controversies in the philosophy of social science.

The *Rationalitätstreit* has proceeded as if refurbishing the unity-of-method thesis or denying that a social science is possible were the exhaustive and mutually exclusive approaches to the study of human behavior. (Max Weber, of course, urged a conception of social science which basically represented an attempt to merge these two strands. His call for explanations that are both "causally adequate" and "adequate at the level of meaning" did not survive him.) I argue that to delimit the options in this way only frustrates debate. Debate is further frustrated by the fact that those emphasizing meaning have never been able to respond adequately to questions about the verification of imputed rules and other mental states, while those advocating the science in social science have been consistently embarrassed by the dearth of results their approach has yielded.

My purpose in this book is to examine the *Rationalitätstreit* in light of developments in contemporary epistemology, particularly, in the writings of Quine, Richard Rorty, and Paul Feyerabend. My claim is that both sides in the *Rationalitätstreit* (the redoers and the undoers) predicate their positions on untenable philosophical assumptions. Put another way, the *Rationalitätstreit* continues a debate over the positivists' unity-of-method thesis—the thesis that there is just one method of inquiry proper to the physical and social sciences. I seek to establish that this debate is fruitless and pointless, at least in its present form. Indeed, I provide a diagnosis of why the debate about rationality has proved to be sterile, and I outline a more fertile approach. The debate concerning standards of rationality should cease to be an issue in the philosophy of social science.

My own claim is that social scientists do best by adopting what is, at least on my account, a pluralist view of rational inquiry. My effort is designed to establish that one can maintain both a type of "methodological anarchism" and a commitment to a Quinean-style holism and empiricism. I conclude by arguing that, if there is no essence to human nature or to scientific method, then a pluralist approach to methodological issues in the social sciences is what is warranted.

## Methodological Pluralism

The *Rationalitätstreit* presumes the truth of a position I dub "methodological exclusivism." This position is centered around the following thesis:

> *Methodological exclusivism* There exists just one proper method for the social sciences.

Methodological exclusivism is championed not only by those, such as Otto Neurath and Richard Rudner, who maintain that there is a unity of method between the natural and social sciences, but also by those, such as Wilhelm Dilthey and Peter Winch, who insist that there exists some fundamental division between the *Geisteswissenschaften* and the *Naturwissenschaften*.

Methodological pluralism, as I argue for it, is just the denial of methodological exclusivism. My claim is this:

> *Methodological pluralism* We cannot make sense of the notion of "one proper set of rules" that defines the study of human behavior.

My argument for methodological pluralism (taken as the denial of methodological exclusivism), and so the argument of the book, proceeds as follows. I begin by explicating and defending those epistemological theses that I take to be fundamental in arguing against exclusivism in its various forms (Chapter 1); I go on to show why rejecting the existence of universal norms of inquiry neither reduces epistemology to empirical psychology (Chapter 2) nor entails epistemological nihilism (Chapters 3 and 4). I then turn to examine and reject various specific formulations of methodological exclusivism: that the one rational method for the social scientist is that of the natural sciences (Chapter 5); that the sole purpose of social inquiry is to uncover the internalized rules governing social behavior (Chapter 6); that epistemology in general and the philosophy of science in particular are just a proper part of the sociology of knowledge (Chapters 7 and 8). The ninth and final chapter sketches an alternative form of explanation (but just one possible alternative) which shows that a methodological pluralist is able to respect what ought to be respected regarding canons of inquiry (as argued in Chapters 2, 3, and 4) but need not insist that just one particular set of methodological canons or normative assumptions defines the rational pursuit of social inquiry (the common error of the positions canvassed in Chapters 5, 6, 7, and 8).

As the preceding makes plain, those seeking some positive theory of social science methodology look to this book in vain. My thrust is primarily negative. The argument for methodological pluralism lies (apart from those chapters devoted to arguing what is and is not implied by rejecting universal norms) in rejecting attempts to underwrite methodological exclusivism. In this respect, my effort is, like John Stuart Mill's defense of liberty which I so greatly admire, to show that we are most likely to do best (in the pursuit of knowledge) by adopting a nonrestrictive view of what to count as a form of rational inquiry. That is, as I argue at length in Chapters 3 and 4, quite far from declaring that we ought to be methodologically indifferent.

One moral of my epistemological inquiry is that what we sacrifice by way of assurance in truth we are duly compensated for by gains in our understanding of freedom. In this regard, I develop some parallels in various chapters between the views I defend regarding the nature of rationality and Mill's notion of liberty as expounded in *On Liberty*. I suggest that a pluralist view of rationality, like a society that tolerates the self-regarding actions of individuals, provides an important bulwark against tyranny. This last point, I emphasize, is not an argument for my position but simply a welcome consequence of it.

## The Quinean Background

In Chapter 1 I provide an interpretation of the Quinean themes I take to be of significance for the study of human behavior. In subsequent chapters I am concerned to explore two questions that arise from the interpretation delineated in Chapter 1:

(i) What is the significance of Quine's critique of positivism and his advocacy of holism for our understanding of rational method in science, and so of rationality in general?

(ii) What is the significance of Quine's views on meaning and rationality for the social sciences?

The central epistemological issue for Quine is whether or not philosophical analysis provides some better justification of beliefs than that provided by scientific inquiry itself. I refer throughout to Quine's negative project and to his positive proposal. His negative enterprise has consisted in arguments for the conclusion that knowledge lacks certainty and that there is no objective basis for determining meaning. Prominent here is Quine's critique of traditional epistemology. "Traditional epistemology" is, in Quine's writings, a blanket term used to refer to any view that seeks to justify knowledge claims (and, in particular, scientifically endorsed beliefs) by appeal to extrascientific methods or knowledge.[4] In this context, a first philosophy is just one that purports to ground scientific truths on truths that are better known than, and independent of, science. Quine's positive proposal has been to argue that epistemological issues are to be pursued from within one or another of the natural sciences. This vision of post-positivist philosophy has not been embraced to the extent that Quine's critical views have.

In the first two chapters of this book I closely examine the negative and positive aspects of Quine's proposals. In the first chapter I focus on two of Quine's critical theses. One, his holism, is not much disputed; the other, his thesis of the indeterminacy of translation, remains among his most controversial claims. Both theses are central to my own argument in later chapters. I confine myself, in the opening chapter, to offering my own interpretation of these theses and, in the course of doing so, I defend Quine's claims, as I understand them, against a variety of criticisms.

I summarize below certain key Quinean themes to which I frequently recur:

(i) *The Duhem thesis* (Quine's holism): the claim that theoretical sentences (within either natural language or more formal theories) have their meaning and their evidence only as parts of a theory.

(ii) *The underdetermination of theories*: the claim that it is possible to formulate empirically equivalent but logically incompatible scientific theories.

[4]See, for example, "Epistemology Naturalized," in *Ontological Relativity and Other Essays* (New York: Columbia University Press, 1969), or the opening section of *Roots of Reference* (La Salle, Ill.: Open Court, 1973).

(iii) *The indeterminacy of translation of theoretical sentences*: the claim that theories of meaning for natural languages, unlike theories in the natural sciences, have no "fact of the matter." This failing distinguishes meaning claims relative to a manual of translation *in kind* from claims that a sentence is true relative to a scientific theory. This failure holds *despite* basic methodological parallels between the analysis of meaning and of truth.

(iv) *The epistemology-naturalized thesis*: the claim that to be an epistemologist is to be an empirical psychologist scientifically investigating man's acquisition of science; epistemology, as such, is contained within natural science, as a chapter of psychology.[5]

Quine's positive program is represented by (iv). Epistemology naturalized is Quine's vision of just what, in light of his negative or critical theses, epistemology ought to become. (The locus classicus here is Quine's essay "Epistemology Naturalized.") Quine's negative theses (for which, I believe, he will be remembered as having done for semantics what Hume did for causality) involve his criticisms of earlier epistemological doctrines. This aspect of his philosophizing includes, at least, his attack on the analytic-synthetic distinction, his claim that the translation of theoretical sentences is indeterminate, his Duhemian view of theories, and his underdetermination thesis. To these critical theses I subscribe, and I am concerned to explicate one of them—the indeterminacy thesis—in the first chapter. The two aspects of Quine's thought—the negative and the positive—are loosely related, or so I argue, insofar as the negative aspect is taken to provide support for (though not to entail) the positive program.

Just how, then, are the canons of rational inquiry to be delineated? Quine insists that the imputation of extrascientific authority to formal analysis and certain conceptions of empirical evidence is hollow. There is, he argues (from "Truth by Convention" onward), no extrascientific basis for authorizing statements believed true.[6] Ultimately, this view leads Quine to declare that "epistemology, for me, is only science self-applied."[7]

[5]Quine, *Roots of Reference*, pp. 2–3.

[6]W. V. O. Quine, *Ways of Paradox* (New York: Random House, 1966).

[7]W. V. O. Quine, "Replies," in *Words and Objections*, ed. D. Davidson and J. Hintikka (Dordrecht: Reidel, 1969), p. 293. This point is also stressed by Quine in a recent collection of his essays; see *Theories and Things* (Cambridge, Mass.: Belknap Press, 1981). p. 21.

Quine's position is that we can do no better in seeking to specify what is rationally justified than by seeing what is confirmed by ongoing scientific inquiry. The argument for epistemology naturalized, in other words, proceeds by way of asking how we are to answer the standard epistemological question, What are we to believe? What is important to note is that where traditional epistemology is concerned to certify knowledge claims against the challenge posed by skepticism, Quine does not believe that such certification is possible. Insofar as Quine entertains any skeptical worries, they arise internal to the scheme of certification he adopts. The reasonableness of moving to epistemology naturalized, on my interpretation of a Quinean position, is contingent on believing that we have no epistemologically favored position from which to explicate scientific concepts by some other means.

Although I agree with Quine and the philosophical tradition that there is more to be made of the notion of objectivity than some post-empiricists allow, there is not enough to be made of that notion to justify attempts to retain the identification of rational inquiry in general with the particular methods of the natural sciences. I therefore ultimately reject Quine's positive proposal insofar as Quine still uses his conception of natural science to delimit what counts as the acceptable warranting of beliefs.

I envision an account of explanation in social science which is finally free of the last vestiges of the positivists' unity-of-method thesis. My position cuts a tortuous path between those, such as Quine, who would retain an essentially positivistic view of the relation of the natural and the social sciences, that is, maintain a unity-of-method thesis, and others, such as Rorty, who take the lesson of philosophy in this century to be that the claim of any method to some special kind of objectivity is just a species of epistemological bad faith. I propose to shed light on the *Rationalitätstreit* first by analyzing how Quine has made the notion of objective evidence problematic and second by indicating how an account of objective evidence *is* sustained within a Quinean framework. For it is the doubts Quine raises about objectivity which seem primarily responsible for opening the door to the alternative views on rationality I explore. The moral of this work is that the attempts to formulate some single post-empiricist model of rational explanation, at least for the social sciences, is to misconstrue the lesson to be learned from developments in epistemology and the philosophy of science in the latter half of this century.

CHAPTER I

# Knowledge Denatured

I take Quine's holist view of theories to be central to his reformulation of epistemology (and, as I argue below, fundamental as well to the argument for the indeterminacy of translation). This sets my interpretation at variance with that favored by Quine and that espoused by many expositors of Quine, for on what I take to be the official reading of the interrelation of the positive and negative aspects of Quine's thought, Quine's naturalistic stance is a premise of his argument for certain of his critical theses and, in particular, for the indeterminacy of translation. He has strongly endorsed those who so read him.[1]

Although I do not deny that Quine writes this way, I want to show that quite a different argument for the indeterminacy thesis can be gleaned from his writings, an argument that does not make any prior appeal to the naturalistic stance. I take this to be crucially important, since otherwise Quine's claim that translation is indeterminate and not just underdetermined by the evidence cannot be sustained.[2] As I show

[1]The most sustained systematic interpretation of Quine in this regard, and the only reading of Quine to receive Quine's official imprimatur, is Roger Gibson's *The Philosophy of W. V. Quine: An Expository Essay* (Tampa, Fla.: University of South Florida Press, 1982) with a foreword by Quine. I discuss my differences with Gibson's reading in "On Missing Neurath's Boat," *Synthese* 61 (November 1984). See especially Gibson, chap. 2, Quine's foreword, and Gibson's discussion in his book of what he calls Quine's naturalistic-behavioristic thesis. A related view is found in R. Schuldenfrei, "Quine in Perspective," *Journal of Philosophy* 69 (1972):5–16.

[2]I have reviewed the problems here and urged my own reading in "Paradox and Indeterminacy," *Journal of Philosophy* 75 (July 1978); "Reconstructing Quine: The Troubles with a Tradition," *Metaphilosophy* 14 (July/October 1983); "Semantics

below, the need to differentiate indeterminacy and underdetermination is an issue of philosophical importance if Quine's proscriptions on meaning are to have the force Quine intends. And since I argue in later chapters that the indeterminacy thesis (like its philosophical doppleganger, Wittgenstein's complaints against private language) is of central philosophical significance, there is particular need to show the viability of my form of the argument for the indeterminacy thesis.

More generally, I argue in this chapter and the next that the received reading is wrong with regard both to what is and is not unproblematic in Quine's philosophy and to the logical relations among Quine's theses. On my reading, what is problematic and widely misunderstood in Quine's thought is (a) the nature of Quine's empiricism (this is a topic of Chapter 2), (b) the significance of the epistemology-naturalized thesis (Section II of this chapter), and (c) how the indeterminacy thesis may be derived without appeal to either one or both of naturalism and underdetermination (Section I of this chapter). By providing a reconstruction of the argument for the indeterminacy of translation which does not depend on the problematic assumption of theoretical underdetermination or on the controversial thesis that epistemology ought to be naturalized, I show how Quine's views on meaning and justification can be sustained by appeal to his less problematic holistic views. This allows me, moreover, in Chapter 2, to separate and criticize Quine's thesis concerning epistemology naturalized from those theses on meaning and reference which I retain and use in later chapters.

In Section I I detail some of Quine's negative theses and what I take to be their logical interconnections. Special attention is given to Quine's argument for the indeterminacy of translation. In Section II I examine certain criticisms of Quine's positive program—in particular, the views of Barry Stroud, Hilary Putnam, and Ernest Sosa. These discussions broach critical issues with regard to how Quine has changed the emphasis in the analysis of knowledge from a concern with

---

without Foundations," *The Philosophy of W. V. Quine*, ed. L. Hahn (Library of Living Philosophers Series; La Salle, Ill.: Open Court, 1987), pp. 433–458.

I am not unsympathetic to those who find a Kantian strain in Quine's writings; see Manley Thompson, "Quine and the Inscrutability of Reference," *Revue Internationale de Philosophie* 26 (1972); Kenton Machina, "Kant, Quine, and Human Experience," *Philosophical Review* 81 (October 1972); Rudiger Bübner, "Kant, Transcendental Argument and the Problem of Deduction," *Review of Metaphysics* 28 (March 1975); Henry B. Veatch, "Is Quine a Metaphysician?" *Review of Metaphysics* 31 (March 1978).

justifying science to a concern with using science to explain the beliefs we hold. In Chapter 2 I argue for the independence of the negative and the positive aspects of Quine's views and criticize Quine's arguments for epistemology naturalized.

## I

Quine's position evolves in the course of his attempts to salvage what he deems important and viable from the old empiricist notion of evidence. Evidence is, for an empiricist such as Quine, what ultimately justifies scientific claims and what ties our language to the world. The positivist account of empirical evidence is inadequate because it takes too sanguine a view of our ability to categorize statements as either observational or nonobservational. The important point is that the problems facing such a salvage attempt are the ones Quine so forcefully poses for the old empiricism—the problems raised by his critique of the analytic-synthetic distinction, on the one hand, and, on the other, his embrace of Duhemian holism. The result of this critique is to make problematic whether there is an account of facts distinct from what current science endorses, whether there is a notion of evidence which validates the intuition that science is tied to the natural world. A defense of such a concept of evidence would be philosophically significant because it would provide an objective touchstone for inquiry; in other words, it would explain how our beliefs about the world are objectively anchored in our experience of the natural world. Moreover, with the appropriate concept of evidence in hand, one could hope to adjudicate the claim that translation lacks an objective basis.

Why does the issue of the status of the "museum myth" (as Quine refers to any view that holds that meanings are fixed by archetypes, e.g., in the head[3]) arise given Quine's other assumptions? As I read Quine, the issue develops in the following way. Given Duhem, we must drop the claim that our scientific theory is isomorphic with, or somehow a mirror of, reality. Quine explicitly rejects, for example, the Peircian view that we approach truth as a limit by continuous application of scientific method to experience.[4] We are left with a very prob-

[3]W. V. Quine, "Epistemology Naturalized," in *Ontological Relativity and Other Essays* (New York: Columbia University Press, 1969), p. 27.

[4]W. V. O. Quine, *Word and Object* (Cambridge, Mass.: M.I.T. Press, 1960), p. 23.

lematic type of "realism" with Quine; he calls scientific posits "real," certainly, but quickly adds that all this means is that statements affirming the existence of such posits are assigned "true" under the intended interpretation of current theory.

Even though Duhemian considerations suffice (at least for Quine) to prevent us from being realists of some classical stripe, this consideration does not obviously undercut what might be called "intentional" or "meaning realism"; we can accept the Duhem thesis and accept the Peircian claim that the meaning of a sentence is a function of whether it is possible to have evidence for its truth and yet insist that translation is determinate, even if unknowable. But Quine is not content to view synonymy relations, as established by, for example, a scheme of translation, as parallel to theoretical constructs in the physical sciences. Nor is an individual's own conviction that he or she knows what is "in his or her mind" sufficient to establish that there is one right way to translate that person's remarks. What must be established, in other words, is why evidence does not support translations as it supports theories in science and why individuals do not have any privileged access to understanding what they mean. What must be shown is how the premises Quine cites (Duhem and Peirce)[5] count against intentional realism.

An interpretation of the indeterminacy thesis might run as follows. Assume that the choice of physical theory is settled, that is, that one has opted for a particular scientific view and ignores competitors. The chosen theory determines, for us anyway, which sentences are true. However, or so Quine claims, settling the question of which sentences are true leaves undetermined the question of what meaning to attribute to these sentences. Meaning remains unsecured, according to this reading of Quine, because even in the situation just imagined we are free to attribute different and incompatible meanings to the same sentences. Consequently there can be incompatible claims about meaning which fail to correspond to *any* difference in microphysical states of affairs. Put another way, there may be imaginable differences in meaning which require no redistribution of claims about the physical facts. With respect, then, to arbitrating between such differences of meaning, there is no fact of the matter. The physical world remains unchanged despite the fact that different meanings are attributed to at least some

[5]Quine, "Epistemology Naturalized," p. 81.

of the true sentences in it. Since differences in meaning prove impervious to arbitration by the facts, meaning is indeterminate.

Perhaps the single most important reason for seeking an alternative to this argument for the indeterminacy of translation is that such a reading does not suffice to undercut Quine's target in his discussions of indeterminacy, the museum myth view of meaning. According to the museum myth, meanings are determined by what the speaker "has in mind" or by virtue of some correspondence between words and the world (the "Fido"-Fido principle). This consideration, however, shows that a choice of physical theory does *not* suffice to limit one's choice to all but one translation manual. Even worse, the argument for the indeterminacy of translation as stated is at best a hypothesis concerning what further scientific inquiry will uncover. The issue becomes, on this way of putting the argument, a question of whether or not science, as it advances, will discover a correlation between certain types of assertions and certain types of physical states. As Michael Friedman puts it, Quine is simply betting that determinations of meaning will escape the nomological net of physics.[6] Hence the argument noted at the outset of this section need not worry a confirmed believer (a meaning realist) in determinacy of translation. Such a thinker remains free to accept the account sketched above and still insist, consistent with what Quine has to say, that there could be a science of intentions on a par with physical science. If the point of Quine's argument is to scotch the museum myth, then the museum myth should somehow be shown to conflict with the claim that translation suffers some peculiar lack of objectivity due to being doubly underdetermined (once qua theory, and again even after a physical theory has been decided on). But the museum myth is not inconsistent with science as we know it. For either Quine is just hypothesizing about what sort of entities (intentional ones, in this case) physics can do without, or he is legislating ontological limits to scientific speculation. On the first alternative, Quine's antagonism to the notion of meaning is based on conjecture and so cannot sustain the "in principle" cast he characteristically gives his own argument; on the second alternative, Quine transgresses his naturalism. If Quine is read as arguing in effect that, since no one has yet established that semantic notions are necessary for doing physics,

[6]See Michael Friedman, "Physicalism and the Indeterminacy of Translation," *Noûs* 9 (November 1975):369.

therefore they are unnecessary, the argument for the indeterminacy thesis reduces to an *argumentum ad ignorantium*.

Intentions, another reply to Quine might go, are not part of the physical furniture of the world, but they are critical in determining what you, I, or anyone means. If verbal behavior is part of what wants explaining, then the initial argument sketched is not an argument for excluding a science or intentions, much less for the indeterminacy of meaning. Quine's argument only reflects an unargued bias for physicalism.

Can a reading of the argument for indeterminacy which sustains the case against meaning realism be formulated? Consider the following formulations of Quine's claim that translation is indeterminate:

A conviction persists, often unacknowledged, that our sentences express these ideas rather than those, even when behavioral criteria can never say which. There is the stubborn notion that we can tell intuitively which idea someone's sentence expresses, our sentence anyway, even when the intuition is irreducible to behavioral criteria. This is why one thinks that one's question 'What did the native say?' has a right answer *independent* of choices among mutually incompatible manuals of translation. In asking "But why should all of this occasion any surprise or concern?" Chomsky did not dismiss my point. He missed it.[7]

May we conclude that translational synonymy at its worst is no worse off than truth in physics? To be thus reassured is to misjudge the parallel. In being able to speak of the truth of a sentence only within a more inclusive theory, one is not much hampered. . . . In short, the parameters of truth stay conveniently fixed most of the time. Not so the analytical hypotheses that constitute the parameters of translation. We are always ready to wonder about the meaning of a foreigner's remark *without reference* to any one set of analytical hypotheses, indeed even in the absence of any.[8]

The question whether . . . the foreigner *really* believes A or believes rather B, is a question whose very significance, I would put in doubt. This is what I am getting at in arguing the indeterminacy of translation.[9]

[7]W. V. O. Quine, "Replies" in *Words and Objections*, ed., D. Davidson and J. Hintikka (Dordrecht: Reidel, 1969), p. 304; emphasis added.

[8]Quine, *Word and Object*, pp. 75–76; emphasis added.

[9]W. V. Quine, "On the Reasons for the Indeterminacy of Translation," *Journal of Philosophy* 62 (March 26, 1970):180–181. Quine also says, a little later in this article, that the problem is not one of "hidden facts."

What do I take these remarks to suggest? On my account, they hint that Quine's claim need not be read as an epistemic one vis-à-vis incompatible manuals of translation tied for first place on the basis of available evidence; that is, the issue is not a variant of the underdetermination of theories by the evidence, nor is the problem that there exist no criteria by which to choose among such manuals.

The argument for indeterminacy, if it is to be compelling, should show that this worry about which translation properly captures what the native (or I) "really" mean is pointless. And the argument, in order to do this, must show that the assumption that there is a determinate meaning beyond dispositions to respond is implausible. To show that there exist competing translations (which Quine never actually shows) would only underscore the difficulty of the supposed problem of finding the correct translation; it would not show that the intuition that there exists one such translation is one whose significance is to be doubted.

The issue, on my reading, is whether a certain intuition people have concerning the determinacy of their own beliefs ("I know what I intend even if others don't") has rational justification. The point in each of the passages cited may be understood as denying that, among various alternative translation schemes (or some translation as yet unknown), one must be the correct translation. A belief in the existence of such a translation is unwarranted because there is no rational basis for assuming that there even need be some uniquely correct translation. (I argue below that there is rational warrant for believing the contradictory of this belief.) We are apt to believe that people know what they themselves mean, even if we do not, and that the best translation is precisely the one that captures just their meaning. But to believe this is to accept the museum myth.

We think we know what we mean (in the sense Quine opposes) when we make certain statements. To be told that there is "no fact of the matter" seems to suggest that, perhaps, behavioral evidence does not suffice to determine interpretation, and that there is no evidence beyond the behavioral. But Quine's claim that this indeterminacy applies to homophonic translation—our understanding of our own utterances[10]—is deeply counterintuitive.

Few of Quine's critics have been convinced that Quine's naturalism

[10]See remarks on homophonic translation, "Epistemology Naturalized," pp. 46–47.

is sufficient to support the various theses he advocates. Indeed, there has developed in the professional philosophical literature a distinct tradition of interpreting and reconstructing Quine's epistemology. The tradition has its roots in Gilbert Harman's influential interpretation of Quine as an empiricist and in Harman's reconstruction of Quine's views on meaning.[11] Richard Rorty, and others influenced by this "Princeton School" of Quine scholarship, have elaborated and extended this tradition.[12] Critical to this tradition as I understand it, and what separates my account from theirs, is that they take the proscription on meaning to be based on Quine's views concerning naturalism; that is, Quine is read as assuming the adequacy of an extensional interpretation of theories in physical science and arguing from there to the superfluity of the notion of meaning.

The members of this school are unified in an attempt to offer a synoptic view of Quine's epistemological project, that is, to specify how the leading themes of Quine's epistemology are (or are not) to be integrated into a comprehensive and systematic account of the nature of human knowledge. This is not to deny that important differences exist within this tradition. Nevertheless, it is possible to specify three fixed theses that together constitute what I take to be the received reading of Quine: (a) Quine is a holist; (b) Quine is an empiricist (of some stripe); and (c) Quine's views on scientific method and on the underdetermination of theories are integral to an understanding of his view on meaning and reference. The first two theses unproblematically appear to belong to Quine's thought. The tradition holds that the reconstruction of Quine's thought (i.e., determining what Quine either meant to say or did say but ought not have said) begins with (c), an explanation of Quine's exclusion of theories of meaning and reference from the range of objectively determinable theories. Most important, these three themes are taken by the tradition to be both mutually consistent and the unproblematic starting points for reading Quine.

How do the theses of the received reading "map onto" the reading of

[11]Gilbert Harman, "Quine on Meaning and Existence," pts. I & II, *Review of Metaphysics* 21 (1967):124–151, 343–367.

[12]Rorty's views are presented in "Indeterminacy of Translation and of Truth," *Synthese* 23 (1972):443–462, and forcefully developed in *Philosophy and the Mirror of Nature* (Princeton, N.J.: Princeton University Press, 1979), especially pp. 191–209; see also Schuldenfrei, "Quine in Perspective," and "Dualistic Physicalism in Quine: A Radical Critique," *Philosophical Forum* 10 (Fall 1978):37–54.

the Quinean theses I have been discussing up until this point? Quine's commitment to the Duhem thesis is indisputable, and to say Quine is a holist is just to say that he affirms the Duhem thesis. Problems arise because underdetermination together with Quine's commitment to an empiricism constrained by his naturalism is thought to yield the indeterminacy thesis.[13] Thus Quine's commitment to a certain way of doing epistemology is believed by those who subscribe to the received reading to engender the initial constraints that, when taken with the other premises, yield the distinction between meaning and truth. Thus, on the received reading, underdetermination and a commitment to a naturalized epistemology are necessary for the argument for the indeterminacy thesis. A close examination of some of Quine's own remarks suggest, however, a rather different view of the relation between the Duhem and epistemology-naturalized theses:

> The crucial consideration behind my argument for the indeterminacy of translation was that a statement about the world does not always or usually have a separable fund of empirical consequences that it can call its own. That consideration served also to account for the impossibility of an epistemological reduction of the sort where every sentence is equated to a sentence in observational and logico-mathematical terms. And the impossibility of that sort of epistemological reduction dissipated the last advantage that rational reconstruction seemed to have over psychology.
>
> Philosophers have rightly despaired of translating everything into observational and logico-mathematical terms. They have despaired of this even when they have not recognized, as the reason for this irreducibility, that the statements largely do not have their private bundles of empirical consequences. And some philosophers have seen in this irreducibility the bankruptcy of epistemology.[14]

What "dissipated" the advantage of old-style epistemology over simply taking scientific method as the unreduced paradigm of rational inquiry is just the fact that the "unit of empirical significance" is our whole system of beliefs. We are now free to make use of the resources of science when studying science (Quine's recommendation to the "liberated" epistemologist)[15] because we have no better model of rational

[13]See especially Rorty, *Mirror of Nature*, pp. 194–204.
[14]Quine, "Epistemology Naturalized," p. 82.
[15]Quine, *Roots of Reference* (La Salle, Ill.: Open Court, 1973), p. 3.

inquiry to go by. We cannot achieve the sort of reconstruction the positivists hoped for, because the units of significance are not, as they thought, given in neatly verifiable statements.

In order to integrate Quine's various themes, I present them as part of an argument. The conclusion states, in effect, that there are no "facts of meaning" as there are facts of nature. Such an argument precludes assuming the epistemology-naturalized thesis or the exclusive correctness of any method that rules out intentional entities. This argument represents the core of my proposed reconstruction of Quine. The argument in outline is as follows:

(i) Given holism, there is no sense to the notion of truth or to the notion of meaning apart from one or another theory. (The concept of truth is, as Quine likes to say, immanent, i.e., explicated only within a given scientific theory.)

(ii) From within our "web of belief," we discern intersubjectively available stimuli to which speakers or potential speakers of a language are capable of responding alike. This shared stimulus is a necessary condition of language learning; that is, in order to explain the social and public character of language, and the fact that it is teachable, we assume that there are shared stimuli to which we respond and around which our use of language is initially coordinated. (The argument for this claim involves appreciating what I call the "paradox of language learning" and understanding the significance of this paradox for anyone who subscribes to a holist cum empiricist view of knowledge. This argument is detailed in Chapter 2.)

(iii) Given that an intersubjective stimulus is a necessary condition of language learning, there is a warrant for a belief in objective evidence which arises from considerations *within* our language qua theory.

(iv) Natural science is about this intersubjective, public domain. Hence theories in natural science posit a fact of the matter (the ontology of a theory) by way of explaining the intersubjectively available evidence that provides the basis for language acquisition.

(v) A belief in a fact of the matter for semantic theories is not warranted by appeal to any absolute standards, given (i); moreover, such a belief is not warranted within the Quinean web as a necessary condition for a public and teachable language. We "misjudge the parallel" between even the relativized notions of truth and of meaning if we think that the *internal* considerations that mandate the attribution of objectivity to scientific theories also extend to semantic theories.[16]

(vi) Since there is no warrant, either internal to theories or external to them, for believing there need exist some special intentional evidence for which semantic theories must account, such theories are indeterminate, that is, not ultimately about a shared environment in the way we must assume that scientific theories are.

Together, (i) – (vi) represent the argument that I suggest a Quinean (although Quine himself does not) assert in defense of the indeterminacy thesis.[17] This argument proceeds without appeal to a *methodological* distinction between science and translation, thus avoiding the pitfalls encountered in the traditional formulation. Indeterminacy obtains, on my account, due to an absence of an assumption in the case of translation which is warrantable for the natural sciences. The argument, in effect, shifts the burden of proof to the meaning realist. Meaning realism is shown to be unwarranted; indeed, and more strongly, the assumption of its truth is inconsistent with the available evidence. The warranting in the one case and not the other is the explanation for the asymmetric relation between truth relative to natural science and meaning relative to semantic theory. We "misjudge the parallel" between science and translation when methodological similarities are taken to be all important—when we believe that from within the web of belief all posits look alike, be they mental or physical, extensional or intensional. The "in principle" cast to the argument is provided by the fact that, given our understanding of how language is learned, no additional evidence suffices to make meaning realism plausible. Rather, meaning realism requires wholesale revisions in our beliefs about language acquisition.

The project of interpreting and ultimately integrating Quine's themes has been transformed, in light of the above considerations, into a problem about the preconditions of a theory which are germane to establishing the presence or absence of objective evidence for intratheoretically affirmed beliefs. What sense can be made of "objectivity" apart from an appeal to the conventions and canons of one or another

[16] I first broached parts of this argument in "Paradox and Indeterminacy." See Quine, *Word and Object*, p. 75.

[17] I show in "Semantics without Foundations" that Quine is not consistent in his characterizations of his own argument. The version I favor is the one Quine gives at "Epistemology Naturalized," pp. 80–81.

discipline? By establishing that the relevant notion of objective evidence can be argued for without appeal to received scientific theory, my argument offers a path to the conclusion that translation is indeterminate other than that path marked by the Princeton School of interpretation. The objectivity of evidence is established by adducing what preconditions are necessary for there to be a language like ours, a language that is socially shared and teachable and yet comprises a theory in the Duhemian sense—recall premise (ii) above. It is the learnability-teachability of language which Quine himself consistently points to as the epistemologically significant trait.[18] But why is the teachability of language of such moment for my interpretation of Quine's position? The answer lies in what I have called the "paradox of language learning."[19] The paradox is as follows: We cannot explain how, on the basis of the available evidence, a child arrives at his or her mastery of the more theoretical portions of language; there is no rational reconstruction of the process which takes us from sentences learned first to accomplished language use. Since we cannot reconstruct how we form our "web of belief" by some sentence-by-sentence analysis of this process, Quine's claim that only sentences taken as an interrelated group have meaning and evidence for their truth seems plausible. If we maintain, however, that the sentences accepted as true in both natural language and natural science have their meaning and their evidence only as a related block, then someone with no knowledge of a language (e.g., an infant) should find any single sentence to be meaningless, and so incomprehensible. But children initially learn to speak by learning single sentences. So Quine must be wrong in claiming that sentences have significance only within a theoretical context. The paradox, in short, is generated by contrasting how language is normally learned with our inability to reconstruct this learning process given the available evidence.

A resolution to the paradox involves Quine's notions of stimulus

[18]See the following works by Quine: "Nature of Natural Knowledge," in *Mind and Language*, ed. S. Guttenplan (Oxford: Clarendon Press, 1975), p. 79; "Grades of Theoreticity," in *Experience and Theory*, ed. L. Foster and J. W. Swanson (Amherst: University of Massachusetts Press, 1970), p. 4; "On Empirically Equivalent Systems of the World," *Erkenntnis* 9 (1975):316; *Word and Object*, Preface, "Facts of the Matter," *American Philosophy from Edwards to Quine*, ed. K. Merrill and R. Shahan (Norman: University of Oklahoma Press, 1977), p. 179.

[19]See Roth, "Paradox and Indeterminacy," pp. 355–356.

meanings of observation sentences (much of what I say below simply adumbrates or anticipates the arguments of Chapter 2). The positing of observation sentences includes the assumption that these sentences have theory-independent causal meanings (whatever the stimulus meanings are), although, as I argue, we can *never* say what the cause is. Holism precludes the possibility of looking past the veil of theory. The philosophically critical point is this: The claim that there are some sentences that are observation sentences is defended by arguing that they are a necessary condition for our language to be as it is. This is the essence of the argument for premise (iii). What makes observation sentences observational, however, is some unknown and unknowable source of shared stimulations. The thing-in-itself that makes observation sentences observational is promulgated as a necessary condition of learning.[20] The claim that any *specific* sentence is an observation sentence, however, is subject to correction and revision, as are all our scientific statements. The Duhemian constraint is epistemological—we cannot know independently of a theory which sentences have theory-independent meanings.

The paradox of language learning raises a question of how an account of the meaningfulness of single sentences—an account suggested by Quine's notion of an observation sentence—can be compatible with a commitment to holism. Quine qua empiricist adheres to the belief that all evidence is sensory evidence,[21] yet his advocacy of holism suggests that there is no way to discriminate, as empiricists traditionally have, between the sensory contribution to knowledge and other sources such as cultural conditioning. An answer to this question is available. Granting (as the fact of language learning requires us to do) that there must be sentences that function more or less as Quine says observation sentences do, the tenets of empiricism to which Quine subscribes need not conflict with his Duhemian outlook. The claim that there are observation sentences represents an inference to the best explanation about the necessary conditions for a natural language.

Insofar as the language we learn to speak, and which natural science sets out to refine, is about what there is, the scientific study of language attempts to articulate those factors that first give shared signs their

[20]See Quine's remarks on empiricism qua theory of evidence: *Theories and Things* (Cambridge, Mass.: Belknap Press of Harvard University Press, 1981), pp. 39–40.

[21]Quine, "Epistemology Naturalized," p. 75.

*social* dimension—what Quine calls the stimulus meaning of an observation sentence. Of course any attempt to explain actual language acquisition occurs within the theory we accept as true, and there is no path back to the sensory starting points. This is how acceptance of the Duhem thesis transforms empiricism. But if the stimulus-meaning-in-itself is fated to remain a transcendent object of scientific inquiry, there remains nonetheless a formal guarantee that there is a fact of the matter about which to inquire; the existence of a theory-independent world is a necessary condition for a language like ours. Insofar as natural science probes what is essentially public, it has a fact of the matter. This science is Duhemian in nature; whether this science is also genuinely underdetermined, that is, whether there can be logically incompatible and empirically equivalent theories that cannot be made equivalent by any possible reconstrual of their predicates, is another question.[22] But even if theories are not what I have just called genuinely underdetermined, this does not affect their Duhemian nature. The Duhemian thesis does not require that theories be underdetermined, for single theoretical sentences (e.g., "protons have mass") lack empirical content qua single sentences whether or not there is a genuine alternative to current theoretical physics. Nor does the Duhem thesis of itself entail that theories will be underdetermined, for the Duhem thesis is a thesis about the truth conditions for single theoretical sentences, whereas the underdetermination thesis is one about the ability to formulate entire theories that satisfy certain desiderata, in particular, that the competing theories account for all the available evidence in logically incompatible fashions.

The saving grace of science is found in an argument for a necessary condition of language. The sin of semantics, conversely, is that no parallel necessary condition can be adduced in its favor. The failure to show that a shared semantic theory (Fregean senses, Platonic Ideas, and other artifacts of the museum myth view of meaning) is a necessary condition for language learning is precisely where the parallel between physical theory and semantic theory ceases;[23] that is, we need not assume that there exists, prior to our efforts at "translation"—our attempts to formulate a semantic theory—a semantic theory possessed by speakers of the language. What frustrates the search for the right

[22]See Quine, "On Empirically Equivalent Systems of the World," pp. 313–328.
[23]Quine, *Word and Object*, pp. 75–76.

translation is not the bounds of sense. The point is that there is no meaning in itself which, were we more godlike, we might glimpse lying beyond the veil of human perceptual capacities.

The necessity of a shared semantic theory is not established by the argument that applies to scientific theory. The considerations that give sense to calling science objective are simply not germane to the sense of objectivity wanted in semantic theory, that is, to showing that there is a "right" translation, even if both unknown and unknowable. The reading I develop above, unlike the Princeton School account, does not reduce the indeterminacy thesis to a case of underdetermination; my interpretation, if viable, establishes just the "in principle" distinction between truth and meaning—between physical science and translation—that makes Quine's indeterminacy thesis of philosophical interest. It does so by establishing that we have no basis for assuming that there is objective evidence for semantics. The central epistemological issue becomes one of determining the necessary conditions of a teachable language given the Duhem premise and the attendant paradox of language learning.

What I attempt to do is to pursue a way of interpreting Quine's thought with regard to where the parallel fails between physical theory and translation theory. I do this by suggesting that there is one metaphysical (or metaphysical-like) claim that arises given that one accepts Quine's Duhemian view of physical theory and that one denies that a parallel claim is supported within translation theory. If this account is plausible, then I have shown (a) why physical theory and not translation theory has a fact of the matter; (b) why observation sentences, which are the evidence for physical theory, are simply not relevant in the case of translation theory; (c) why we are mistaken to think that there is an answer to the question, What did the native mean?—a question we are tempted to ask even in the absence of a specific manual of translation for natives; (d) that the parallel between physical theory and translation fails for deep reasons and not because of some methodological quirk or a priori restriction that Quine places on translation schemes; (e) that my reconstruction of Quine's argument would defeat the intentional realist, or, at least, show why the assumption of intentional realism (and so an important variant of the museum myth) is not consistent with Duhem and Peirce; and (f) that the argument for the indeterminacy thesis need make no appeal to Quine's views on underdetermination or epistemology naturalized.

## II

In this section I further elaborate the philosophical consequences that follow from adopting, as Quine does, a holistic Duhemian view of theories, and the consequences of Quine's views that are tied more particularly to his proposal to collapse epistemology into empirical psychology—epistemology naturalized. As I detail below, there is considerable confusion in the philosophical literature concerning the nature of epistemology naturalized. Each of the critics of Quine whom I consider in this section—Barry Stroud, Ernest Sosa, and Hilary Putnam—tends to evaluate improperly the constraint on any epistemological program imposed by Quine's holistic outlook.

A failure to appreciate the radical break with traditional epistemology which the Quinean proposal represents is, I suggest, at the heart of Stroud's complaints against epistemology naturalized.[24] As Stroud views the matter, Quine's relation to the philosophical tradition is difficult to understand. The question Stroud believes the epistemologist is duty bound to answer is that posed by the skeptic who doubts the legitimacy of seemingly well-founded beliefs. The problem is how to clarify Quine's views on skepticism and the validation of knowledge claims:

> The "old" epistemology asked how any of us know anything at all about the world around us, and it recognized that most of what we know is based somehow on the senses. The problem was given its special philosophical character by certain facts about sense-perception . . . which seem to imply at least the possibility of the world's being quite different in general from the way it is perceived to be. The philosophical problem was then to explain how anyone can know that such a possibility does not obtain. . . . Only then would the possibility of human knowledge have been explained. [p. 455]

Put another way, Stroud takes the epistemologist's task to be one of *validating* knowledge claims. Insofar, then, as Quine assumes the role of epistemologist, the problem for his epistemological program is to generate the appropriate sort of validation.

[24]Barry Stroud, "The Significance of Naturalized Epistemology," *Midwest Studies in Philosophy*, vol. VI (Minneapolis: University of Minnesota Press, 1981). Quine's "Reply to Stroud" is contained in the same volume (pp. 473–475). References cited in the following discussion are to this work.

Stroud's general question concerning the Quinean approach may be put as follows. Either an epistemologist is or is not concerned with the validation of knowledge claims. If the former, then Quine must show how knowledge is possible. If the latter, then Quine must show why the traditional problem is ill framed or otherwise worthy of rejection. But, Stroud claims, Quine does neither of these things: "I will try to show that (i) given Quine's conception of knowledge, his program of a naturalized epistemology cannot answer what appears to be the most general question of how any knowledge at all of the world is possible . . . [and] (ii) there is in Quine no demonstration of the incoherence or illegitimacy of that question" (p. 460). In either case, the significance of naturalized epistemology appears open to serious doubt. It seems that Quine must take one or the other stance toward validation, and, whichever he takes, his account is found wanting.

What does Stroud take to be Quine's conception of knowledge, and how does it preclude his responding satisfactorily to skepticism (and so answering the general question concerning how knowledge is possible)? At first glance, Stroud's characterization of Quine's conception of knowledge appears unobjectionable; it identifies, as it ought, two components—the evidence of the senses and the perceiving subject's own contribution: "Quine's conception of human knowledge and therefore of his epistemological project shares with earlier philosophers the idea of human knowledge as a combination of two quite general but distinguishable factors—the contribution of the world and the contribution of the knowing or perceiving subject" (p. 456). And, Stroud insists, this conception of knowledge commits Quine to answering the traditional question noted above: "Quine himself seems committed to the coherence of that traditional conception by his very conception of knowledge" (p. 468).

Stroud's phrase "general but distinguishable factors," however, hints at his misunderstanding of what Quine is about. For this "bipartite conception of knowledge," as Stroud likes to call it, commits its holder to something like a correspondence conception of truth; yet, as is well known, Quine constantly denies that we can make sense of such a correspondence relation. Stroud observes that it is a

> truism that we could not explain how someone's knowledge, or even true belief, is possible unless we could observe that person's assertion on the one hand, and observe or otherwise know about the world they are about on the

other, and thereby ascertain, independently of his asserting them, whether those assertions about the world are true. But although that is an uncontroversial truism, I think it presents a problem for Quine's conception of naturalizing epistemology. [p. 463]

Stroud's worries regarding Quine's inability to make sense of the correspondence relation, and so to respond to the skeptic, are made explicit in the following passages:

If we tried to think of *all* our own beliefs as a "construction or projection from stimulations" [as Quine does], we would at most have access to what we know to be our assertions or beliefs about the world, but we would not in addition have *independent* access to the world they are about on the basis of which we could determine whether they are true. [p. 463, emphasis added]

If objective "input" from the world can always in general be isolated from everything we believe about the world as a result of that "input," it does not seem possible for Quine to expose and therefore defuse or get rid of the traditional question in the right way. The traditional bipartite view of knowledge leaves open the general possibility that the objective world is different from the way we take it to be, and so the question of how we know that possibility does not obtain will always be in place. [p. 468]

What is noteworthy here is that Stroud looks Quine's position in the face, and says, no, this cannot be what Quine means. Although my reasons, at least as they apply to Stroud, are speculative, I suggest an explanation of Stroud's rejection of what Quine "obviously" seems to be saying.

Stroud balks at accepting the implications flowing from the Quinean epistemologist's commitment to making sense of the input-output relation from *within* an ongoing scientific theory. Once this is appreciated, Quine's rather casual attitude toward skepticism (which receives fuller discussion in Chapter 2) ceases to be so surprising. Concomitantly, his views concerning the justification of knowledge claims are put in proper perspective.

As noted earlier, Stroud puzzles over Quine's position on skepticism. Either Quine is responding to standard skeptical questions concerning how one validates knowledge claims or he is not. It seems unlikely that Quine is attempting to refute skeptical doubts, since he shows no interest in establishing that our beliefs correspond to independent states of affairs. Yet if Quine is to profess to be unconcerned with skepticism, then he owes an explanation, or so it would seem, of why the skeptic's doubts may be dismissed. But Quine does not do this either. What sort of epistemologist simply feels free to ignore skepticism?

Stroud is puzzled specifically by Quine's seemingly cavalier attitude toward skeptical challenges to scientific method. Quine apparently grants the skeptic's right to challenge scientific results, yet he insists that the only answer that can be given these doubts is by the scientist using the very methods on which the skeptic has cast aspersion. Thus, Stroud writes, "I conclude that even if Quine is right in saying that skeptical doubts are 'scientific' doubts, the 'scientific' source of those doubts has no anti-skeptical force in itself. Nor does it establish the relevance and legitimacy of a scientific epistemology as an answer to the traditional epistemological question" (p. 467). Having let the skeptic throw science into doubt, the Quinean epistemologist has no resources left by which to show that any knowledge is possible. The skeptical conclusion, which Quine seems both unwilling and unable to forestall, is "that nothing we believe about the physical world amounts to knowledge, so it would then be to no avail to appeal to some of those very beliefs about the physical world in the hope of showing how they all amount to knowledge after all. We would find ourself precluded from using as independently reliable any part of what we had previously accepted as physical science" (p. 467). So, far from denying the legitimacy of the skeptic's challenge, Quine acknowledges its legitimacy and then strips, in effect, the scientific epistemologist of the resources needed to mount a response to skepticism. Stroud observes that this is not a counsel of despair; it is no counsel at all.

Quine is not averse to the idea of justifying scientific beliefs by appeal to, for example, the resources of logic, mathematics, and sensory evidence. But, he remarks, "[My] only reservation is that I am convinced, regretfully, that it cannot be done" (p. 475). Moreover, in his reply to Stroud he simply reiterates his refusal to be bothered by skepticism. The skeptic, Quine willingly concedes, just might be right; everything that we think we know might turn out to be mistaken. "Experience might, tomorrow, take a turn that would justify the skeptic's doubts about external objects. Our success in predicting observations might fall off sharply, and concomitantly with this we might begin to be somewhat successful in basing predictions upon dreams or reveries" (p. 475). Yet, Stroud insists this attitude is inconsistent with Quine's "bipartite" conception of knowledge. This conception seems, on Stroud's reading, to require that we distinguish the world's contribution to what we know from our own bit of "free creation." Once that is done, does it not follow that we can reasonably ask whether what we believe corresponds to what there is?

Stroud has seriously misunderstood just what Quine's conception of knowledge implies. For although Quine does hold that knowledge is a combination of sensory evidence and subjective creation, he emphatically denies that we can separate or distinguish these two elements in any analysis of knowledge:

> A philosopher may have rejected phenomenalism in the full reductionistic sense, in favor of admitting that statements for the most part are laden with an irreducibly extra-phenomenal burden over and above their phenomenal import. But he may continue to hold (a) that the statements do still possess their phenomenal import, what there is of it, as separate statements one by one; or he may hold rather (b) that the statements are tied to the testimony of the senses only in a systematic or holistic way which defies any statement-by-statement distribution of sensory certificates. . . . [If] his position is (b), he may be expected to find no way of putting some truth into empirical quarantine and judging the remainder free of infection. For him the contribution which linguistic meaning makes to knowledge and the contribution which sensory evidence makes to knowledge are too inextricably intertwined to admit of a sentence-by-sentence separation.
>
> My own position is (b).[25]

Epistemology naturalized is subject to the same holistic constraint that weighs upon all attempts to evaluate beliefs. This constraint does not allow one to erect standards of justification which somehow supersede the web of belief. The scientist, too, is in Neurath's boat. In other words, validation in the sense which Stroud desires is foreclosed to the Quinean epistemologist because there are no standards independent of and firmer than those that our theory offers for the evaluation of knowledge claims. Granted holism, as I argued in Section I, a Quinean (remembering that Quine does not see things quite my way) has, on the face of it, reason enough to retreat to the natural sciences as the method of epistemology. There is no philosophically higher ground that one can hope to occupy.

[25]W. V. O. Quine, *Ways of Paradox* (New York: Random House, 1966), p. 137.

Skepticism is, as Quine says, best understood as a question about the capacity of science to be self-justifying—about its capacity to explain, using only the resources of science, how the selfsame science is possible.[26] Knowledge, in the sense in which that term implies some correspondence with reality, is just not possible according to the Quinean scheme. When Stroud complains (as he does on p. 465) that Quine offers no way to tell if one theory is true and another false, he is quite right. As Quine puts it, "Immanent truth, à la Tarski, is the only truth I recognize. But . . . the question has often be posed rather as an epistemological question, *viz.*, how can we know that the one theory is true and the other false? . . . There is an obstacle still in the verb 'know'. Must it imply certainty, infallibility? Then the answer is we cannot."[27] The skeptical question is simultaneously accepted and rejected; if we change the conception of knowledge, then the skeptical complaint concerning how knowledge is possible loses its point. Quine defeats skepticism by having a conception of knowledge which is indifferent to the skeptical challenge (and, so, to most of traditional epistemology). Quine has shifted to a variant of a pragmatic conception of knowledge; knowledge, on this account, is whatever explanation of experience is certified by the current best standards of justification—the standards most likely to provide correct predictions of future experience. This is knowledge worth having to whatever extent scientific knowledge is, in fact, worth having.

But why should Stroud think otherwise? What is it about Quine's bipartite conception of knowledge that causes him to miss the important fact about Quine's holism noted above (and that allows Quine to reject just the concept of validation with which Stroud attempts to refute Quine)? The answer, in part, is that Stroud takes the bipartite conception of knowledge to imply that we have access to some form of "unvarnished news" of the world; hence it does seem reasonable to insist that Quine take validation more seriously than he does.

What is bound to puzzle an epistemologist such as Stroud is Quine's holist view. For holism commits Quine to the denial that we have any access to just the sort of evidence that, in the first place, is required by the claim that Quine has a bipartite conception of knowledge. A

[26]Quine, *Roots of Reference*, pp. 2–4.

[27]W. V. Quine, "Replies to Eleven Essays," *Philosophical Topics* 12 (Spring 1981):238.

Duhemian view does not allow for a distinction, it would seem, between sensory input and subjective creation, for how is the appropriate notion of sensory evidence to be specified from within the web of belief? If Quine allows, however, that certain individual sentences are empirically meaningful, then he is liable to the sort of charges Stroud brings against him. So it seems that Quine must either give up his bipartite conception of knowledge or answer Stroud. To do the former would be to cease to be an empiricist, which Quine does not consider; and he obviously believes he need not do the latter. But why? This question indicates why, the received reading notwithstanding, the nature of Quine's empiricism is problematic. A beginning of an answer is indicated in the previous section, where I argued that the existence of objective evidence does not require that one maintain that some specific beliefs about matters of fact are incorrigible.

The considerations raised by Stroud lead to a more general question regarding epistemology naturalized. It might be urged that actual debates in the philosophy of science with respect to the appropriateness of certain methodological restraints are not themselves part of or a result of scientific inquiry;[28] practicing scientists are characterized, on this view, as concerned with substantive issues, with testing specific hypotheses and formulating laws. If we identify science with, perhaps, a statement of accepted method plus such substantive inquiry, then methodological controversies appear to help shape scientific inquiry without being, in the Quinean sense, a part of it. Yet arguing for the appropriateness of certain norms of inquiry counts, surely, as epistemology. So a Quinean is faced with the following dilemma: Either explain what the philosopher of science is doing as something other than epistemology or give up the claim that epistemology is just a "chapter" of scientific inquiry.

For the dilemma to stick, however, one must justify a view of natural science which excludes methodological disputes from the practice of science. Thus, on the view scouted above, disputes between, for example, those holding different views about the standard by which to evaluate scientific progress or the appropriate sample size in clinical tests are not part of science. Selection of a model takes place in some netherworld of inquiry which we are to call epistemology.

It is certainly not analytic that methodological disputes and concerns

[28] I owe this objection, and an appreciation of its force, to Teddy Seidenfeld.

over the proper constraints on scientific procedure cannot be counted as part of science proper. Moreover, it is clear that for Quine science is not just the search for substantive laws; it also includes debate on how best to proceed with the business of formulating such laws: "For we can fully grant the truth of natural science and still raise the question, within natural science, how it is that man works up his command of that science from the limited impingements that are available to his sensory surfaces. This is a question of empirical psychology, but it may be pursued at one or more removes from the laboratory, one or another level of speculativity."[29] This stance, in turn, is perceived by Quine as a direct consequence of rejecting first philosophy.[30]

In asserting that there is no distinction in kind between competing hypotheses or models and competing methodological norms, am I foisting upon Quine's account of scientific method some unwanted and unnecessary normative component? If Quinean science is not objective with regard to the determination of norms, does this not vitiate the ideal of an empirical and relatively value-free discipline? This challenge, I suggest, ignores Quine's claim that the only way to evaluate the norms of scientific inquiry is by the practice of science. Given that Quine denies that there are extrascientific constraints on scientific method, a scientist must modify the scientific ship while afloat in the sea of inquiry: "Our speculations about the world remain subject to norms and caveats, but these issue from science itself as we acquire it. . . . The norms can change somewhat as science progresses."[31] A parallel might be drawn here with the fact that there is no clear way to mark off what is "purely observational" from what is not; the parallel is that we cannot clearly mark off what is purely normative from what is not. Concerns about the justification of theoretical entities or norms of inquiry are subject to a general holistic constraint; we go with what seems required or what works best now, given current purposes.

Does this mean that it is possible that other norms of inquiry, radically different from (perhaps antithetical to) our own, might prove as efficacious in scientific practice? Would we, faced with the success of

[29]Quine, *Roots of Reference*, p. 3.

[30]Quine also distinguishes between the "methodological facet" of science and those special sciences that deal in substantive issues (e.g., biology or zoology); "Replies," p. 294. J. J. C. Smart, whose characterization of Quine's view is strongly endorsed by Quine (ibid., p. 292), reads Quine's position here as I do; see especially ibid., pp. 3–4.

[31]Quine, *Theories and Things*, p. 181.

some alien science that proceeded by different principles, have to admit that their results were justified? "Yes, I think that we must admit this as a possibility in principle; that we must admit it even from the point of view of our own science. . . . I should be surprised to see this possibility realized, but I cannot picture a disproof."[32] What is relevant to the pursuit of scientific truth is whatever promotes this pursuit.

Quine's methodological constraints are selected, not by reference to what satisfies some a priori standard of justification or some extrascientific ideal of inquiry, but by what promotes, as a matter of fact, the ends of science. By the "ends of science" I mean the goals (at least) of explaining the observed evidence and of making successful predictions. Epistemology, understood for the moment as a concern with constraints on scientific method, is then part of the general scientific enterprise, since it shapes the constraints of science only in light of the acknowledged ends and purposes of natural science. The touchstone of correct epistemology is the better achievement of scientific goals based on the changes in scientific method. The traditional epistemologist looks for guidance—for standards of justification—elsewhere than in the practice of science. The Quinean epistemologist looks to science, even when seeking to improve it, in order to know what justifies changes in practice. And just so long as we hold science (and epistemology) liable to no other standard than what smoothes the way for ongoing research, we sustain the Quinean thesis that epistemology is best viewed as a part of natural science.

If we accept, following Quine, that analyticity and related notions do not illuminate the notions of logical truth, and if we accept Quine's claim that the sentences of a theory face the tribunal of experience together and not individually, then science self-applied yields the deepest understanding of our beliefs, jointly shared or individually held. There is no evaluating our theory from without, so we must try to account for it from within, using the resources it offers. In asking epistemological questions from within science, we attempt to explain our belief in the science of which that epistemological enterprise is a part. In this sense, epistemology contains all of science while being contained within it. Stroud is surely correct to note how different this is from what has heretofore counted as epistemology. What he misses is the force of Quine's reasons for reconceiving the task of epistemology.

[32]Ibid., p. 181.

The force of the position lies in pointing out that, in the absence of a first philosophy, natural science provides the best standard of rational justification.

The deeply radical flavor of Quine's proposal is just that it leaves unclear what parts of traditional philosophy of science and of traditional epistemology can be retained. Stroud's puzzlement is how to fit one part of the old tradition within Quine's scheme. Quine is not insensitive to such distinctions; the problem is whether the traditional concepts have any place in the epistemological enterprise as Quine conceives it. If epistemology cannot be the "science of justification," what is it? This reconception is understood by Quine as a consequence of two of his widely accepted positions—his critique of analyticity and his Duhemian view of theories (for these are his reasons for denying first philosophy). To attempt to measure the adequacy of Quine's proposal merely by whether or not it accords with traditional epistemology is to miss the point of the proposal.

One might still grant all that has been said so far concerning Quine's reconception of the epistemological project and still feel doubtful that epistemology naturalized has much to offer. In particular, one might ask what sort of recommendations, if any, a Quinean epistemologist can make? It is with this question that Hilary Putnam claims to be particularly troubled.[33] Putnam finds two problems that he believes obfuscate the function of an epistemologist who attempts to follow Quine's proposal. The problems arise in connection with Quine's accounts of truth and of justification. On the one hand, Putnam claims that Quine's conception of truth is too narrow—so narrow, in fact, that it prohibits Quine from proving true the very precepts that Quine endorses. On the other hand, Putnam argues that Quine's conception of justification is too broad—so broad, it seems, that it is unable to exclude anyone's views on warranted assertibility. This particular failure, in turn, leaves Quine unable to distinguish sense from nonsense, and so, ironically, with an epistemology that makes epistemology impossible. Moreover, these problems concerning truth and justification occur, on Putnam's account, because Quine has eliminated any special vantage point from which to conduct normative inquiries. With respect to each of these points, Putnam is mistaken—or so I argue below.

[33]Hilary Putnam, "Why Reason Can't Be Naturalized," *Synthese* 52 (1982):16. Page numbers cited in the following discussion are to this work.

Quine, as has been noted, opts for what he terms an immanent notion of truth, that is, truth defined in accord with the Tarskian paradigm. But one might also ask just what it is that makes one or another *theory* true? It is Quine's answer here (briefly examined in the discussion of Stroud) that puzzles Putnam. Quine's position, to recall, is this: "What is it that makes one complete physical theory true and another false? I can only answer, with unhelpful realism, that it is the nature of the world. Immanent truth, à la Tarski, is the only truth I recognize." But, Putnam protests, this attitude toward questions regarding the truth of theories will not do, for it proves too narrow.

The problem here, Putnam claims, is that on Quine's own model of an ideal scientific theory, certain sentences—the self-referential kind that Gödel showed us how to construct—are true (for the theory under consideration) but not provable or refutable in it. And this fact, or so Putnam avers, conflicts with Quine's adherence to the principle of bivalence: "If being *true* were just being a theorem in the system, such sentences would be neither true nor false, since neither they nor their negations are theorems. But Quine holds to bivalence" (p. 16). Yet such sentences, being statements of arithmetic, must be either true or false. The point, in other words, is that the true sentences outrun what is provable in any given consistent system. But Quine cannot say that such sentences are neither true nor false, given his adherence to bivalence. Neither can he maintain that they are true but not provable, since that would suggest, against everything else Quine has said, that there is some method for determining truth other than what is provable within the theory.

Putnam speculates on Quine's behalf as to how the foregoing problem might be resolved. The solution he proposes is that we view bivalence as a metalinguistic device: "I hazard the following interpretation: bivalence has *two* meanings for Quine: a "first order" meaning as viewed *within* the system of science (including its Tarskian metalanguage) and a "second order" meaning, a meaning as viewed by the philosopher. In effect, I am claiming that Quine too allows himself a "transcendental" standpoint which is different from the "naive" standpoints that we get just taking the system at face value" (p. 17). The efficacy of this move is supposed to be that it allows Quine to pronounce on the truth value of sentences that are not also theorems of the system in which one is working: "From *within* the first order system, '*p* is true or *p* is false' is simply true; . . . Statements that are provable are true in *all* intended models; undecidable statements are true or false in each intended model, but not *stably* true or false. Their truth value varies from model to model" (p. 17). It is, as it were, a matter of transcendental decree which settles the fate of the undecidables for a given theory.

This metalinguistic move, however, is not obviously open to Quine. And, in fact, after having foisted this particular perspective on Quine, Putnam worries how well all this fits with Quine's proscriptions on "philosophical" perspectives. Putnam is sensitive to the fact that this "transcendental" standpoint is subject to the same *methodological* constraints as any other: "For Quine, what the philosopher says from the 'transcendental' standpoint is subject to the same methodological rules that govern ordinary first order scientific work. . . . Quine emphasizes that there is no room for a special status for philosophical utterances" (p. 17). It is just here, however, in resolving his question concerning bivalence (by making it a metalinguistic principle), that Putnam contends that Quine is foiled by his own narrow notion of how to establish what is true.

On Putnam's account (and, if one replaces "sensation" with "experience," I would agree with Putnam here), Quine follows Ernst Mach in holding that the "business of science is *predicting regularities in our sensations*; we introduce 'objects' other than sensations only as needed to get theories which neatly predict such regularities" (p. 15). But what of those principles, such as the principles of bivalence, that have no predictive import? In general, "whether we say that some statements which are undecidable in the system are really rightly assertible or deny it does not have any effects (that one can foresee) on prediction. Thus, *this* statement [i.e., any statement concerning what is rightly assertible] *cannot* itself be rightly assertible" (p. 18). Once a Quinean moves away from a strict truth-as-provable-in-a-system account, it seems as if nothing can be legitimately said concerning the rules that stipulate which inference procedures may be used. "Truth is, to be sure, an acceptable notion for Quine, if defined à la Tarski, but so defined, it cannot serve as the primitive notion of epistemology or of methodology" (p. 19). Putnam neatly sums up his criticism here as follows: "[Quine] produced a conception of rationality so narrow as to exclude the very activity of producing that conception" (p. 18). (Putnam intends this criticism to apply to positivists in general as well as to Quine in particular.)

Before detailing Putnam's other criticism of Quine, it behooves us to ponder what has been argued by Putnam so far. Putnam effects his conflict of Quinean principles by assuming a certain rigidity in Quine's view on the matter of bivalence. And although Quine is known to give short shrift to multivalued logics, it is still worth considering what he actually does say concerning bivalence.

The title of an article Quine devotes to this issue—"What Price Bivalence?"[34]—contains an important clue to Quine's position. The article is, as its title suggests, simply an examination of whether, and under what conditions, bivalence is a desirable methodological principle. Bivalence is *not* touted by Quine as an unassailable tenet of his program. Indeed, he begins the piece in question by rehearsing some of the considerations and trade-offs involved in theory construction. Moreover, he freely admits that there is no neat (or even not so neat) algorithm by which to decide which trade-offs to effect. Taste and temperament are ineluctable influences on the final form a theory takes: "The values that we thus trade off one against the other—evidential value and systematic value—are incommensurable. Scientists of different philosophical temper will differ in how much dilution of evidence they are prepared to accept for a given systematic benefit, and vice versa."[35]

It is in this pragmatically tempered context that Quine raises, in similar voice, the question of the value of the principle of bivalence. "I propose in the present pages neither to defend bivalence nor to repudiate it. My inclination is to adhere to it for the simplicity of theory that it affords, but my purpose now is to acknowledge the costs."[36] In this context, what worries Quine is the price of adhering to bivalence when confronted with certain traditional paradoxes, such as the paradox of the heap (when does a heap cease to be one as it is diminished grain by grain). It is the case, given any pile, or whatever, that it is a heap or that it is not. But the truth of a statement of the form "x is a heap" is not settled, as Quine notes, "by the distribution of microphysical states, known or unknown; it remains an open option."[37] In general, Quine worries about statements concerning matters of fact whose truth is not determined by any matter of fact.

[34]W. V. Quine, "What Price Bivalence?" originally published in *Journal of Philosophy* 78 (1981); reprinted in *Theories and Things*. Page references are to the latter work.

[35]Ibid., p. 31.

[36]Ibid., p. 32.

[37]Ibid., p. 35.

Quine proposes no solution to the problem; by implication, he has no solution to Putnam's. But examining what Quine does write allows us to appreciate, I suggest, that the problem put to Quine by Putnam is unacceptably contrived. Recall that Putnam's charge is that Quine has different principles, which, on the face of it, are not fully self-consistent. In addition, Putnam explicitly burdens Quine, as noted above, with the tired charge that Quine's conception of rationality is inexplicable on the grounds Quine permits for rational explanation. But from where do these principles come? When this question is considered, Putnam's critique appears in a different light. And this light reveals, or so I argue, that Quine's grounds are not so narrow; nor are the origins of the principles he considered so obscure, as Putnam's remarks suggest.

If we are concerned with successful prediction, with discovering a method by which to say, from one moment to the next, what will or will not be the case, science is what commands our attention. And we deem rational what scientists do because it aids us in regularly making successful predictions. Rationality is concerned, in one way or another, with the rules and procedures for promoting reliable inferences. What favors bivalence, as with every other rule that finds favor with Quine, is that it promotes the scientific search for truth, either at the substantive level or as a normative precept.

> One might then despair of bivalence and proceed disconsolately to survey its fuzzy and plurivalent alternatives in hopes of finding something viable, however unlovely. Or one might dig in one's heels—recalcitrate, in a word—and accept this demarche as a lesson rather in the scope and limits of the notion of linguistic convention.
>
> Bivalence is a basic trait of our classical theories of nature. It has us positing a true-false dichotomy across all the statements that we can express in our theoretical vocabulary, irrespective of our knowing how to decide them. In keeping with our theories of nature we have viewed all such sentences as having factual content, however remote from observation. In this way simplicity of theory has been served. What we now observe is that bivalence requires us further to view each general term . . . as true or false of objects even in the absence of what we in our bivalent way are prepared to recognize as objective fact. At this point, if not before, the creative element in theory-building may be felt to be getting out of hand, and second thoughts on bivalence may arise.[38]

[38]Ibid., p. 38.

What I take Quine to be saying here is just that there are problems—"costs," if you like—associated with bivalence. What pleases him, however, is that bivalence suits well logical systems whose properties are extensively explored and which fit the purposes of scientific inquiry. But whether to adhere to bivalence or to some other principle turns, in the end, on what considerations are adduced in favor of the overall theory that results. Putnam notwithstanding, Quine's conception of rationality is certainly broad enough to include within itself an account of its basis for accepting its own precepts. He requires no transcendental perspective from which to impose bivalence; consideration of what affects and advances scientific inquiry suffices. Neither is Quine caught in any mindless conflict of precepts dictated to scientists, and for just the same reason.

Putnam's reflections on justification, in turn, lead him to ponder what is left, in the context of Quine's epistemology naturalized, of normative considerations. Since Quine denies that there exists any special philosophical perspective by which to evaluate or pronounce upon methods of reasoning, it seems that the Quinean epistemologist is precluded from offering any normative recommendations. This is odd in that epistemology has traditionally been concerned to distinguish legitimate and illegitimate modes of establishing and securing knowledge claims. Even worse, Quine's approach seems to make each person the standard of rational acceptability—and broadly democratic principles bode ill in epistemology. In this regard, Putnam offers the following characterization of Quine's account of justification: "I believe that, in fact, this is what the 'normative' becomes for Quine: the search for methods that yield verdicts that one oneself would accept" (p. 20). Yet, Putnam observes, this seems to have unacceptable consequences. For if the preceding is an apt characterization of Quine's "eliminationist line" with respect to normative considerations, Putnam asks, "could it be a superstition that there is such a thing as reason?" (p. 20). If we accept the characterization of the Quinean position given above, then apparently I am the only arbiter of what is reasonable and what is not. And this goes, of course, for every thinking person. "If the *only* kind of rightness any statement has that I can understand is 'being arrived at by a method which yields verdicts I accept,' then I am committed to a solipsism of the present moment" (p. 20). Such a solipsistic view leaves us in the position of believing "that there is *no* sense in which any thought is *right* or *wrong* (including the thought that no thought is right or wrong) beyond being the verdict of the moment. . . . This is a self-refuting enterprise if there ever was one" (p. 21). Since the Quinean epistemologist eschews normative considerations, such a person is left without any resources by which to distinguish sense from nonsense. And so the broadened account of justification reduces Quine's position to nonsense.

There are at least two serious problems with Putnam's account. First, as is clear from discussions above, it is simply false that a Quinean epistemologist is precluded from debating or otherwise speculating about normative considerations. The constraints on normative reflections are quite different, admittedly, from the type entertained by an epistemologist whose primary worry is skepticism. The traditional epistemologist is concerned to safeguard a certain conception of knowledge. Quine has given that up; his worries about justification take a distinctly pragmatic turn.

What is particularly irksome with regard to Putnam's characterization is that it is inconsistent with the characterization of Quine's position he provides earlier in his essay. Note that in order to convict Quine of solipsism, Putnam must insist that Quine can say no more about justification than that it reduces to the question of what some one individual, at some one moment, would accept. How easy it is to show that such a view is lacking. Yet Putnam correctly notes that a cornerstone of Quine's conception of rationality is the notion of an observation sentence; this is what ties the formal considerations to the social sphere and so makes knowledge claims intersubjectively checkable, that is, objective. An observation sentence, in turn, is defined "in neurological and cultural terms," that is, "for a community" (p. 15). "The key idea is that observation sentences are distinguished . . . by being keyed to the same stimulations *intersubjectively*" (p. 15). In fact, Putnam explicitly distinguishes Quine's position from that of a methodological solipsist (p. 17). The foregoing suggests that Quine, even on Putnam's own characterization of Quine's position, is not guilty as charged. Finally, I note in passing that a textual basis for Putnam's imputations of solipsism are not made clear.

Putnam is not alone in his worries about the internal coherence of Quine's conception of epistemology. Like Putnam, Ernest Sosa is troubled by Quine's commitment to an immanent notion of truth. As defined in accord with the Tarskian paradigm, this account of truth might seem unproblematic. This is not, however, the case. Sosa charges that Quine's reflections do not clearly add up to a coherent epistemology.[39] Coherence eludes Quine because, it seems, he allows science to be the "last arbiter of truth" and yet denies, as noted previously, that we can say of theories that they are true. The result, Sosa complains, is a "fictional realism" (p. 68) that does not bear critical examination.

Sosa mounts his charge of incoherence by attributing to Quine the following three theses, whose conjunction, he argues, is inconsistent:

> (Q1) What then does our overall scientific theory claim regarding the world? Only that it is somehow so structured as to assure the sequences of stimulations that our theory gives us to expect.
> (Q2) Yet people, sticks, stones, electrons, and molecules are real indeed.
> (Q3) [It] . . . is within science itself and not in some prior philosophy, that reality is properly to be identified and described.
>
> . . . . .
>
> We cannot have it all three ways: (Q1), (Q2), and (Q3) form an incoherent triad. If we trust science as the measure of reality, and if we think there really are sticks and stones, then we can't have science accept only a world "somehow so structured as to assure" certain sequences of stimulations or the like. Our science must also claim that there really are sticks and stones.
>
> What is more, if science is really the measure of reality, it cannot undercut itself by saying that it really isn't, that it is only convenient "manners of speaking" to guide us reliably from stimulation to stimulation. [p. 69]

Obviously, Quine has no trouble with claiming that there really are sticks and stones. The problem arises, rather, with Sosa's final point. Quine accepts truth as defined *intratheoretically* by science and yet declares himself a nonbeliever with regard to the claim that some one theory is true. Does Quine heartily affirm the reality of things, on the one hand, but, on the other hand, deny sotto voce their reality? In short, Sosa's complaint is that immanent truth is not truth enough.

Sosa believes that Quine's inconsistency is exposed when Quine's position is confronted with the following reductio ad absurdum (from Russell). The scientific picture is, in broad outline, either true or false. If false, then we lack scientific knowledge of the world around us. If true, we still lack scientific knowledge, because by Quine's account we cannot noncircularly justify our belief in this science. Therefore we lack scientific knowledge of the world around us (p. 66–67). Sosa observes that Quine would reject the conclusion that there is no scientific knowledge; but in saying this, Quine would become caught, as noted

[39]Ernest Sosa, "Nature Unmirrored, Epistemology Naturalized," *Synthese* 55 (1983):70. Page references cited in the following discussion are to this work.

above, in the charge of the inconsistency of (Q1)–(Q3): in order to escape the argument, he must claim that scientific theory, in broad outline, is true; but this undercuts his view (also emphasized, as we saw, by Putnam) that scientific theories are just a means of predicting the course of experience.

Sosa's claim to discern an inconsistency at the heart of the Quinean epistemological program is contingent on his view that "Quine certainly rejects the conclusion that we have no scientific knowledge" (p. 67). But there is a critical equivocation in this argument. What does it mean to say that Quine rejects the assertion that there is no scientific knowledge? Surely Quine does believe that there is scientific knowledge, if by this is meant only that a rational person will accept as true those statements affirmed by scientific theory. But if this is all that there is to Quine's account of knowledge claims, there is no argument for Sosa to make against Quine, for the term "knowledge" in his argument is ambiguous. The intended sense of knowledge could be an immanent one, or it could be a "realist" sense, one that maintains that scientific theories picture the world seen sub specie aeternitatis. It is clear that it is the realist sense Sosa intends, at least as he sets up the key premise of his reductio: "If the scientific account of the (supposed) world around us is true at least in broad outlines, that rules out any possibility that we really know such a world even in broad outline" (p. 67). Sosa's confident claim that Quine must accept this premise because Quine believes that there is scientific knowledge is simply based on a conflation of the very senses of knowledge in question. Of course Quine affirms that there are truths of science *immanently affirmed*. But why is this inconsistent with the claim that there is no one true scientific *theory*? Sosa begs the question against Quine by simply assuming that by "scientific knowledge" Quine means "true scientific theory." As Sosa himself recognizes elsewhere, Quine intends no such meaning (p. 66). Construed realistically, as I have termed it, Quine *does* accept the conclusion of the Russellian reductio rehearsed by Sosa; he accepts that "we lack scientific knowledge even in broad outline of the world around us" (p. 67). But unless equivocation counts as a valid move in argumentation, there is no inconsistency in accepting both the premise cited above and the claim that we possess scientific knowledge in the form of truths affirmed by received scientific doctrine. Sosa clearly opposes the suggestion that epistemology should be naturalized, but he nowhere confronts the serious arguments that favor this proposal.

Rather than continue to defend epistemology naturalized on a case-by-case basis, I conclude this discussion with a sketch of a general argument which is meant to undercut the worry voiced by Putnam and others about whether a naturalized epistemology can address normative issues. Recall the parallel noted previously between, on the one hand, questions of how to distinguish matters of scientific practice tainted with normative considerations from those that are value-free and, on the other hand, the dispute over whether it is possible to distinguish between theoretical and observational entities. This latter dispute was resolved, not by successfully drawing a line between the two types of entities, but by acknowledging that there is no line to be drawn. Likewise, it should be acknowledged that there is no meaningful distinction between what is a normative concern and what is not. As a justification of such a claim, I urged that general holistic concerns mitigate against such distinctions. What I now add is that the fact-value distinction is itself of a piece with the analytic-synthetic distinction; and as goes the analytic-synthetic distinction, so goes any hard and fast distinction between what counts as a norm and what counts as a purely factual concern.[40] If we could satisfactorily distinguish between normative considerations and substantive ones in science, then we would also have in hand the class of statements that are just the empirically meaningful ones. But with this class demarcated, the analytic statements too could be sorted out; presumably, the analytic statements would be those we identified as true "come what may." This sort of sorting, however, is precisely what we cannot do. Therefore it is pointless to worry where to draw the line.[41] What is worth the worry is how to advance research. In accepting the holistic constraint on evaluating scientific rationality, we accept that the standard of evaluation becomes what fosters the aims and goals of this science. This acceptance, in turn, both provides a working standard to appeal to when statements need adjudication and frees one from worries about what is normative and what is not.

[40]This develops a suggestion made to me by Roger Gibson. Quine, it is worth noting, does not find the normative-substantive distinction worth drawing, although he does not make his reasons for this explicit; see the previously cited comments on these matters in *Theories and Things*, p. 181 and "Replies," pp. 3–4, 292, 294.

[41]It is interesting to note, in this regard, that on Quine's account both epistemic and moral principles are grounded on human predispositions to pleasure; see *Theories and Things*, p. 57, and *Roots of Reference*, secs. 8, 13.

CHAPTER 2

# Epistemology Socialized

In the preceding chapter, holism is presented as the central tenet of Quine's epistemology and the indeterminacy of translation as the crucial implication of this position. Chapters 5 through 9 are devoted to exploring what holism and indeterminacy imply for methodological disputes in the social sciences. Chapters 2 through 4, however, assess varying interpretations of the position outlined so far in order to justify my particular interpretation applied in the later chapters. Two specific interpretations of holist epistemology are examined and, in their extreme forms, rejected. One interpretation—Quine's own—argues that epistemology ought to be viewed as part of neurophysiology. Another interpretation—so-called irrationalist or anarchist views—denies that there is any satisfactory way to evaluate knowledge claims. My own position develops in response to each of these extremes.

In this chapter I examine arguments for the claim that Quine has not extended his own criticism of traditional epistemology far enough. In addition, I engage in reinterpreting and "correcting" Quine's own account of what follows from the dissolution of epistemology as an autonomous discipline.

With regard to extending or radicalizing (in a sense to be specified below) Quine's views, the central figure is Richard Rorty. Rorty insists that Quine's commitment to holism is incompatible with the program to naturalize epistemology. Any attempt to formulate a general model of rationality (and especially one using natural science as *the* model) is, in Rorty's view, a species of bad faith; given what we have learned from Quine (among others) about the nature of knowledge, no such formulation is ever warrantable. Rorty believes that the only constraints on warranting beliefs are internal to a theory; I argue that he is wrong on this point.

With respect to correcting Quine, my particular concern is to argue that Quine's account, if it is to function in place of traditional epistemology, must avoid what I call "linguistic solipsism." Linguistic solipsism obtains when an explanation fails to explain the *social* dimension of language development and use. The core of my complaint against Quine is that, while, for Quine, the basis of knowledge lies in whatever stimulations people share, his epistemological program fails to explain how sensory stimulations account for the public or shared basis of knowledge. Yet it is just such an analysis of the social basis of language and knowledge which Quine sets as the task of a naturalized epistemology. Hence Quine's positive program cannot explain human knowledge in Quine's chosen terms and so cannot count as epistemology.

The central thrust of what I have called Quine's negative program ("Two Dogmas of Empiricism," the attack on modal operators, the Duhemian view of theories, and indeterminacy) is to deny that there exists some special method (a first philosophy) by which to noncircularly legitimate our current favorite set of justificatory canons.[1] Quine transmutes the old epistemological question about the justification of standards of rational inquiry into a question of how to use our current best methods—those of natural science—to explain the genesis of the beliefs we currently accept.

In what follows, I outline the central role of behavioral and social criteria in Quine's analysis of knowledge and evidence. In subsequent sections I develop my argument that the sort of causal scientific explanations Quine apparently favors cannot function to answer the type of epistemological questions he asks.

## I

Quine has been taken to task for a seeming refusal to fully acknowledge the consequences of his Duhemian views. The charge may be

[1]Or, as he puts it in a number of places, skeptics may raise doubts about scientific method, but these, if they are to be taken seriously, will be doubts that arise because of the failure of scientific methods to meet the appropriate scientific standards; see Quine's "Replies to Eleven Essays," *Philosophical Topics* 12 (Spring 1981):238.

forcefully stated as "the dilemma of a Duhemian empiricist." The dilemma develops as follows. Quine views his philosophical efforts as a continuation of the empiricist tradition. Whatever changes he has rung on the empiricist tradition from Hume to Carnap, Quine holds as an article of faith that "two cardinal tenets of empiricism remained unassailable, however, and so remain to this day. One is that whatever evidence there is for science *is* sensory evidence. The other . . . is that all inculcation of meanings of words must rest ultimately on sensory evidence."[2] The positivists were right in believing that the evidence is sensory and not otherwise. They erred, rather, in thinking that there existed techniques that would allow them to make explicit the sensory content of individual scientific statements.

One consequence of the Duhem thesis, however, is the denial that there exist any clear-cut observational notions. The notions of truth and of factuality seem, on Quine's account, to be purely internal (immanent) to the theory with which one is working. But if this is the case, then Quine's distinction between truth and meaning—theories in science and theories of translation—cannot be right. For the distinction appears to appeal to a notion of evidence which Quine is otherwise committed to denying.[3] Evidence, as Quine understands the term, consists of whatever it is that triggers our nerve endings (see his remarks in his "Reply to Cresswell" cited in n.1). Explanations of what the evidence is are provided in terms of the facts a theory posits. But if, as Quine states, the evidence for both the translator and the scientist is sensory evidence, then it appears that Quine is arbitrarily favoring the theoretical constructs of the scientist over those of the semanticist. How can it be that hypotheses in natural science have a "fact of the matter" that hypotheses about translations lack, since statements of fact are based, in both cases, on the same type of evidential considerations? The dilemma, then, is how there can be no facts for a linguistic theory for which we nonetheless have evidence.

The problem may be extended in the following way. Some state-

[2]W. V. Quine, *Ontological Relativity and Other Essays* (New York: Columbia University Press, 1969), p. 75.

[3]See Paul Roth, "Paradox and Indeterminacy," *Journal of Philosophy* 75 (July 1978); "Reconstructing Quine: The Troubles with a Tradition," *Metaphilosophy* 14 (July/October 1983); "Semantics without Foundations," *The Philosophy of W. V. Quine*, ed. L. Hahn (Library of Living Philosophers Series; La Salle, Ill.: Open Court, 1987).

ments of scientific fact refer to theoretical entities. Inasmuch as not all statements of fact are observational, not all statements of fact are part of what counts as evidence for the theory. Quine's complaint cannot be just that the ontology of current science does not include intentional objects, for this is to presume a distinction in kind and not to prove one. At base, the issue must be that our theories of truth are tied to objective evidence and that theories of translation are not. But holism seems to deny that it is possible to specify any nonimmanent notion of evidence. For the fact-evidence distinction on which Quine relies to preserve his empiricism is itself immanent, that is, part of our current theory of the world. But what then is to be made of this bedrock notion of empiricism by which to distinguish physics and semantics? Clearly Quine cannot insist that the fact-evidence distinction is, on his view, not part of current theory, for that would be to take a stance reminiscent of first philosophy. Yet without the fact-evidence distinction, Quine's empiricism comes to naught. The further problem for Quine, then, is this: either he must renounce the two "unassailable" tenets of empiricism or he must give up the Duhem thesis, for the latter appears inconsistent with the former.

In order to ultimately resolve the apparent dilemma, it is necessary to attend to Quine's remarks on language learning. Language learning involves the acquisition of knowledge. The basis for Quine's claim that meaning and truth finally diverge with respect to their epistemological status should be reflected in his explanation of the process of language acquisition. Quine's new epistemological question concerns what is open to scientific treatment via empirical psychology; this is a question that, in its epistemological moment, concerns how people acquire and use language. In particular, by studying how language is acquired by children, that is, by learning how the paradigm cases of know-nothings are integrated (the majority of them, anyway) into the speech community, one learns how the standards actually employed (plastic though they may be) come to have the status they do.

In what terms must one answer this central question of Quinean epistemology—the question of the social basis of language learning? Quine sometimes speaks as if epistemology naturalized is just empirical psychology; his program is, in fact, much more aggressively reductionistic than that. The reductionistic side of the program comes out clearly when he distinguishes three levels of explanation. The key to the distinction is the type of entity or mechanism to which each level of explanation appeals. Quine terms the levels the "mental," the "behavioral," and the "physiological." The first of these Quine disparages as explanation in name only, and this because of an inherent lack of clarity in the mental notions invoked. In contrast is the last named of the three; the "physiological is the deepest and most ambitious, and it is the place for causal explanations."[4] It is no surprise that Quine views the three levels as levels of reduction—from terms first known but poorly understood to the terms of science, which are last in the order of knowing but well understood: "Our three levels thus are levels of reduction: mind consists in dispositions to behaviour, and these are physiological states."[5] Real, as distinct from purported, explanations are framed in the idiom of natural science.

Quine's official doctrine is that behavioral or dispositional accounts are halfway houses, explanations for which we settle until something better comes along. And the "something better," in this case, is going to be an explanation in neurophysiological terms. Yet the question of how to salvage Quine's fact-evidence distinction from the difficulties noted above does not concern the mechanics or the vocabulary of explanation. The issue, rather, is whether explanations at one level can serve the *purpose* Quine intends for them. What is lost, I suggest, when explanation is moved from the behavioral to the physiological level is the epistemological value of the behavioral explanation.

My disagreement with Quine, and my focus in reconstructing his views, concerns not his naturalism per se, but rather his insistence that naturalism favor explanations in neurophysiological terms. It is in his reductionistic proclivities that Quine goes wrong. As I argue below, in order to preserve empiricism, explanation at the behavioral level is necessary. At the behavioral level, an argument for the fact-evidence distinction can be made; conversely, this is what is lost if we insist that the third level of reduction represents the sole legitimate level of explanation. And it is this loss that counts against Quine's claim that epistemology naturalized should strive for the third level of explanation.[6] Naturalism, on my account, must rest with both levels as basic.

[4]See Quine's "Mind and Verbal Dispositions," in *Mind and Language*, ed. S. Guttenplan (Oxford: Clarendon Press, 1975), p. 87.

[5]Ibid., p. 94.

[6]My account here bears certain resemblance to the strategies deployed in Alan Garfinkle's *Forms of Explanation* (New Haven, Conn.: Yale University Press, 1981) and Peter Achinstein's *The Nature of Explanation* (New York: Oxford University

In what follows, I argue that a behavioral account of language learning is central to establishing a fact-evidence distinction and, further, that the basis for accepting this distinction cannot be maintained at Quine's third level of explanation.

Quine does not distinguish between the acquisition of language and the acquisition of knowledge; the activities are coeval:

> I had characterized science as a linguistic structure that is keyed to observation at some points. . . . There is the beginning, here, of a partnership between the theory of language learning and the theory of scientific evidence. It is clear, when you think about it, that this partnership must continue. . . . We have here a good reason to regard the theory of language as vital to the theory of knowledge.[7]

> I have now sketched the nature of the connection between the observations and the labyrinthine interior of scientific theory. I have sketched it in terms of learning of language. . . . The paths of language learning, which lead from observation sentences to theoretical sentences, are the only connection there is between observation and theory.[8]

This acquisition process, in turn, is socially fostered and guided. "Language is a social art. In acquiring it we have to depend entirely on intersubjectively available cues as to what to say and when."[9] Yet in order to be socially fostered and taught, people need to share a sense of when they are being similarly stimulated. If they did not have this shared sense of the physical environment, people could not begin to teach one another what they were talking about: "If substantial agreement in similarity standards were not there, this first step in language acquisition would be blocked."[10] In learning how we learn to use

---

Press, 1983). My specific strategy is different from the attack Garfinkle favors, although I believe our positions are consistent. The complexity of Achinstein's account, and his use of the notion of propositions, dissuade me from here attempting a comparison of our accounts.

[7]W. V. O. Quine, "The Nature of Natural Knowledge," in *Mind and Language*, ed. S. Guttenplan, pp. 74–75.

[8]Ibid., p. 79.

[9]*Word and Object* (Cambridge, Mass.: M.I.T. Press, 1960), p. ix. This general emphasis on the importance of language learning is demonstrated as well in writing more recent than *Word and Object*; see, for example, "Facts of the Matter," in *American Philosophy from Edwards to Quine*, ed. K. Merrill and R. Shahan (Norman: University of Oklahoma Press, 1977).

[10]Quine, "Nature of Natural Knowledge," p. 73.

language, we learn how we come to know what we know. Epistemology merges with the study of how children acquire language.

The ability of people to perceive similar stimulations as similar is the sine qua non of language acquisition. The relevant notion of similarity, it is important to note, is not defined by appeal to objects. Such an appeal would build into the foundations of Quine's account an ontology, but ontological commitments are to be purely immanent (and so derivative). Perception here is, rather, to be understood in terms of social conditioning and other theoretical considerations.[11]

In later writings, Quine *identifies* the processes of language acquisition and the study of knowledge; they are two sides of the same phenomenon.[12] The study of language acquisition is critical for epistemology because it isolates what evidence there is for our knowledge claims. Something like observation sentences, with their stimulus meanings, "afford the only entry to a language," and "any treatment of language as a natural phenomenon must start with the recognition that certain utterances are keyed to ranges of sensory stimulation patterns; and these ranges are what stimulus meanings are." Thus "observation sentences are the gateway to language, as to science."[13] There is, in other words, no separating Quine's proposal to naturalize epistemology via the scientific study of language use and the social arena in which this language is acquired. The key to science and so to the study of knowledge is just what will be publicly acknowledged under particular conditions to which people are jointly exposed. Language learning is the first case in which this publicity condition is seen to be manifestly important. Since, on Quine's view, scientific language is just a refinement of ordinary language, the question of how ordinary language is acquired is critical for any full account of human knowledge and beliefs. Hence, what makes this scientific study of language of *epistemological* significance is just the claim that studying the social aspect of language acquisition is another way of asking those questions about the nature of knowledge which trouble epistemologists.

The analysis of language learning is what makes plausible, in turn, the development of a notion of objective evidence consistent with Quine's Duhemian scruples and yet which also preserves a notion of

[11]Quine, "Facts of the Matter," p. 176.

[12]See W. V. Quine, *Roots of Reference* (La Salle, Ill.: Open Court, 1973), p. 138, and "Nature of Natural Knowledge," pp. 74–75, 79.

[13]Quine, *Ontological Relativity*, p. 89; ibid., p. 157; *Roots of Reference*, pp. 39–40.

evidence satisfying the tenets of empiricism. To show this involves the paradox of language learning.[14] The paradox, which obtains for anyone holding a holist view of language, may be formulated as follows: On a Duhemian (holist) view of language, the theoretical sentences of one's native tongue are taken to be an interrelated group, and to have their meaning and their evidence only as such. Yet, for example, infants learn language only a bit at a time, and so in isolation from the containing theory that, ex hypothesi, alone provides each linguistic bit with whatever semantic and evidential import it may have. Thus, it would seem, verbal stimulations consisting of individual sentences must be meaningless for a child. But this suggests the paradoxical situation in which each person learns meaningful discourse by parroting what must always be, for the learner, meaningless verbal segments.

Quine, in fact, is aware of and sensitive to this paradoxical consequence of holism: "Such relativity would be awkward, since, conversely, the individual component sentences offer the only way into the theory."[15] Since Quine is certainly quick to concede that there are no continuous derivations from the observational to the theoretical levels of language, the problem posed by the paradox must be (and is) taken very seriously by Quine.

How does the proof for the existence of theory-neutral evidence turn on the resolution of the paradox of language learning? As I read Quine, his response to the paradox is basically this: since most people do become fluent members of their linguistic community, some linguistic device must be available to help bridge the paradoxical gap. This bridge is provided by sentences that allow an "entry-way" into language and, so, that must function, roughly, as observation sentences are said to. To explain why such sentences are not mere counterexamples to holism, one needs to explain how they play an important evidential role and yet do not undermine the general semantic interdependence asserted by a holist.

Observation sentences, as Quine develops the notion, are to express whatever evidential connection there is between language and "nonlinguistic reality."[16] Observation sentences are the point at which sentences of the theoretical structure impinge on the world; they "are

[14]See Roth, "Paradox and Indeterminacy," and "Reconstructing Quine."

[15]W. V. O. Quine, "Meaning and Translation," in *Challenges to Empiricism*, ed. H. Morick (Belmont, Cal.: Wadsworth, 1972), pp. 74–75.

[16]Quine, "Facts of the Matter," p. 156.

the repository of evidence for scientific hypotheses. [Their] relation to meaning is fundamental, too, since observation sentences are the ones we are in a position to learn to understand first, both as children and as field linguists."[17]

Central to Quine's account of an observation sentence is the notion of a stimulus meaning, for competent speakers must agree that the putative observation sentence is true only in the presence of the appropriate stimulations. "What distinguishes [the observation sentence] is just that the general usage of it conforms to concurrent observation in about the way that it would if everyone had learned it ostensively. . . . Such sentences are necessarily our entering wedge into our first language; for clearly we can begin only by connecting heard utterances with concurrent stimulation, and by being confirmed in our utterances by speakers who share the concurrent stimulation."[18] An observation sentence must be keyed to stimulations so as to "elicit assent from any competent user of the language on the occasion of its use in the presence of appropriate stimulations." Stimulus meanings are said to "isolate a sort of net empirical import of each of various single sentences without regard to the containing theory." The important point to remember in this regard is the claim that in order to penetrate the web of theoretical discourse, "some such device [as stimulus meaning] is indispensable." Emphasis is on the need to explain how language learning is possible: "The really distinctive trait of observation terms and sentences is not to be sought in the concurrence of witnesses [one of Quine's criteria for identifying observation sentences] but in ways of learning."[19] If observation sentences are just a definitional matter, there is no nonimmanent notion of evidence to be salvaged, and so nothing remains of philosophical interest from empiricism.

The foregoing digression on observation sentences and the notion of stimulus meaning is meant to establish that Quine both recognizes the paradox of language learning and proposes a solution. According to

[17]Quine, *Ontological Relativity*, pp. 88–89.

[18]W. V. O. Quine, "Grades of Theoreticity," in *Experience and Theory*, ed. L. Foster and J. W. Swanson (Amherst, Mass.: University of Massachusetts Press, 1970), p. 4.

[19]Quine, "Nature of Natural Knowledge," p. 73; "Meaning and Translation," p. 75; ibid., p. 75; "On Empirically Equivalent Systems of the World," *Erkenntnis* 9 (1975): 316. For a detailed analysis of Quine's position which also recognizes the importance of language learning in Quine's epistemology but does not otherwise agree with the view taken here, see Roger Gibson, *The Philosophy of W. V. Quine: An Expository Essay* (Tampa, Fla.: University of South Florida Press, 1982), especially chap. 2.

the solution, which I examine further in Section II, certain sentences must function, for child and for teacher, as observation sentences do, as those sentences we coordinate with the appropriate sort of stimulations apart from any knowledge of the rest of the language.

The contention that there is objective evidence need not, then, conflict with Quine's Duhemian view of theories, since the argument that there must be observation sentences never assumes that they can be identified. In short, we distinguish between arguments that some sentences must play this role and arguments that purport to tell us which sentences do. Arguments for the former point turn on a need to settle the paradox of language learning in a way that makes empirical sense; arguments for the latter are always couched from the standpoint of one specific theory and so are open to revision. My position is that, while there must be observation sentences, they cannot be identified with certainty.

Due to his unusual conjunction of doctrines—the holism and observation sentences—Quine has been accused by Donald Davidson, who is otherwise very sympathetic to Quine's position, of adhering to an illicit scheme-content dichotomy.[20] As Quine has urged in rebuttal of Davidson, however, this charge confuses empiricism as a theory of truth and empiricism as a theory of evidence:

> If empiricism is construed as a theory of truth, then what Davidson imputes to it as a third dogma is rightly reputed and rightly renounced. Empiricism as a theory of truth thereupon goes by the boards, and good riddance. As a theory of evidence, however, empiricism remains with us, minus indeed the two old dogmas. . . . It has both a descriptive and a normative aspect, and in neither aspect do I think of it as a dogma. It is what makes scientific method partly empirical rather than solely a quest for internal coherence.[21]

Indeed, without empiricism as a theory of evidence, one would "[part] the last mooring of empiricism."[22] As noted above, on Quine's use of the notion of an observation sentence, truth remains a matter that is immanent—internal to the theory. Observation sentences are also

[20]See Davidson's "On the Very Idea of a Conceptual Scheme," *Proceedings and Addresses of the American Philosophical Association* 47 (1973–74):12–13.

[21]W. V. Quine, *Theories and Things* (Cambridge, Mass.: Belknap Press, 1981), p. 39.

[22]Ibid., p. 38.

determined internally in the sense that the sentences specified as observational are so specified intratheoretically. But the claim that there are stimulus meanings guiding and directing our use of certain sentences is a claim about what *evidence* is needed in order to teach a language. "The proper role of experience or surface irritation is as a basis not for truth but for warranted belief."[23] For Quine (and Quineans) a key aspect in determining which beliefs are rational is how the justifications incorporate the appropriate notion of evidence. Put another way, the notion of evidence—observation sentences in Quine's preferred terminology—is central to our scheme of justified belief. And the pragmatic test that indicates this central role is that, like logical laws, we cannot surrender certain observational statements without, as a rule, greatly altering a good many other beliefs.

How do these points concerning evidence reflect on Rorty's claim that Quine's holism and his distinction between truth and meaning conflict? Rorty does, to be sure, deeply appreciate certain aspects of Quine's reformulation of conventional epistemological inquiry. Quine, he notes, subverts those interests that traditionally have motivated epistemologists. By assimilating the tasks of justification and causal explanation, Rorty observes, Quine does not so much answer

[23]Ibid., p. 39. Davidson, if I read him correctly, has moved closer to Quine on this point than he was in "On the Very Idea of a Conceptual Scheme." Davidson is not, however, as specific as Quine is in the discussion of how to preserve empiricism as a theory of evidence. Davidson has nevertheless insisted that the basis of shared beliefs is *causally* determined. What is noteworthy, for the view being defended here, is that Davidson too seeks to preserve an account of empirical evidence which, nonetheless, does not require identifying some actual class of sentences as epistemologically privileged. He argues, rather, that we can (as I have argued that Quine does) simply point to the ways in which the possibility of communication *presupposes* something like stimulus meanings of observation sentences: "Neurath, Carnap and Hempel were right, I believe, in abandoning the search for a basic sort of evidence on which our knowledge of the world could rest. None is available, and none is needed. What they perhaps failed to appreciate is *why* it is not needed. It is not needed because the causal relations between our beliefs and speech and the world also supply the interpretation of our language and of our beliefs. In this rather special sense, 'experience' is the source of all knowledge. But this is a sense that does not encourage us to find a mental or inferential bridge between external events and ordinary beliefs. The bridge is there all right—a causal bridge that involves the sense organs. The error lies as Neurath saw in trying to turn this causal bridge into an epistemological one, with sense data, uninterpreted givens, or unwritable sentences constituting its impossible spans" (Donald Davidson, "Empirical Content," *Grazer Philosophische Studien* 16/17 [1982]:488). Evidence there is, and it connects our talk of the world, not to any indubitable facts about or truths of the world, but, as the epistemological twist has it, to others when speaking about the world.

skepticism as refuses to take it seriously as an epistemological problem: "Quine's remoteness from skeptical concerns is shown by his assimilation of elements of experience to elements of knowledge, and of explanation to justification. . . . Nobody would assimilate epistemology to psychology unless he were so little frightened by skepticism as to regard 'grounding human knowledge' as a bit of a joke."[24] In short, Rorty correctly understands that what Quine has done in his proposal to naturalize epistemology is to change "the motive of inquiry" (p. 225).

Epistemology naturalized is, as Rorty perceives, traditional epistemology ended. It results not in new answers to old questions; rather, Quine is willing to let traditional epistemology "wither away. For if we have psychophysiology to cover causal mechanisms, and sociology and history of science to note the occasions on which observation sentences are invoked or dodged in constructing and dismantling theories, then epistemology has nothing to do" (p. 225). The key point in Rorty's reading of Quine is that he believes that evidence, in the guise of observation sentences, is what the community of scientists currently accept on this score; observation sentences are taken to be a purely sociological phenomenon. Rorty, unlike Quine, sees internal coherence as the only constraint on the warranting of beliefs.

Indeed, Rorty is puzzled by Quine's intransigence in refusing to explicitly acknowledge that evidence is a sociological concept, and not one tied to any philosophical considerations. Quine defines observation sentences by appealing both to agreement of joint witnesses and to stimulus meaning; Rorty questions what the notion of stimulus meaning can add to the joint-witnessing condition:

> What is puzzling is that we have defined "observation sentence" in terms of the *consensus gentium*; we divide observation from theory without knowing or caring which bits of our body are the sensory receptors. . . . We do not need any psychophysiological account of causal mechanisms to isolate what is intersubjectively agreeable—we just do this in ordinary conversation. . . . To put it another way, once we have picked out the observation sentences conversationally rather than neurologically, further inquiry into "how evidence relates to theory" would seem to be a matter for Polanyi, Kuhn, and Hanson. [p. 227]

[24]Richard Rorty, *Philosophy and the Mirror of Nature* (Princeton, N.J.: Princeton University Press, 1979), p. 229. Page references in the following discussion are to this work.

Yet, as Rorty knows, Quine specifically rebukes Polanyi et al. for making light of the notion of observationality.[25]

Rorty also senses the conflict between evidence and holism developed above. He takes the prima facie conflict between holism and empiricism as evidence that Quine has not fully confronted the implications of his (Quine's) own criticisms. Quine, Rorty claims, cannot reconcile his preference for the methods and ontology of physical science "with his holistic claim that there is no 'first philosophy' higher than and prior to ordinary scientific inquiry" (p. 199). Rorty suggests that a Quine cleansed of his unjustified preference for science would appear as an expositor of "epistemological behaviorism." Epistemological behaviorism, as Rorty develops this position in *Philosophy and the Mirror of Nature*, holds that socially endorsed standards of knowledge are all there is to work with when evaluating knowledge claims; there is nothing more to go on:

> Explaining rationality and epistemic authority by reference to what society lets us say, rather than the latter by the former, is the essence of what I shall call "epistemological behaviorism." . . . This sort of behaviorism can best be seen as a species of holism—but one which requires no idealist metaphysical underpinnings. It claims that if we understand the rules of a language-game, we understand all that there is to understand about why moves in that language-game are made. [p. 174]

> For the Quine-Sellers approach to epistemology, to say that truth and knowledge can only be judged by the standards of the inquirers of our own day is not to say that human knowledge is less noble or important, or more "cut off from the world," than we had thought. It is merely to say that nothing counts as justification unless by reference to what we already accept, and that there is no way to get outside our beliefs and our language so as to find some test other than coherence. [p. 178]

Rorty's conception of epistemological behaviorism, unlike Quine's holism, involves a rejection of the science-nonscience distinction. Rorty insists that knowledge is simply a matter of measuring up to the standards of a discipline; but there is no marking off either the standards of one particular discipline, say, physics, or a favorite set of axioms as paradigmatically rational. On Rorty's analysis, Quine's

[25]See Quine, *Ontological Relativity*, p. 87, and "Grades of Theoreticity," pp. 4–5.

indeterminacy thesis is founded only on Quine's prejudice for the ontology of physics. Rorty attacks the claim that there remains any epistemological significance to empiricism once one has acceded to a Duhemian account. Rorty's view here has struck a responsive chord; even Richard Bernstein, who is otherwise critical of Rorty's final position, finds his analysis of Quine praiseworthy. As Bernstein puts it, "many critics have argued that Quine's later work, especially his reflections on the indeterminacy of translation, reveals a blatant contradiction—or at least a deep tension—with his own pragmatic and holistic arguments. Rorty locates and specifies this tension better than anyone else."[26]

To be sure, Rorty does not deny the efficacy of natural science as a means of warranting beliefs; what he does deny is that it is *the* means. He rejects Quine's view, in other words, that scientific method is the final arbiter of truth. And the reason for this difference, in turn, is that the two disagree about whether there is any objective—theory-neutral—evidence for beliefs. Rorty maintains that standards of justification and evidence are purely theoretical matters; the relevant standards, and the evidence to which these standards apply, vary from discipline to discipline (or culture to culture). If revelation counts as good evidence for warranting belief in one group but not in another, there is no gainsaying the first group's preferences in this matter. Rorty refuses to acknowledge that there is any *evidential* constraint on the rationality of conversation. Since, on his account, factuality is determined intratheoretically, to call a sentence observational is merely to designate the role it plays in a particular form of life and does not indicate that the sentence has some particular epistemologically privileged status; its rank is purely a matter of convention.

What Rorty overlooks, however, is the important distinction between empiricism as a theory of truth and empiricism as a theory of evidence. Although truth may be a matter settled within the constraints of a theory, the question of when the belief in the truth of a statement is warranted, that is, whether there is evidence for the belief, is not just a matter of convention. Quine (and now Davidson) argues that the learning of language has, as a necessary condition, a public and shared sense of the environment. The notion of evidence to

[26]Richard Bernstein, "Philosophy in the Conversation of Mankind," *Review of Metaphysics* 33 (June 1980):757.

which they ultimately appeal is a necessary condition for people to speak the language they do. Rorty's offhanded references to the history of science alert or remind us how the internal account of factuality has changed; but the notion of evidence Quine employs is not tied to one or another scientific theory (or paradigm). Of course, what are taken to be the facts is a matter of the accepted theory. But the evidence central to the case of language learning does not depend on any particular account of the facts. Insofar as the physical sciences appeal to such a concept of evidence, they can be adjudged to have an objective evidential basis.

Briefly put, if Rorty wishes to mount an effective challenge to Quine's distinction between meaning and truth, he must show either that the notion of evidence Quine assumes (in the form of stimulus meaning) is *not* a necessary condition for communication or that we must assume the existence of a shared meaning in order to explain the possibility of communication (contra my exposition of Quine's argument for the indeterminacy thesis in Chapter 1). To simply assert, as Rorty does, that the holist assumptions rule out the notion of objective evidence to which Quine appeals is both to miss the import of the paradox of language learning and to mistake an empiricist theory of evidence for a theory of truth.[27]

Rorty believes that he can wring his brand of pragmatism from Quinean holism, but in this assumption he is mistaken. The burden of proof in this case remains with Rorty; he might be able to show that the Quinean account of evidence is mistaken, but simply confronting Quine with a holist perspective is not sufficient to show anything illicit about the theory of evidence to which Quine resorts.

## II

The problem I have been exploring is how to salvage empiricism by formulating a fact-evidence distinction that is consistent with a holist view of theories and that also preserves a theory-neutral account of evidence. My chief claim against Quine, and the focus of my efforts in reconstructing his views in this area, is that he commits himself to an

[27]This confusion is explicit, for example, in *Philosophy and the Mirror of Nature*, pp. 194–95.

unduly narrow notion of naturalism, a type of reductionism that, in fact, leaves him unable to do justice to both his empiricist tenets and his holist outlook. The requisite fact-evidence distinction can only be established, on my account, at the behavioral level.

Agreement in reactions explained by the appropriate concept of sameness of stimulation is the crucial concept for a Quinean epistemologist. Quine's proposal to provide a scientific account of the generation of science, which includes an account of how language is learned, requires an explanation of the public basis for language acquisition.[28] Yet if Quine explicates sameness of stimulus meaning at an "anontological" level and also tries to cater to his preference for physiological explanations, the public basis for language acquisition becomes inexplicable. In order to maintain that a philosophically adequate account of sameness of stimulus meaning is possible within natural science, Quine faces the following problem: either he has to make assumptions about the word-world relation which, based on other views that he holds, cannot be justified, or he has to surrender the claim that physiological explanations can accomplish his epistemological task.

The challenge facing Quine's proposal to collapse epistemology into neurophysiology can be sharpened in the following way. Quine explicitly contends that a "private language" is not possible; that is, he denies that one could develop a social form of communication epistemically based on experiences whose descriptions could be used to communicate with others and yet which a person had learned to notice without the aid of any socially acquired teachings. As Quine insists, "[language] is a social art which we all acquire on the evidence *solely* of other people's overt behavior under publicly recognizable circumstances."[29] The important point is that a private language, if such there be, would be of no interest to an epistemologist who studies how people manage to successfully communicate. If a scien-

[28]See, for example, Quine, *Ontological Relativity*, pp. 114–138; "Grades of Theoreticity," pp. 6–7; *Roots of Reference*, p. 19; *Word and Object*, p. 83.

[29]See Quine, *Ontological Relativity*, pp. 26–27 (emphasis added). The deep parallels between Quine's argument for the indeterminacy of translation and Wittgenstein's critique of the possibility of a private language are noted by Saul Kripke in *Wittgenstein: On Rules and Private Language* (Cambridge, Mass.: Harvard University Press, 1982), pp. 55–57. Kripke is, I believe, quite correct in his intuition that the two philosophers are concerned with basically the same issue.

tifically adequate account of language learning yields a view of language that is essentially private, then it fails to serve Quine's epistemological purpose.

Natural science, in order to fulfill its promise as epistemology, must enlighten us with regard to how people make shared sense of the world and the language used to discuss it. Otherwise, and despite whatever else science tells us regarding perceptual mechanisms, we remain ignorant as to why shared discourse is possible.

> The crucial logical point is that the epistemologist is confronting a challenge to natural science that arises from within natural science. The challenge runs as follows. Science itself teaches that there is no clairvoyance; . . . How, the challenge proceeds, could one hope to find out about that external world from such meager traces? In short, if our science were true, how could we know it? . . . His problem is that of finding ways, in keeping with natural science, whereby the human animal can have projected this same science from the sensory information that could reach him according to this science.[30]

In sum, the study of what humans know is to be pursued by adopting the strategy of learning how language is learned.

As noted in Section I, it is observation sentences that "afford the only entry to a language." Yet, with regard to acquiring the meaning of even an observation sentence, it is the case that "you cannot learn, ostensively, a term or observation sentence with just any stimulus meaning."[31] Rather, "any treatment of language as a natural phenomenon must start with the recognition that certain utterances are keyed to ranges of sensory stimulation patterns; and these ranges are what stimulus meanings are."[32] Observation sentences, in other words, are partially defined by their stimulus meaning. It is the stimulus meaning that provides the causal connection between language and the world. Yet, if what science seeks is to understand this causal connection as a basis for warranted belief, then what needs explaining is how people are stimulated the same. The explanation must proceed, moreover, without appeal to any assumptions regarding the word-world relationship. A failure to analyze the social basis for

[30]Quine, *Roots of Reference*, p. 2.
[31]Quine, "Grades of Theoreticity," p. 6.
[32]Quine, *Ontological Relativity*, p. 157.

sameness of stimulation would leave us without any distinctively empiricist insight into the epistemological question of how beliefs about the world gain social warrant, and so epistemology naturalized would not be capable of even answering the epistemological issue it raises. Put another way, if one subtracts Quine's account of stimulus meaning from his views on epistemology naturalized, the result is, in essence, Rorty's epistemological behaviorism.

Stimulus meanings are occurrences to and for individuals, yet these occurrences must yield a social basis for communication. To Quine's credit, he directly confronts the fact that his own account of stimulus meaning places a special burden on the naturalized epistemologist: "It seems vital that in correlating one subject's verbal behavior with another's, for instance as a basis for translating one language into another, we will be able to equate one subject's stimulation to another's. Yet how are we to do so?" And while he notes that this is rarely a practical problem, he concedes that "theory, however, must be articulate."[33] Articulation here, recall, is explanation at Quine's third level of explanation, the neurophysiological. And while Quine concedes that it is the behavioral level—the second level of explanation—that we in fact "settle for in our descriptions of language, in our formulations of language rules, and in our explication of semantical terms," he cannot rest with this sort of explanation.[34] A definition of sameness of stimulus meaning on a behavioral basis would not be the sort of explanation Quine expects from an epistemology naturalized.

What is wanted is an explanation of Quine's theory of knowledge which makes consistent his remarks about the web of belief and his remarks about there being objective evidence. When we turn to examine Quine's positive proposal, however, we find that in order for it to function as an epistemology *and* to provide the level of explanation Quine desires, his version of epistemology naturalized requires making sense of the shared world intratheoretically. Sameness of stimulus meaning is to explain why we prompt or elicit certain behavior (e.g., assent or dissent in the case of observation sentences). But "same stimulus meaning" is itself only identified, in the Quinean scheme, by

[33]Quine, ibid., pp. 157, 159–160 (see also *Roots of Reference*, p. 24); *Roots of Reference*, p. 22.

[34]Quine, "Mind and Verbal Dispositions," p. 87. See Bryan Magee, ed. *Men of Ideas* (London: BBC Pubs., 1978), p. 174, for a particularly clear statement of Quine's views on behaviorism.

reference to a behavioral criterion. What this establishes, I claim, is that the epistemological question—How do people learn to become members of their speech community?—only allows of a behavioral-level explanation. Nevertheless, the notion of there being objective evidence remains intact, because the argument for there being objective evidence depends on what is necessary in order to have a language like ours. The very ability to use a language—and so to have a knowledge—is mediated by the ability to similarly perceive a world that is, nonetheless, unknowable in itself.

## III

In the preceding section I argued that central to Quine's version of epistemology naturalized is the explication of the notion of sameness of stimulus meaning.[35] The ability to formulate answers to the epistemological questions inherent in the study of language acquisition presupposes that the relevant account of sameness can be formulated at the neurophysiological level. In this section I develop the problems latent in Quine's exposition.

The study of language learning is to clarify the notion of stimulus meaning. In particular, when it comes to teaching infants how to speak, not just any stimulus meaning will do. Quine distinguishes between episodes a subject finds *perceptually* similar and those a subject finds *receptually* similar. The former hinge only on subjective considerations; here it is appearances to the individual that count. The latter, however, are objectively based; receptual similarity is defined in terms of sameness of stimulation of nerve endings. Quine acknowledges that it is shared perceptual similarity that counts for providing meaning and evidence with whatever empirical ties they have:

> The child's success in learning . . . observation sentences depends on substantial agreement between his similarity standards and those of the adult, . . .

[35]It is worth noting that Quine's position on the notion of stimulus meaning has shifted in his writings. In, for example, *Word and Object*, pp. 44–45, "Grades of Theoreticity," pp. 3, 6, and *Ontological Relativity*, p. 87, Quine maintains that the notion of stimulus meaning can be explicated independently of any behavioral criterion. By *Roots of Reference*, however, he appears to drop this claim. I forego any analysis of the vagaries of Quine's position on this point since, on either reading of his account, my criticisms hold.

clearly, therefore, the similarity concerned here is perceptual similarity, that being fairly uniform over society. . . . The learning of an observation sentence amounts to determining, as we may say, its *similarity basis*. By this I mean the distinctive trait shared by the episodes appropriate to the observation sentence; the shared trait in which their perceptual similarity persists. [p. 43; see also pp. 39–40][36]

The shared trait common to all perceptually similar episodes Quine terms the *salient* feature of these episodes. Of course to rest the explication of the notion of evidence on an appeal to salience is to employ a "conspicuous instance of mentalistic idiom, however behavioral in intent" (pp. 33, 25). Salience, for this reason, is best understood as a "place marker." An appeal to salience signals that an area is presently unoccupied by advancing science. "Mental entities are unobjectionable if conceived as hypothetical mechanisms and posited with a view to the systematizing of physical phenomena" (pp. 33–34). Such terms are "unredeemed notes; the theory that would clear up the unanalyzed similarity notion is still to come."[37]

Sameness of stimulation must be understood not for one individual but for groups, differently oriented, over time: "Language depends on associating utterances with stimulations that can be publicly identified in their recurrences from occasion to occasion and speaker to speaker." Yet Quine is also careful to insist that the stimulations be defined in a way that is ontologically neutral—anontological.[38] Otherwise, his claim to have isolated a theory-neutral notion of evidence is inconsistent with his claim that ontological notions are theory-dependent and that reference is inscrutable. Finally, if the public basis of communication is not identified, then Quine is left with a form of linguistic solipsism which is unacceptable given the social explication sought by epistemological inquiry.

Quine's problem can be best appreciated by looking closely at his accounts of perceptual similarity and receptual similarity. These notions, Quine believes, allow him to avoid or otherwise expunge mentalistic terms from his explanations of human information processing: "Reception is flagrantly physical. But perception, for all its mentalistic overtones, is accessible to behavioral criteria. It shows itself in the

[36]In the following discussion, page references are to *Roots of Reference* unless otherwise noted.

[37]Quine, *Ontological Relativity*, p. 138.

[38]Ibid., p. 158; "Grades of Theoreticity," pp. 6–7.

conditioning of responses. . . . When conceived thus in behavioral terms, the notion of perception belongs to the psychology of learning: to the theory of conditioning, or of habit formation" (p. 4). Ideally, a Quinean epistemologist should be concerned only with the "conditions for the triggering of verbal stimulations" (p. 17); this keeps explanation in the appropriate receptual vocabulary. Perceptual similarity, in contrast with receptual, demands only behavioral conformity (p. 17); Quine understands the notions to be independent of one another (p. 16, 21). Perceptual similarity is what is critical to Quine's account of observation sentences. But since one cannot infer one type of similarity from the other, how is the Quinean epistemologist to proceed?

A salient feature, it was earlier observed, is what perceptually similar traits have in common; it is what catches the perceiver's eye, other differences notwithstanding. "Perhaps *a* is receptually more similar to *c* than to *b*; still salience has the power to swing perceptual similarity the other way" (p. 25). But the notion of salience, since it appeals to the mentalistic notion of awareness, is itself in need of purification.

Quine suggests that salience might be analyzed on the model of the mathematical notion of "neighborhood." This would allow receptual similarity to be stated in a less rigorous way than that demanded by identity of stimulations. Roughly stated, the notion of a neighborhood of points would allow Quine to establish that some specified range of stimulation patterns count as receptually similar. Perceptual similarity, in turn, would now be explicated in a way that did not appeal to strict receptual similarity but that was nonetheless expressed in terms of what is receptually specifiable (p. 17).

This suggestion is unsatisfactory for at least two reasons. First, judgments regarding perceptual similarity might shift without any corresponding change in the receptual situation. This much Quine concedes: "But perceptual similarity is not to be expected of receptually similar episodes either, because of changes in standards of perceptual similarity, changes in second-order dispositions. . . . Our trouble is that we are groping for a notion of perception just here, with no other to check against" (p. 21). This leaves Quine in the unacceptable situation where "a subject's standards of perceptual similarity are to be known only from his behavior" (p. 20); that is, sameness of stimulation, in the crucial case of explaining how observation sentences are learned, is being analyzed only by appeal to behavioral congruences.

The key notion of external stimulation has been eliminated, itself analyzed away in terms of behavior. Even worse, receptual likeness is to be discounted if it does not pass the perceptual test. Indeed, behavior, far from being "reduced" to an analysis of receptual similarity, becomes the reference point for determining if receptual similarity is relevant to the perceptual situation at hand. Since perceptual standards change with experience (p. 20), salience is subject to an ad hoc definitional standard. Such standards, needless to say, do not serve Quine's epistemological purposes.

A second problem with this use of the notion of a neighborhood is that it relativizes to the receptual standards of an individual. But individualized accounts will not do for what was earlier termed a philosophically adequate account of sameness of stimulation. In fact, Quine admits, receptual similarity is ill suited for social purposes:

> Receptual similarity was defined . . . in terms of how close the class of all the receptors that were activated in one episode came to matching the class of those activated in another episode. At that point we were thinking of the episodes and receptors as all belonging to one subject. But now we have appealed to receptual similarity between episodes *a* and *a′* of two subjects. The subjects share no receptors, so it is no longer a question of matching the two classes of receptors on the score of their sharing most of their members. . . . Vagueness mounts, since the receptors of different subjects are far from homologous. [pp. 23–24]

The notion of neighborhood will not make receptual similarity philosophically respectable, since it is unable to do without reference to a behavioral criteria. Receptual similarity, for epistemological purposes, is unable to stand alone.

Perceptual similarity was to have been explicated in terms of receptual considerations; Quine's conception of explanation in naturalized epistemology demands as much. This cannot be done straightforwardly, it turns out. Nor do the notions of salience or of a receptual neighborhood prove to be of much avail for making sameness of stimulation independent of the behavioral criterion. Indeed, even though in *Roots of Reference* Quine identifies three levels of similarity—behavioral, perceptual, and receptual (p. 21)—which roughly parallel (in terms of explanatory efficacy) his three levels of explanation, the distinctions go nowhere toward resolving his problem. Rather, they serve to emphasize that the "official" view is that behavioral explanations are considered inadequate for epistemological purposes. Analogously, it does not help to claim that talk of salience is to mark some physiological feature when there is no hint of how the feature for some one individual is to serve the social purpose for which it is required.

The conclusion that suggests itself here is that the behavioral level of explanation is as fine-grained as can be hoped for when it comes to asking for an analysis of people's shared basis of knowledge of the world. The social basis of knowledge requires, for a Quinean, sameness of stimulus meaning. But this notion, if carefully examined throughout Quine's writings, proves (again, contrary to Quine's explicit beliefs concerning what he takes himself to have established) inseparable from some behavioral element as a defining condition for sameness of stimulus meaning in the perceptually relevant sense.

There are certain parallels between the criticism I am here developing of Quine and Chomsky's classic critique of Skinner's theory of verbal behavior,[39] but the parallels between Quine and Skinner (and so the parallel between my critique and Chomsky's) are easily overestimated. Among other things, Quine does not take behavior to define or explain mental states; rather, he takes behavior to be symptomatic of a disposition, which, in turn, is to be explained in some other way—specifically, in neurophysiological terms:

> We have here an illustration of what I consider the proper function of behaviorism. Mental states and events do not reduce to behavior, nor are they explained by behavior. They are explained by neurology, when they are explained. But their behavioral adjuncts serve to specify them objectively. When we talk of mental states or events subject to behavioral criteria, we can rest assured that we are not just bandying words; there is a physical fact of the matter, a fact ultimately of elementary physical states.[40]

It is also worth noting how Quine's notion of salience distinguishes his notion of stimulus meaning from that of the classical behaviorist. Salience appeals to stimulations that are perceptually alike and relies on an anontological notion of stimulus meaning:

[39]Noam Chomsky, "Review of B. F. Skinner's *Verbal Behavior*," *Language* 35 (1959):26–58. For an informed analysis of how some of Chomsky's criticisms of Quine qua behaviorist simply miss the mark, see chap. 4 of Gibson's *The Philosophy of W. V. Quine*.

[40]Quine, "Facts of the Matter," p. 194; see also Magee, *Men of Ideas*.

> Psychologists ordinarily speak simply of the stimulus, where I am speaking of what is salient in the episode. One reason for my speaking this way is that there can be multiple salience, and in varying degrees, within an episode. In classical terms one would speak, in such a case, of simultaneous stimuli of unequal strengths. But the salience version suggests a field of gradations rather than just one or several clean cut stimuli, and this I find good. Further, the salience version encourages us to think of the overall episode as basic, and to think of its operative components or features as abstracted from these episodes by the psychologist on the basis of collations of the subjects behavior. [p. 25]

And while Quine does not specify what he means here by "clean cut" stimuli, one may take a lead from his discussion of the problems surrounding the "radical separation" of stimulus and response (p. 30). It is clear, in this context, that "clean cut" stimuli would have to be *receptually* specified, not identified ad hoc in light of behavior. Yet even ignoring all the problems noted so far with identifying "sameness of stimulation" receptually, a more fundamental difficulty looms: "clean cut" stimuli, in the desired sense, would require specification of the precise (receptually defined) worldly basis of a single sentence. And this, in turn, contradicts what the Duhem premise says (and Quine agrees) can be done. Better to speak only of an anontological "field of gradations" than to satisfy classical behaviorism at the expense of the Duhemian view of theories.

In light of the foregoing considerations, then, we must say that Quine is simply equivocating on the term "explain." If by an explanation in epistemology naturalized Quine means one that explicates the social basis of knowledge—the question Quine originally addressed—then his "elementary physical states" explains nothing. As Quine's own analysis makes perfectly plain, to insist just or primarily on receptual similarity is to block the account of shared meaning the epistemologist seeks. "Radical separation of the stimulus and response would have obstructed this account" (p. 30). But if by explanation of an individual's beliefs Quine means one in terms of the best type of scientific explanation available, then, indeed, what is wanted is just the sort of account to which he alludes. His mistake is to think that the latter type of explanation, should we have it, answers the epistemological question with which we began—the question concerning the social basis of language acquisition. The scientific type of explanation (understanding this to be Quine's third level of explanation) is a form of linguistic solipsism. And linguistic solipsism, in turn, is unacceptable, since it would generate within science precisely the type of skepticism Quine is anxious to fend off. If science is to be used to explain science, as Quine proposes, then part of what is to be accounted for is just those scientific beliefs that are objectively warranted (or, the belief in the theory that warrants the statements held true). But if the social status of the theory or of the beliefs cannot be explained, then Quine is confronted with the sort of skeptical objection he not only cannot sidestep but also cannot answer.

In the rough and ready situations of everyday life in which people learn to communicate, Quine recognizes that "radical separation" of stimulus and response proves futile. Yet our judgments regarding perceptual similarity are good enough (for evolutionary reasons?) that, for speakers and learners, the salient element is regularly reidentified. The deep problem is, not only that the idealized radical separation obstructs the account of what it is in the stimulus situation which one person shares with other members of the speech community, but also that this concern with receptual similarity proves to be irrelevant. The important point is that communication is achieved just because the differences of perspective of a receptual nature are regularly "transcended."

Ironically, the point on which I am insisting seems to be one that Quine explicitly acknowledges. The irony is that the acknowledgment brings him no recognition of the disturbing implications this concession implies for his notion of how epistemology is to be naturalized. Faced with such facts as that people's nerve endings are dissimilar, Quine sanguinely reflects that "such differences are bound to be transcended in the learning of words."[41] Indeed, just so long as we keep one eye on the environment and the other on our neighbor's behavior, most of us achieve agreement in our talk about what there is:

> Unaided by language, we might treat a great lot of sensory events as recurrences of one and the same sensation; simply because of a similarity between each event and the next; and yet there can have been a serious cumulative slippage of similarity between the latest of these events and the earliest of them. But if we have learned society's word for the sensation, the social intercourse will arrest the drift and keep us in line. We will be saved by the statistical fact that the speakers have not all drifted in the same direction.[42]

[41]Quine, "Facts of the Matter," p. 181.
[42]Ibid., p. 176.

Slippage induced by sensory considerations alone, in other words, is arrested provided that there is another's behavior to keep the aspiring conversationalist's perception of events in social line.

Before completely giving up on Quine's attempts to separate the account of the stimulus meaning of observation sentences from the behavioral criterion, one other option broached by Quine needs to be explored. In a number of places, Quine suggests that the relevant account of perceptual similarity (relevant, that is, to the epistemological issue of identifying the community basis for perceptual similarity) might be found by appealing to innate standards. These innate standards, in turn, are to be explained by the appropriate physical mechanism, evolutionarily refined.[43] Quine puts the matter as follows: "If then I say that there is an innate standard of similarity, I am making a condensed statement that can be interpreted, and truly interpreted, in behavioral terms."[44] The behavioral criterion, of course, is to be explained ultimately by appeal to the appropriate microscopic structures:

> When I posit an innate disposition I am assuming some specific though unspecified arrangement of cells or perhaps some combination of such arrangements. It could be a nerve tract or a gland. It could consist of several structures, variously situated in the organism. It could be one structure in one individual and some different structure to the same specified effect in another individual. Its innateness consists in its being complete at birth. . . . The attribution of a behavioral disposition, learned or unlearned, is a physiological hypothesis, however fragmentary. [p. 13]

Do we now have a third-level explanation that also promises to be epistemologically adequate? Do the above speculations regarding the future course of physiology solve the problem of how we are to make sense of the world people share when they learn to communicate with one another?

Suppose that scientific inquiry broke Quine's way, that the appropriate innate standard qua physiological mechanism were found. The epistemological problem would remain unsolved, at least in the terms Quine demands for its solution. The problem here is not akin, for

[43]See, for example, Quine, "Facts of the Matter," p. 179; *Ontological Relativity*, p. 126; *Roots of Reference*, p. 19.

[44]Quine, *Ontological Relativity*, p. 123.

instance, to an inverted spectrum problem; the puzzle with the Quinean scheme does not concern whether or not people, when subject to *identical* stimulations, "see the same." The puzzle, rather, concerns how it is, given different perspectives and so different stimulations altogether, that a socially relevant salient feature comes to loom on each person's perceptual horizon. Let innate standards be as alike as they can be; this alleviates the problem not a whit. The point remains that receptual considerations give way to perceptual ones. This is not a problem of seeing the same thing differently, but of seeing sameness despite differences. This notion of sameness remains explicable only insofar as one has the behavioral criterion to appeal to. Without the agreement of joint witnesses, there is no vouchsafing that the stimulations are appropriate for the job of communicating what one wants.

The fact that perceptual consensus is achieved is not a fact that the natural scientist explains. Learning to participate in this perceptual consensus is, to be sure, a process to be studied empirically: but to assume that neurophysiology holds the answer is to ignore how the question got going in the first place. The problem in Quine's exposition is this: innate standards are genuine hypotheses—have observational implications—only on the condition that they can be given a behavioral interpretation. And since innate standards are to be used in explicating perceptual similarity, there appears to be no prospect of excising the behavioral condition from the analysis.

The problem of explaining how language is learned is a problem of explaining how behavior is coordinated under certain circumstances. If the foci of the analyses become neurophysiological states, then the public character of what is learned (and so the public character of what we know) remains mysterious. Surely Quine is correct to insist that the basis of language learning is to be explained by reference to publicly shared reference points: "It is in the observational vocabulary that language makes its principal contact with experience. It is this part of language that we first learn to apply, and to which we retreat when a check point is needed."[45] Such a check point must exist, or so I have argued, if language is to serve its communicative function. Given the paradox of language learning, "somewhere there have to be nonverbal reference points, nonverbal circumstances that can be intersubjectively appreciated and associated with the appropriate utterance on the spot"

[45]Quine, "Facts of the Matter," p. 180.

(p. 37). The question I have raised—the Quinean claim on which I have sought to cast doubt—is whether it is reasonable to expect that this intersubjectively checkable point is to be best understood from the standpoint of neurophysiology. The problem is, to repeat, not that such reductions cannot be carried out, but that once carried out, the neurophysiological explanations are not suited to answer the epistemological questions.

The linguistic solipsism with which the neurophysiological account leaves us marks a critical limit of the Quinean attempt to show that science can be self-validating. Quine dreams of a science that can do what traditional epistemology failed to accomplish—validate science by showing it to be in accord with the best standards available. Against this, I have argued that the study of our shared use of language (and so of knowledge) is not only inescapably social but also irreducibly so. Our behavioral conformity is, I would like to say, empirically mediated but neurophysiologically inexplicable.

I have indicated that none of Quine's formulations succeed in making sense of "sameness of stimulus meaning" without appeal to "same behavior." Yet, if there is no defining sameness of stimulus apart from behavioral conformity, then my claim is that the behavioral criterion is shown to be fundamental *if we want to do epistemology*. Epistemology naturalized becomes epistemology socialized, that is, a study of the social and cultural conditions under which people acquire shared beliefs. As I put the complaint earlier, Quine cannot have it both ways: he cannot preserve ontological neutrality in his notion of evidence and also define sameness of stimulus meaning by appeal to nerve endings alone. Epistemology, at least for a Quinean empiricist, "looks out"—to the social conditions of knowledge. Neurophysiology "looks in"—to what is going on inside some one individual. It should come as no surprise that the object of epistemological explanation is lost when explanations are no longer behavioral but are, rather, stated in terms of the triggering of nerve endings.

One way of viewing my strategy here is as an application of Quine's own "maxim of minimum mutilation."[46] Having distinguished Quine's critical and his positive projects, and having endorsed his various critical proposals, including his theses with regard to ontology,

[46]W. V. Quine, *Philosophy of Logic* (Englewood Cliffs, N.J.: Prentice-Hall, 1970), p. 7.

I am opting for the least drastic revision within Quine's overall account. In modifying his notion of what counts as a warrant for belief, I surrender none of his critical theses and none of his empiricist tenets.

The paradox facing a Quinean naturalized epistemologist is that, if our information about the world we live in and know about is as science says, then we do not, in any scientifically explicable sense, share a world; that is, we do not share a common fund of information about which to talk. And so, just as Quine modified the Duhem premise in the face of the paradox of language learning, I propose modifying Quine's views on rational explanation. Confronted by the linguistic solipsism implied by taking to heart the third level of explanation, the analysis of knowledge becomes a question of understanding the empirical *and* social conditions under which knowledge claims are made and evaluated. The conditions for objectively warranting beliefs cannot, however, be purely social; empiricism qua theory of evidence thus retains a place. This view of evidence is what separates my epistemology socialized from Rorty's epistemological behaviorism. We return, in this way, to a Kantian picture in which the focus of epistemological inquiry is the knowing subject and not what is said to be known.[47]

[47]See Manley Thompson's discussion of these matters in "Things in Themselves," *Proceedings and Addresses of the American Philosophical Association* 57 (September 1983).

CHAPTER 3

# The Rites of Rationality

Our problem so far has been to assess what is implied by the epistemological position defended in Chapter 1. If, as just argued, Quine's version of epistemology naturalized is not a plausible interpretation of what the position implies, what is? Another line of interpretation which allegedly develops from a holist epistemology is the so-called irrationalist or anarchist position. Its chief advocates are Paul Feyerabend and Richard Rorty. In this chapter and the next I assess their views and in response develop what I call "methodological pluralism." Methodological pluralism, understood as what is implied by holism in contrast with the more extreme implications canvassed and rejected in Chapters 2–4, is the philosophical basis for the issues analyzed in the remainder of the book.

In the previous chapter, I defended a version of naturalized epistemology. Is this consistent with the epistemological position of Chapter 1? So-called anarchist or irrationalist interpretations of holism deny that it is possible to rationally favor one set of justificatory practices over any other. Hence, the sort of behavioral emphasis I advocate is inconsistent with the philosophical premises I endorse. So even if I am correct in arguing that Quine's constraints on epistemology are too rigid, even my more modest version cannot be derived from my premises. If methodological pluralism follows from holism, my naturalism cannot be part of it.

Methodological pluralism, on my account, does entail a rejection of any unity-of-method thesis. The general problem is whether any epistemology is possible if there are no absolute standards. Irrationalist responses are negative. I devote this chapter and the next to demonstrating why this response is mistaken.

I construct my particular interpretation of methodological pluralism by examining three conceptions of rational inquiry: Quine's, Feyerabend's, and Rorty's. Each addresses the traditional epistemological question of how to account for the success of science; each rejects the traditional ways of framing an answer. What unites Quine and Feyerabend is a respect for what science has accomplished and an interest in providing guidelines that will help to facilitate and perpetuate such accomplishments; what divides them is their differing beliefs about how to further scientific success.[1] I also argue that methodological pluralism is not tantamount to saying "anything goes." We should be methodological pluralists in the social sciences, I maintain, because it is in the interest of *both* freedom and knowledge to do so.

## I

What is the substance of the charge, often leveled explicitly against Feyerabend, Rorty, and Kuhn, that they are "irrationalists"? Motivating the charge, as I discuss below, is the belief that to abandon traditional epistemology is to take an irresponsibly laissez-faire view of how beliefs may be validated. (This view of the consequences of foresaking traditional epistemology parallels the complaints concerning the consequences of turning one's back on traditional morality.) Is there merit to the charge that to abandon traditional epistemology is to court a position that leaves one without anything to say about the respective merits of one or another scheme of justification?

Rational inquiry, as I understand it, is that that incorporates whatever procedures are most likely to facilitate or guarantee the achievement of one's end. Questions about rational inquiry are questions about the basis or breadth of proposed rules for guiding inference.

[1]Both Quine and Feyerabend, in turn, are at odds with Rorty just because Rorty has no interest in or concern with what science has accomplished. Rorty believes that nothing very interesting or deep can be said to explain this accomplishment. I discuss in Chapter 4 why Rorty holds this view and, moreover, why, given the reasons Rorty accepts, it is not the view he ought to hold. What is to be gained from Rorty's discussion of epistemological issues is an explanation of why there is no methodological divide between the natural and the human sciences.

Epistemology has traditionally been concerned with uncovering and critiquing such rules.

Frustration among philosophers of social science with the failure of philosophers of science to produce the requisite methodological dicta has led to skepticism about the possibility of a science of society; the pessimists suggest that the "cargo-cult view of the 'about to arrive science' just won't do."[2] My skepticism with regard to defining the notion of rationality, however, is *not* a doubt about the efficacy of science or the possibility of a social science. My question, rather, is how to function in a philosophical environment where the usual landmarks are lacking, where there is no agreed delimitation of rational procedure.

My suggestion that we should be methodological pluralists is based on a very different set of considerations than those urged by David Thomas in defense of a seemingly similar multiple-paradigm approach. Thomas is also concerned about the relation of values and rationality. His primary concern, however, is to argue that it is possible to have a naturalistic approach to the study of society and to accommodate a plurality of methods. The reasons he offers in support of this conclusion are that there is no clear separation between observational and theoretical statements and that theories are, in any case, underdetermined (so there can be logically incompatible but empirically equivalent theories):

> Two propositions of post-empiricist philosophy of science are crucial to my analysis of values and social science. First, theoretical and factual statements cannot be radically separated; that is, facts are theory-laden. Secondly, what theory we accept is underdetermined by the world. These two propositions are crucial because both are necessary for us to argue that every element of a social scientific theory is value-laden. . . . These value commitments act as an extra criterion of theory choice.
>
> . . . . .
>
> But the argument that social science is value-laden is, in fact, neutral between different possible value bases. More than that, it positively welcomes value diversity. For the values underlying different theories may direct each of them to a comprehensive analysis of some area of social reality. . . . Hence, the project, occasionally mooted, of finding a single philosophy for the study of society is intellectually misguided.

[2]P. Rabinow and W. Sullivan, eds. *Interpretive Social Science* (Berkeley: University of California Press, 1979), p. 4.

> The reason for theoretical plurality in social science deriving from its distinctive moral relevance is additional to the *a priori* point about the underdetermination of theory by the world, and to the pragmatic point that criteria of theory choice . . . are unlikely in the foreseeable future to yield unanimity in theory choice.[3]

Differing values ensure different initial assumptions among researchers; underdetermination permits logically incompatible theories to account for the available data. The result is multiple research paradigms for the study of human behavior.

My complaint against Thomas is that his analysis does not accurately assess the philosophical situation. It is not just that differing values make multiple paradigms possible; the whole question is what is to count as a *rational* method. Indeed, his remarks on paradigms betray a naive belief in a unity of method across paradigms:

> My rough, working definition makes less the notion of a paradigm equivalent to the central concepts and ideas of a scientific theory. It would be wrong to include what I have called methodological elements within this notion. For methodology—the principles of scientific reasoning and validation—is not specific to any particular paradigm. Indeed, if we are to have principles which at least in part determine choices between paradigms, then these will be drawn from general scientific methodology.[4]

Thomas, in effect, accepts the unity-of-method thesis; the syntax of justification remains the same across paradigms. As I have argued, however, it is precisely this point that has been thrown into question. The rejection of meaning realism and the acceptance of holism force on us the question of just what sense to make of the notion of rationality.

To even suggest that there exists a problem about standards of rationality such as has been discussed, however, is considered by some people tantamount to abandoning the claim that there are any guidelines for rational inquiry.[5] With regard to the philosophers with whom

[3]David Thomas, *Naturalism and Social Science: A Post-Empiricist Philosophy of Social Science* (Cambridge: Cambridge University Press, 1979), pp. 126, 148–149; see also 149–151 and 161–180.

[4]Ibid., pp. 162–163.

[5]A recent instance is David Stove, *Popper and After: Four Modern Irrationalists* (New York: Pergamon, 1982). For a number of references to similar criticisms of Feyerabend et al., see those cited (and responded to) by Feyerabend in "Conversations

I am concerned—Quine, Feyerabend, and Rorty—the charge of irrationalism seems to arise in at least two ways. In one case, critics such as David Stove are perplexed by the fact that Feyerabend and Kuhn deny what he takes to be obvious—that scientific knowledge is cumulative.[6] Stove correctly perceives that this denial is intimately linked with a holist view of theories; hence Quine comes in for criticism.[7] The other problem is that holism denies that there is any special epistemic license for our rules of inference; holism also seems to preclude telling the sort of story about the development of science which Stove deems appropriate and correct. Since Quine et al. deny what Stove takes to be obvious, they are irrational. Put another way, Stove's position appears to be that if our knowledge claims are only historical accidents, then this is tantamount to denying that rules of inference have any special legitimacy and so is equivalent to denying that rational thought is somehow special or privileged. Reason rules by divine right or it does not rule at all. (Stove, like Thomas, assumes that canons of justification remain unchanged; the error of modern irrationalists is one of confusing changes of content with questions concerning the syntax of justification in the sciences. The latter, Stove seems to believe, is not subject to the whims of history as is the former.)

Kuhn and Feyerabend have led the assault on the belief that scientific knowledge is cumulative; Quine and Rorty have argued that we are unable to justify as incorrigible any of our beliefs, including our confidence in our canons of justification. The former pair relativize scientific knowledge; the latter two relativized our standards of inference and evaluation. It is the historicizing of seeming certainties by these thinkers which has engendered the wrath of their fellow professionals.

What I find most interesting about the charge of irrationalism against Feyerabend, Rorty, and Quine is the extent to which it echoes the charge that Socrates "makes the weaker argument defeat the stronger." Stove claims that it is by clever rhetorical strategies that the irrationalists make their points. He wonders how "these writers succeeded in making irrationalism about science acceptable to readers,

with Illiterates," *Science in a Free Society* (London: New Left Books, 1978). A sympathetic discussion of Feyerabend's position which appropriately downplays the charges of irrationalism is Denise Russell's "Anything Goes," *Social Studies of Science* 13 (1983):437–464.

[6]Stove, *Popper and After*, p. 1.

[7]Stove, ibid., p. 35.

most of whom would reject it out of hand if it were presented to them without disguise."[8] Feyerabend et al. purvey this beguiling, dangerous doctrine by making acceptable doctrines that are, on the face of it, unacceptable. Thus they are guilty of making weak—indeed absurd—arguments appear the stronger—or at least plausible to the unwary.

In what follows, I examine an interpretation of Socrates' reply to his accusers, in particular, his failure to explicitly reply (in the *Apology*) to the charge that he makes the weaker argument defeat the stronger. The interpretation I offer here provides a framework by which to understand the charge of irrationalism discussed so far. The line of interpretation I develop draws on an inspired reading of the *Apology* offered by Alexander Sesonske.[9]

Sesonske notes that, of the various charges pressed against Socrates at his trial, the only charge to which Socrates does not directly reply is the charge that he (Socrates) makes the weaker argument defeat the stronger (p. 222). Before asking just what the significance of this omission is, we need to determine the precise nature of the charge against Socrates. The force of this indictment stems from differences in intellectual style characteristic of literate and preliterate societies. The point here is, not to postulate some distinction in kind between the domesticated and the savage mind, but to speculate about what significant differences arise between learning dependent on memorization (characteristic of preliterate cultures) and learning that allows perusal of texts (where what is asserted is preserved and so subject to recurrent scrutiny). This contrast is important, as Havelock, Goody, Watt, and Sesonske have all noted, because what is involved are differing accounts of knowing and what counts as acceptable argument or proof. The transition from preliterate to literate culture is one from identifying knowledge with rote or brute memorization to equating knowledge

[8]Stove, ibid., p. viii.

[9]Alexander Sesonske, "To Make the Weaker Argument Defeat the Stronger," *Journal of the History of Philosophy* 3 (July 1968):217–231. Page references in the remainder of this section are to Sesonske's work. Issues relevant to my concerns here are further illuminated in Jack Goody and Ian Watt, "The Consequences of Literacy," *Comparative Studies in Society and History* 5 (1962–63):304–345 and in Goody, *The Domestication of the Savage Mind* (Cambridge: Cambridge University Press, 1977). Sesonske's analysis, however, is specifically indebted to Eric Havelock's work. See, in particular, Havelock's *Preface to Plato* (Cambridge, Mass.: Belknap Press of Harvard University Press, 1963), and his essays collected in *The Literate Revolution in Greece and Its Cultural Consequences* (Princeton, N.J.: Princeton University Press, 1982).

with what survives critical scrutiny and examination by abstract standards:

> The development of literacy frees the mind from this massive task of memorization. Its energies may now be used to develop and practice other modes in which the object known is distinct from the knower and can be dispassionately viewed—in short, critical inquiry and analysis, the modes of thought which Socrates and Plato pursued in Athens. In a pre-literate community, the occurrence of a question is an occasion for the exercise of memory. . . . But with literacy a new technique disputes the propriety of the old; a problem may be met by working out the solution in abstract thought. The full utilization of this technique requires a new form of education, though, with memorization being supplemented or replaced by a method which fosters the understanding of abstract terms . . . a method which teaches men 'to think about what they say, instead of just saying it.' [p. 223; see also p. 228][10]

If Havelock et al. are correct not only about the differences in argumentation and education between preliterate and literate societies but also in their suggestion that Socrates/Plato is a central figure in the Greek transition in this area, then the charge against Socrates is symptomatic of a general problem concerning the nature of justification.

Socrates, his accusers charge, is guilty of deception; yet they cannot say just how. This is not surprising, for, as anyone who has studied Plato's dialogues appreciates, the arguments Socrates characteristically develops are, at least, prima facie logical. Yet, ironically, if it is by virtue of their logic that his arguments are compelling, then that is also their problem—for such arguments are not (yet, anyway) recognized as legitimate. Indeed, they can hardly be understood as arguments, for the canons for articulating such arguments are still in the process of being formulated; it was not, as we now know, until Aristotle that any canons of logic achieved articulation.

> We must, then, try to state what 'strength' in argument would be for those who accuse Socrates. It will not do to say 'persuasiveness,' for what men are persuaded by will differ with their modes of thought. . . .
>
> A strong argument for any man will at least be one he seems to understand, one couched in familiar terms that he can comprehend and proceeding in patterns he recognizes as appropriate to the subject at hand. Assuming that

[10]In addition, see Goody, *Domestication*, esp. chap. 3; Goody and Watt, "Consequences," p. 311.

> Socrates' accusers were men still close to the oral tradition, we can say what such argument would be for them. . . . In an oral culture the wise man earns that name through his power of memory and speech. He is the man who most completely and readily recalls the poetic narrative with which the tradition is retained. [p. 224]

The problem faced by Socrates, then, is to account for why his arguments compel assent and yet do not belong to the recognized repertoire of argument forms. "In these terms the claim that someone 'makes the weaker argument defeat the stronger' asserts that the accused speaks in terms and forms quite different from those familiar to the tradition, *and yet somehow compels* assent. All of Plato's early dialogues proclaim that this was true of Socrates!" (p. 224).

Socrates makes the weaker argument defeat the stronger by forcing his interlocutors to agree to arguments that, inevitably and understandably, they find unpersuasive. They are unpersuasive because they are not part of the standard stock of accepted modes of argument; they compel assent because those whom Socrates questions cannot find exceptions or objections to his reasoning.

> For in their step-by-step procedure Socrates' arguments have a *logical strength* that even the most analytically untrained mind must feel. However, the argument is completely unpersuasive; the conclusion cannot be believed even though it cannot be denied. It wholly lacks the persuasive psychological strength of the traditional wisdom. Hence, Meletus' reluctance to answer, hence the shouted interruptions by the crowd; and hence the charge that Socrates makes the weaker argument defeat the stronger. [p. 228]

Socrates' ability to make the novel overthrow the accepted without anyone understanding how or why this should be is, then, the substance of the charge against him.

The suggestion is that the charge against Socrates is actually based on his introduction of abstract modes of reasoning, modes characteristic of a literate society, into a preliterate society that does not recognize the acceptability of such modes. This point, if correct, allows us to explain Socrates' otherwise puzzling silence with respect to this charge. For Socrates, ever the teacher, takes the opportunity of his trial to construct a test for his jurors. The test is whether or not the jury is prepared to distinguish between logic and rhetoric, between what compels assent although unfamiliar and what is persuasive because part of the established repertoire. The issue to be decided is no less than that of choosing the basis on which to validate beliefs. To pass the test, the jury must agree to change the going standard.

The test is formulated with characteristic irony and literary skill; for Socrates' defense against this charge is, in effect, to turn the charge against his accusers, that is, to suggest that they seek to make the weaker argument defeat the stronger.

> Socrates' response to the charge is, as we have seen, first to define his trial as a confrontation of linguistic forms and to make a counter charge, i.e., the *same* charge, but understood in what I have called Platonic terms. The contest is between truth and persuasion, but the jury must decide which form of speech expresses truth and *then accept this as the basis of belief*. The question with which Plato's Socrates faces Athens is: have you so learned the lesson that I teach that you now recognize the strength of abstract argument and *believe* in its conclusions?
>
> . . . . .
>
> In his first words Socrates testifies to the persuasiveness of his accusers. And in his defense he takes great care not to compete with them on this ground. Here we have an explanation for the suicidal tone. Socrates' speech is not devoid of persuasive devices, but all of them are used to weigh the psychological balance against himself. His stance before the jury is: I have told you the truth; I have replied to the charges. . . .
>
> The irony then is that in his defense Socrates does his best to make the weaker argument defeat the stronger. He builds the logically weak case of his accusers to maximum psychological strength, leaves his defense with mere unpersuasive truth to recommend it; then says, "Now judge!" [pp. 230–231]

What I take to be particularly significant about the charge against Socrates is that it highlights the following state of affairs: if accepted criteria of knowledge or reasoning are challenged, one likely response is the charge that the challenger is engaging in some form of intellectual nihilism or deceit. (Socrates, of course, was also charged with corrupting the youth.)

Turning back to Stove's book, one notes that despite his witty and amusing fulminations against those he identifies as irrationalists, Stove is at a loss to explain why anyone would believe such a position. His clever stylistic parodies, his suggestion that a rather "frivolous" and "harmless" skepticism underlies the apparent challenge by Popper et al. to traditional philosophy of science,[11] is evidence that he simply cannot make sense of the changes in rational evaluation these proposals seem to involve. Indeed, my suggestion is that nothing less is at stake here than a change in the repertoire of accepted modes of evaluation.

## II

A positive aspect of the thesis of methodological pluralism, as I formulate it, is that it maximizes opportunities for humans to exercise freedom of thought. I show this by developing a basic parallel between the open-ended notion of rationality I am supporting and John Stuart Mill's notion of liberty. My claim is that the problem Mill develops with respect to perpetuating liberty in a society, namely, the question of how to balance constraint and experimentation, is precisely the problem with which thoughtful individuals are now faced with respect to the notion of rationality. For the study of human behavior, I suggest that there is, at best, a blurred distinction between what is rational (on what bases we should accept statements as true) and what is moral (what we ought to do).

Methodological pluralism, or my version of it, is also similar to Mill's position insofar as there is an absence of clear guidelines just where one believes such guidelines are needed. Mill's position demands a tolerance for self-regarding actions and also mandates that there be no harm to others; yet Mill offers no fixed procedure for distinguishing illicitly harmful from self-regarding actions. Similarly, both Quine and Feyerabend urge that we promote those scientific methods that have helped our science achieve its notable successes. Yet they deny that there is any fixed procedure by which to do this; even worse, they strongly disagree among themselves, or so it appears, with respect to what position one should contingently adopt.

The problem, in short, is that the Quine-Feyerabend view of rationality is anomic; it precludes the formulation of a definitive criterion for separating the rational and the irrational. This view is not, however, to be confused with the denial that there exists such a distinction. Central to assessing their views is discerning how one can deny that

[11] Stove, *Popper and After*, pp. 19–20; 101ff.

there is a fixed rational standard and yet retain a belief that there is some sense to be made of the notion of rational inquiry. The question of whether we are intellectually eviscerated by rejecting absolutist epistemology is the issue I explore below.

What little Quine has to say directly about rationality and rational inquiry belies the radical implications of his views which others have seized upon and developed. The point of science, on Quine's account, is to help us anticipate experience: "Our overall scientific theory demands of the world only that it be so structured as to assure the sequences of stimulation that our theory gives us to expect. More concrete demands are empty."[12] The standards of scientific justification are, as was discussed in Chapter 2, also the criteria of rational justification.

Even though Quine identifies justification with the going scientific standards, he attaches no cosmic significance to these standards. The standards recommend themselves insofar as they allow us to anticipate what will happen next. Yet should some alternative scheme, radically unlike the science we know (say, employing ouija boards), prove more accurate, then, Quine suggests, we would replace science, and so change our whole notion of rational justification, to incorporate the more efficacious standards:

> Experience might still take a turn that would justify [the skeptic's] doubts about external objects. Our success in predicting observations might fall off sharply, and concomitantly with this we might begin to be somewhat successful in basing predictions upon dreams or reveries. At that point we might reasonably doubt our theory of nature in even fairly broad outline.[13]
>
> The utility of science, from a practical point of view, lies in fulfilled expectation: true prediction.[14]

What determines reasonableness is adherence, not to timeless standards, but to whatever rules abet our intellectual goals (in this case, successful prediction). The traditional distinction between observa-

[12] W. V. O. Quine, *Theories and Things* (Cambridge, Mass.: Belknap Press of Harvard University Press, 1981), p. 22.

[13] Ibid., p. 22.

[14] W. V. O. Quine, "The Nature of Natural Knowledge," in *Mind and Language*, ed. S. Guttenplan (Oxford: Clarendon Press, 1975), p. 68.

tional and theoretical entities is not a concern for Quine; he accepts the going account of scientific evidence for the same reason that he celebrates scientific method. What remains untouched by revisionist histories of science is the success of science as a predictive device. It is this success that impresses Quine, and because it is successful he is curious to see, granted the epistemological limitations, how one can help perpetuate such an enterprise.

Quine speculates that the success of science is due to its "tunnel vision," to its relentless pursuit of the experimental paths opened by the sciences' way of looking at the world:

> What wants recognizing is that a physical theory of radically different form than ours, with nothing even recognizably similar to our quantification or objective reference, might still be empirically equivalent to ours, in the sense of predicting the same episodes of sensory bombardment on the strength of the same past episodes. Once this is recognized, the scientific achievement of our culture becomes in a way more impressive than ever. For, in the midst of all this formless freedom for variation, our science has developed in such a way as to maintain always a manageably narrow spectrum of visible alternatives among which to choose when the need arises to revise a theory. It is this narrowing of sights, or tunnel vision, that has made for the continuity of science, through the vicissitudes of refutation and correction.[15]

It is this pragmatic view of the purpose of science, together with his conservative intuitions regarding the reasons for the success of science, which leads Quine to see scientific theory as definitive of rational inquiry and knowledge.

In contrast to Popper and (sometimes) Feyerabend, Quine is inclined to a cautious approach to revision of scientific theory. Where revision of theory is called for, he advocates a "maxim of minimum mutilation,"[16] which counsels revising only those tenets that have the least effect on other beliefs. Quine favors conservative, incremental shifts over bold new conjectures; scientific procedure, as he understands it, works best that way.

> Familiarity of principle is what we are after when we contrive to "explain" new matters by old laws. . . . Familiarity of principle also figures when "unex-

[15]Ibid., p. 81.

[16]W. V. O. Quine, *The Philosophy of Logic* (Englewood Cliffs, N.J.: Prentice-Hall, 1970), p. 7.

pected observations" (i.e., ultimately, some undesirable conflict between sensory conditionings as mediated by the interanimation of sentences), prompt us to revise an old theory; the way in which familiarity of principle then figures is in favoring minimum revision.

The helpfulness of familiarity of principle for the continuing activity of the creative imagination is a sort of paradox. Conservatism, a favoring of the inherited or invented conceptual scheme of one's own previous work, is at once the counsel of laziness and a strategy of discovery. Note, though, the important normative difference between simplicity and conservatism. Whenever simplicity and conservatism are known to counsel opposite courses, the verdict of conscious methodology is on the side of simplicity. Conservatism is nevertheless the preponderant force, but no wonder: it can still operate when stamina and imagination fail.[17]

We cannot, however, infer from the predictive success of science to the conclusion that its model corresponds to the world it is about. There is no point of cosmic exile that licenses such a conclusion. Quine counsels defining rational inquiry by reference to accepted procedure and adopting a generally conservative posture toward proposed revisions. The criteria of rational inquiry are vouchsafed, then, by the assumption that they promote scientific success. Should greater success come from other means, then these means would be the rational path (and, presumably, the standard of rationality) to adopt.

What is striking and exceedingly original in Quine's stance is that his approach to the question of accounting for the status of reasoning patterns is fundamentally different from philosophers, such as Frege, Russell, and Carnap, who otherwise share his interest in and respect for formal logic. These three made epistemology a handmaiden to their intuitions concerning the nature of logic. Logical form, one might say, provided them an unquestioned metaphysical basis on which explanations were to be formed; considerations based on matters of logical form, in turn, determined the demands ontology, metaphysics, and epistemology had to satisfy.[18] Quine, in contrast to this approach, reads the nature of logic from his epistemology; logic, on his account, is one more feature of our scientific worldview for which we require a scientific accounting.

The foregoing sketch of Quine's position is sufficient to indicate why

[17]Quine, *Word and Object* (Cambridge, Mass.: M.I.T. Press, 1960), pp. 20–21.

[18]I discuss in greater detail the significance of Quine's orientation on this point in "On Missing Neurath's Boat," *Synthese* 61 (1984):205–231.

he is untroubled by the relativist-historicist implications of his holist view. Rational rules are meant to serve a particular purpose, the promotion and perpetuation of useful patterns of inference (e.g., predictions), and his epistemological position retains just that critical feature. There is no need to make the rules timeless in order to make them useful and rational.

Feyerabend, like Quine, is basically concerned to discern those methodological processes that promise to help perpetuate successful inference, in particular, successful development in the sciences. But Feyerabend and Quine differ, and crucially so, in their reading of the historical data and the lessons concerning scientific method to be drawn from this data. Whereas Quine, as noted above, attributes the success of science to its tunnel vision, its relentless pursuit of a particular methodological strategy, Feyerabend insists, not contradicting Quine but adding to his emphasis on tenacity, that the strategy that promotes our ability to better anticipate experience is the strategy that encourages *several* theories to pursue their goals using the tunnel vision Quine celebrates.

Feyerabend is concerned to promote the growth of our ability to cope with the world, and he has definite views on how this ability is best enhanced. Whatever the field of inquiry is, he insists that "knowledge is obtained from a proliferation of views rather than from the determined application of a preferred ideology."[19] Feyerabend is not rejecting the idea that people should be rational; he is, rather, attempting to redefine what counts as an appropriate strategy to the end of obtaining various goals. He urges, against the tradition, that the identification of rationality as such with scientific method is a perversion of the notion, a misidentification of the necessary conditions for increasing our ability to better get about in the world: "It is possible to *retain* what one might call the freedom of artistic creation *and to use it to the full*, not just as a road of escape but as a necessary means for discovering and perhaps even changing the features of the world we live in. This coincidence of the part (individual man) with the whole (the world we live in), of the purely subjective and arbitrary with the objective and lawful, is one of the most important arguments in favour of a pluralistic methodology."[20]

[19]Paul Feyerabend, *Against Method: Outline of an Anarchist Theory of Knowledge* (London: New Left Books, 1975), p. 52.

[20]Ibid., pp. 52–53.

As previously noted, Quine stresses that tenacity is a central element in the success of science. Feyerabend, I hasten to add, does not dispute this. Indeed, he celebrates this point in the form of his "principle of tenacity."[21] Yet Feyerabend is wont to give greater emphasis to the changing tide of fortune that has beset any number of theories; so, in addition to tenacity, he promotes what he calls his "principle of proliferation," which emphasizes the importance in the history of science of the clash of theories. He does not claim to show that proliferation guarantees progress, but rather that it previously has and that there is no good reason to now claim that proliferation is outmoded or unnecessary as a methodological strategy. "My arguments are rather of a negative kind, they show that reason and science *cannot exclude* such a plurality."[22] Plurality cannot be excluded, because the human intellect in general, and scientific thought in particular, will presumably continue fruitfully to violate accepted methodological norms.

Feyerabend's view of rationality is caught in what, in light of the earlier discussion of Socrates' defense in the *Apology*, might be called the Socratic paradox. On the one hand, if Feyerabend attempts to argue for his pluralistic case by sticking to the conventions of the accepted repertoire, then his strategy will be a symptom of the disease it is intended to cure. Feyerabend, I believe, recognizes this, and he attempts to "play" with the usual conventions of philosophical argument;[23] he mixes, for example, reductio arguments, historical analyses, autobiographical insights, and ridicule among his rhetorical strategies in the course of his writings. Still, on the other hand, if he makes his own argument an example of the cause he is promoting (as I believe he has tried to do), it will not be accepted as legitimate (because he is not playing the game by the usual rules). Feyerabend recognizes the paradox but, I suggest, does not discern an escape. Thus it is a question of how he can succeed in persuading his audience without surrendering the very point he wants to make. (Indeed, as I argue in the next chapter, Rorty is also caught in this paradox, and his arguments are vitiated by his failure to recognize this fact.)

[21]See, for example, Paul Feyerabend, *Problems of Empiricism: Collected Papers*, vol. 2 (Cambridge: Cambridge University Press, 1981), pp. 137–140; see also his "Outline of a Pluralist Theory of Knowledge and Action," in *Planning for Diversity and Choice* (Cambridge, Mass.: M.I.T. Press, 1968), p. 280.

[22]Feyerabend, *Science in a Free Society*, p. 148.

[23]See especially *Against Method*, p. 30.

The solution to the paradox lies, for Feyerabend as for Socrates, in inducing one's audience to alter how it thinks about rational inquiry. A case for redefining rationality as Feyerabend does is developed by appreciating the parallels between his thought and Mill's (at least the Mill of *On Liberty*). Feyerabend's account of rationality is to be preferred, in short, because it holds greater promise for human development without sacrificing what is desirable in the notion of rationality as defined by standards.[24]

Mill remarks at the beginning of Chapter 5 of *On Liberty* that he has devoted his efforts to clarifying "the two maxims which together form the entire doctrine of this essay." These are "first, that the individual is not accountable to society for his actions in so far as these concern the interest of no person but himself. . . . Secondly, that for such actions as are prejudicial to the interests of others, the individual is accountable and may be subjected either to social or legal punishment if society is of the opinion that the one or the other is requisition for its protection."[25]

Briefly stated, I take Feyerabend's view to be that the philosophical (and the scientific) establishment has too high a regard for the ensconced standards of scientific reasoning. The result is to identify rational inquiry with adherence to these standards. Conformity is demanded at the risk of being branded irrational. But this coercive approach to rationality is a confusion of genuine self-regarding actions, that is, actions reasoned according to one's idiosyncratic notions of what ought to be looked into and how, and actions that are prejudicial to the interest of others. In other words, Feyerabend wants to insist that reasoning be regarded more like a self-regarding action—except (as he makes quite clear) should actual harm be threatened. It is interesting and important to note that Feyerabend explicitly distinguishes his epistemological anarchy from any violent, political kind and forcefully endorses a version of Mill's principle prohibiting harm

[24]Discussions with Robert Barrett have greatly enhanced my understanding of Feyerabend's "positive" position. However, Barrett is in no way responsible for any of the ideas I develop here. Although Feyerabend has long stressed his appreciation of and debt to John Stuart Mill's *On Liberty*, my own analysis is, so far as I know, the first attempt to exploit this parallel in explicating Feyerabend's position. A brief appreciation of the parallel and its significance for Feyerabend is offered by Robin Horton, "Tradition and Modernity Revisited," in *Rationality and Relativism* (Cambridge, Mass.: M.I.T. Press, 1982), pp. 224–226.

[25]John Stuart Mill, *On Liberty* (Indianapolis, Ind.: Hackett, 1978), p. 93.

to others.[26] Most of Feyerabend's effort, however, is devoted to arguing that there is no good reason to insist that being rational be equated with toeing a particular logical line. The efficacy of reasoning is best judged (and, if Feyerabend is right, has always been judged) by its results. Thus, experimentation in modes of reasoning should be tolerated just as experimentation in modes of living should be tolerated, for this is most likely to lead to the best results for people both individually and collectively.

This way of putting the matter sharpens the Socratic paradox noted earlier, for one is inclined to think that to liken reasoning to a self-regarding action is to destroy the purpose of rational standards. The value of objective standards that apply generally is to further inquiry. Feyerabend's claim is that people ought to recognize that one may learn by changing the rules as well as by following them. The lesson to be learned is not to disdain standards but to recognize their limits. Feyerabend views rules of reasoning on analogy with act utilitarians' moral rules:

(Incidentally, it should be pointed out that my frequent use of such words as 'progress', 'advance', 'improvement', etc., does not mean that I claim to possess special knowledge about what is good and what is bad in the sciences and that I want to impose this knowledge upon my readers. *Everyone can read the terms in his own way* and in accordance with the tradition to which he belongs. . . . *And my thesis is that anarchism helps to achieve progress in any one of the senses one cares to choose.* Even a law-and-order science will succeed only if anarchistic moves are occasionally allowed to take place.)[27]

For nobody can say in abstract terms, without paying attention to idiosyncrasies of person and circumstances, what precisely it was that led to progress in the past, and nobody can say what moves will succeed in the future.[28]

The idea that science can and should be run according to some fixed rules, and that its rationality consists in agreement with such rules, is both unrealistic and vicious. It is unrealistic, since it takes too simple a view of the talents of men and of the circumstances which encourage, or cause, their development. And it

[26]See, for example, "Against Method," *Minnesota Studies in the Philosophy of Science*, vol. 4 (1970), p. 104 n. 33.

[27]Feyerabend, *Against Method*, p. 27.

[28]Feyerabend, "Against Method," pp. 19–20.

is vicious, since the attempt to enforce the rules will undoubtedly erect barriers to what men might have been, and will reduce our humanity by increasing our professional qualifications.[29]

The notion that human well-being is improved by adherence to scientific method as we presently understand it is, on Feyerabend's analysis, historically inaccurate and fraught with politically undesirable consequences. With respect to the latter point, the adulation accorded scientific method justifies, Feyerabend argues, cultural elitism and a disrespect for those who wish to live their lives another way, for example, rejecting conventional medicine in favor of some other form of treatment.[30] Feyerabend would permit forms of nonstandard treatment—laetrile or voodoo, for instance.

Feyerabend does not claim that advances and breakthroughs made by scientists have been to no good effect. The issue is rather whether the reason for these achievements is that one particular method was followed. In short, on Feyerabend's view, people have drawn the wrong lessons from the success of science. The mistaken lesson is that these procedures have universal applicability:

But on page 32 of AM [*Against Method*] I say quite explicitly that 'my intention is not to replace one set of general rules by another such set: my intention is to convince the reader that *all methodologies, even the most obvious ones, have their limits*' or, to express it in terms just explained my intention is to show that idealism, whether of the simple or of the context-dependent kind, is the wrong solution for the problems of scientific rationality. These problems are not solved by a change of standards but by taking a different view of rationality altogether.[31]

Of course, we may one day find a rule that helps us through all difficulties just as we may one day find a theory that can explain everything in our world. . . . The point is that the development *has not yet started: today* we have to do science without being able to rely on any well defined and stable 'scientific method.'

The remarks made so far do not mean that research is arbitrary and unguided. There are standards, but they come from the research process itself, not from abstract views of rationality.[32]

[29]Ibid., p. 91.
[30]See, for example, *Problems of Empiricism*, vol. 2, pp. 28–30.
[31]Feyerabend, *Science in a Free Society*, p. 32.
[32]Ibid., p. 99.

I argue that all rules have their limits, I do not argue that we should proceed without rules. . . . In my polemics I neither want to eliminate rules, nor do I want to show their worthlessness. My intention is, rather, to expand the inventory of rules and also to suggest a new use for all of them. It is this *use* that characterizes my position and not any particular rule-*content*.[33]

As these remarks make plain, there are definite standards operating "locally" and there are bases for making judgments as to which sets of rules are better or worse. What the "different view of rationality" Feyerabend endorses promises is that, in proceeding from one context of inquiry to another, there is no universal, surefire method to be applied. There exists no cookbook account of rationality on which to draw. We do not, of course, play dumb when faced with a new situation; nothing Feyerabend says counsels forgetting what one has previously learned. Just as people ought to be permitted to experiment with various ways of living their lives, including being allowed to make their own mistakes, so reasoners ought to be allowed to play with different styles. Fruitless options will be chosen, but there is no guard against that in any case.[34]

The goal is not to forego a concern with rationality, but to recognize the limits of any attempt to explicate the term. It is instructive, in this respect, to compare remarks by Feyerabend and Quine:

Epistemology is sick, it must be cured, and the medicine is anarchy. Now medicine is not something one takes all the time. One takes it for a certain period of time, *and then one stops*. . . . *Today* epistemology is sick and in need of a medicine. The medicine is anarchism. Anarchism, I say, will heal epistemology and *then* we may return to a more enlightened and more liberal form of rationality.[35]

For, in the midst of all this formless freedom for variation, our science has developed in such a way as to maintain always a manageably narrow spectrum of visible alternatives among which to choose when need arises to revise a theory. It is this narrowing of sights, or tunnel vision, that has made for the continuity of science, through the vicissitudes of refutation and correction.

[33]Ibid., p. 164. For related remarks, see ibid., pp. 64–65, 145–146; "Against Method," pp. 100–101 n. 27; *Against Method*, pp. 179–180.

[34]Compare what Feyerabend says about the lack of fixed standards of reasoning at "Against Method," p. 22, and what he says about proliferation as "the solution to the problem of life" on page 28 of that essay. The parallel with Mill is quite clear.

[35]Feyerabend, *Science in a Free Society*, p. 127.

And it is this also that has fostered the illusion of there being only one solution to the riddle of the universe.[36]

Because Quine celebrates normal science, the more radical implications of his positions on this point have not been much remarked upon. Feyerabend's challenge comes in more eye-catching verbal dress than Quine's, but the bare doctrine is the same. Rationality is still identified with method, but the notion of method now proves to be Protean. Significant differences remain, however. For Feyerabend, constant change and challenge to existing standards are to be encouraged; for Quine, changes are expected, but normal science remains the method of choice, pending revision.

Intellectual inquiry is now to be understood as a self-regarding action, and so to be left from coercive conformity. Alasdair MacIntyre puts the matter well when he remarks:

What Polanyi has shown is that all justification takes place within a social tradition and that the pressures of such a tradition enforce often unrecognized rules by means of which discrepant pieces of evidence or difficult questions are often put on one side with the tacit assent of the scientific community. . . . (Paul Feyerabend—at first sight so different from Polanyi—agrees with Polanyi in his understanding of tradition. It is just because he so understands the scientific tradition that he rejects it and has turned himself into the Emerson of the philosophy of science; not "Every man his own Jesus," but "Every man his own Galileo.")[37]

What is important is that Feyerabend (and surely Quine) do *not* have Nietzschean aspirations for humans. If the statement "Every man his own Galileo" is read in a Nietzschean way, then Feyerabend appears to be advocating that each person reinvent the logical wheel (just as the Ubermensch is to reinvent morality). Yet the passage just quoted from *Science in a Free Society* clearly suggests that a rather different reading may be distilled from Feyerabend's remarks. As I read Feyerabend here, the lesson is certainly not to cease rule following or to abandon methods found fruitful. Anarchy, Feyerabend insists, is a medicine to

[36]Quine, "The Nature of Knowledge," p. 81.

[37]Alasdair MacIntyre, "Epistemological Crises, Dramatic Narrative, and the Philosophy of Science," in *Paradigms and Revolutions*, ed. Gary Gutting (Notre Dame, Ind.: University of Notre Dame Press, 1980), p. 67.

counteract possible methodological stiffening of the mind. Experimentation and constraint exist, for purposes of rational thought, in an uncertain balance.

Feyerabend's attention is focused rather exclusively on an aspect of the *Rationalitätstreit* which has been waged between Popperians and non-Popperians in the natural sciences. The issue is the status of what Kuhn calls "normal science"; even renegade Popperians such as Feyerabend believe that nonrevolutionary but fruitful science does not follow the Kuhnian pattern. All proper science is a Kuhnian revolution writ small, since what is to be striven for is the falsification of existing beliefs.[38] Whatever the merits of this dispute, it should be noted that the social sciences are a natural area in which to apply Feyerabend's views on rationality (and, of course, Quine's views on meaning). Social scientists are apt to bewail the plurality of paradigms already present in their various disciplines as indicative of a deep *problem* within their field (see Chapter 5). But if my distillation and synthesis of Feyerabend and Quine is correct, then this lack of methodological unity is not a problem.

The basic parallel between liberty and rationality suggested by my analysis and my corresponding doubts about a need for a unified notion of method in the social sciences is echoed in the works of other commentators on the social sciences. For example, Brian Fay, in his thoughtful and provocative *Social Theory and Political Practice*, applies a perspective explicitly informed by Feyerabendian considerations on the relation of theory and practice to his (Fay's) study of the politics of policy science:

> Perhaps the most important point for my purposes is that Feyerabend believes that there is an ideological ingredient in any large-scale theory or basic paradigm. . . . It is in this spirit that he himself discusses the effects of a positivist metatheory of science and epistemology on human communication as well as focusing attention on the social importance of the principle of proliferation which derives from his 'anarchist epistemology.'
>
> . . . . .
>
> For what I am doing . . . is attempting to describe and analyse *the political commitments of the global paradigm which, among other things, seek to give*

[38]Most of the criticisms of Kuhn contained in the much-cited I. Lakatos and A. Musgrave, eds., *Criticism and the Growth of Knowledge* (Cambridge: Cambridge University Press, 1970), concern, in fact, just this point.

*an explanatory account of events in terms of a distinctive, nomological understanding of cause and effect.*[39]

Indeed, Fay affirms a basic Feyerabendian article of methodological faith: that scientific method is informed and influenced by one's views of what is worthwhile in human existence.[40]

By "policy science" Fay means not just the decision theorists' clarifications of economic and social problems but also the administrative procedure by which options are actually selected for consideration (pp. 13–15). Fay sets himself the task of elucidating the normative element contained in apparently objective reasoning in policy making. His argument, in brief, is that a policy-science approach makes assumptions about what the planner (or those for whom planners work) deems appropriate and so is inevitably value-laden:

> *All* political proposals, no matter how instrumental, will alter and shape the personal relations of at least some of the members of a society, and will affect the relative welfare of various classes of people; as such they embody moral notions as to what is permissible, just, or right in human affairs. They are a species of moral statement. [p. 52]

> Assume what I have in fact tried to deny, namely, that a policy scientist could impartially determine the most efficient means to a given end; still my argument runs, to engage in this type of political decision-making itself betrays a certain conception of the purposes and needs of men which the political sphere is supposed to satisfy, and it therefore incorporates certain values. In fact, just because proposals regarding a certain instrumental course of action based on a policy scientific analysis presuppose a theory of politics which incorporates certain values, such proposals themselves cannot be politically neutral. [p. 53; see also p. 64]

Fay wishes to urge, as an alternative model of social inquiry, a psychoanalytic perspective.[41] Such a model takes as its primary data the actor's felt conflicts and then asks for the social and political causes of

[39]Brian Fay, *Social Theory and Political Practice* (London: George Allen & Unwin, 1975), p. 17. Page references in the following discussion are to this work.

[40]Compare Fay, pp. 68–69, and Feyerabend, "Against Method," p. 29.

[41]Fay develops this in his essay "How People Change Themselves," in *Political Theory and Praxis*, ed. T. Ball (Minneapolis: University of Minnesota Press, 1977).

these (p. 94). (Fay, unfortunately, appears committed to a meaning realist account of interpretation; see pp. 80–83).[42]

In an essay with the wonderful title "The Search for Paradigms as a Hindrance to Understanding," Albert O. Hirschman enters a protest against "the tendency toward compulsive and mindless theorizing—a disease at least as prevalent and debilitating, so it seems to me, as the spread of mindless number work in the social sciences."[43] The theorizing he has in mind here is speculation about economic development in backward societies. And what upsets Hirschman, it turns out, is that theorizing that is insensitive to the sort of considerations raised by Feyerabend and Fay concerning the political implications of methodological strategies: "But cognitive style, that is, the kind of paradigms we search out, the way we put them together, and the ambitions we nurture for their powers—all this can make a great deal of difference."[44]

In the case of developing societies, Hirschman's own studies suggest that the particular theory used to study existing social hierarchies invariably determines the nature of the problems faced and the prospects for change: "The initial effort to understand reality will almost inevitably make it appear more solidly entrenched than before. The immediate effect of social analysis is therefore to convert the real into the rational or the contingent into the necessary."[45] What is more interesting, however, is Hirschman's suggestion of a methodological strategy fundamentally akin to Feyerabend's notion of counterinduction—a strategy whereby one proceeds by "introducing, elaborating, and propagating hypotheses which are inconsistent either with well-

[42]It is interesting to find a mainstream philosopher of science such as Hilary Putnam urging that we "enrich" our account of rationality, especially with regard to the study of human behavior; see *Meaning and the Moral Sciences* (London: Routledge & Kegan Paul, 1978), pp. 76–77. Putnam, however, does not seem sensitive to the Socratic paradox in the way in which Feyerabend is. Even more significant is the emergence of such concerns in the writings of social scientists. For example, Fay's argument is given additional force and is provided with an array of interesting examples in a probing essay by economist Michael McPherson, "Want Formation, Morality, and Some 'Interpretive' Aspects of Economic Inquiry," in *Social Science as Moral Inquiry*, ed. N. Haan et al. (New York: Columbia University Press, 1983), pp. 105–110.

[43]In *Interpretive Social Science*, ed. Rabinow and Sullivan, p. 163.

[44]Ibid., p. 174.

[45]Ibid.

established theories or with well-established facts."[46] Hirschman prescribes counterinduction when one "discovers," through one's theory, obstacles to or dead ends in social development:

> In the case of the backward countries, the realization will dawn that certain so-called attributes of backwardness are not necessarily obstacles, but can be lived with and sometimes can be turned into positive assets. . . . This evidence, then, should make us a bit wary when new vicious circles or new development-obstructing personality types or new dead ends are being discovered. Though such discoveries are bound to occur and can be real contributions to the understanding, they carry an obligation to look for ways in which they may play not a reinforcing but a neutral or debilitating role insofar as system maintenance is concerned. Perhaps social scientists could pass a rule . . . that anyone who believes he has discovered a new obstacle to development is under an obligation to look for ways in which this obstacle can be overcome or can possibly be lived with or can, in certain circumstances, be transformed into a blessing in disguise.[47]

Obstacles, then, are to be treated counterinductively, as apparent facts to be explained away by introducing new theories. Indeed, in the true Feyerabendian spirit, social scientists are encouraged to reason against the very facts their research reveals.

Hirschman's advocacy of counterinductive strategies is based on his experience as a researcher of the economies of underdeveloped countries; he has no epistemological axe to grind vis-à-vis the notion of rationality. His remarks on how theoretically mandated results have to be tempered with the experience of research are a nice instance of how practice encourages researchers to throw off the intellectual shackles of their theory. Hirschman urges this approach even when the obstacles perceived by the theory are, in fact, considered enlightening. It is Hirschman's respect for the vagaries of human nature and of human society, moreover, which lead him to this conclusion.[48] And this also is in accord with the general Feyerabendian scheme regarding the interrelation of scientific and human concerns.

My variant of methodological pluralism applies nicely to the social sciences. Methodological pluralism represents an attempt to speculate

[46]See Feyerabend, "Against Method," p. 26.
[47]Hirschman, "Search for Paradigms," p. 175.
[48]Ibid., p. 174–175.

about the nature of rational inquiry in an intellectual landscape where the usual and expected landmarks have been removed. In attempting to forge a version of methodological pluralism which draws on both Quinean and Feyerabendian views, I have emphasized each philosopher's brief against traditional epistemology. Moreover, by adding to this Feyerabend's view that an emphasis on normal science misrepresents the situation concerning how inquiry actually advances, I have suggested that, *in the context of the social sciences*, methodological pluralism would promote both intellectual inquiry and human freedom.

Methodological pluralism promotes intellectual inquiry because the social sciences, unlike the natural sciences, presently contain many competing theories. From the epistemological perspective I have urged, this situation should be viewed as an encouragement to research and not as a hindrance to it. In addition, methodological pluralism is most compatible with Mill's account of liberty insofar as inquiry may be regarded as a kind of self-regarding activity. I have argued, in addition, that a putative disadvantage of this view—that it is tantamount to intellectual irresponsibility because it recognizes no intellectual absolutes—is not a cogent objection. This objection ignores the practical concerns retained by even such alleged relativists as Feyerabend. Central to the concepts of both liberty and inquiry, I have urged, is learning, in the light of ongoing experience, how to balance experiment and constraint. At least as I have interpreted the lessons of contemporary epistemology for the notion of rationality, the moral of the story is that, while scientific method might be the first word in rational inquiry, it is a mistake to take it as the final word.

CHAPTER 4

# Methods Unbound

Methodological pluralism, as I have developed it, argues for a third way between traditional epistemology and "anything goes." By merging Quine's objections to traditional epistemology and the notion of meaning with Feyerabend's strategy of inquiry, we gain a conception of rational justification and inquiry well suited to the social sciences. Before considering some of the ramifications of my views for the *Rationalitätstreit* in the social sciences, I want to consider a final objection to methodological pluralism. Methodological pluralism is not radical enough, this objection runs, because it does not adhere to the full implications of the Quinean premises it accepts. This objection represents, as I understand it, the position developed by Richard Rorty; it is to an evaluation of Rorty's position vis-à-vis my own account of methodological pluralism that I now turn.

Rorty shares with Quine and Feyerabend their criticism of traditional epistemology. Yet his own position, in particular, as developed in Sections II and III of *Philosophy and the Mirror of Nature*, is importantly at variance with theirs in at least three ways.[1] First, unlike Quine and Feyerabend, both of whom remain convinced that there is something to be said concerning how inquiry may best proceed even after the demise of traditional epistemology, Rorty denies that such speculation serves any positive purpose. Indeed, he maintains that such philosophizing only fosters dehumanization.

Second, Rorty maintains a contrast between the role assigned to

[1]Richard Rorty, *Philosophy and the Mirror of Nature* (Princeton, N.J.: Princeton University Press, 1979). Page references to Rorty in this chapter are to this volume.

"hermeneutic" or "edifying" philosophy, on the one hand, and epistemology, on the other. My third and final concern focuses on Rorty's interesting remarks with regard to the supposed methodological divide between the *Geisteswissenschaften* and the *Naturwissenschaften*; he claims that no such theoretical distinction can be sustained. I agree, but I show that this position is detachable from Rorty's doubts about the efficacy of speculation about rational inquiry and his contrast between inquiry and edification.

In the previous chapter I indicated that, for the sort of philosophical project undertaken by Quine, Feyerabend, and Rorty, there exists what I termed the Socratic paradox. The paradox, to recall, concerns how to change the accepted repertoire of argument without either using the techniques one is intent on rejecting or using argument forms that are inevitably unpersuasive. Feyerabend, I suggested, appreciates just this paradox, and his stylistic experiments are part of his struggle to solve it. Rorty, I argue below, misunderstands the import of the paradox, and this because he has not appreciated the full changes rung by Quine on epistemological inquiry (this despite the fact that Rorty has understood better than even Quine himself the radical implications of Quine's holist position). This misunderstanding, in turn, creates a difficulty in Rorty's account, since it leads him to adopt an inconsistent metaphilosophical stance.

Rorty's odd attitude toward scientific success is manifested in his claim that what is to be learned about modern science from historians of science is that scientists have no "secret of success."[2] Indeed, Rorty not only denies that there is some secret to the success of science, but he also is apt to characterize apparent advances in scientific knowledge, such as Galileo's, as cases of luck: "Scientific breakthroughs are not so much a matter of deciding which of various alternative hypotheses are true, but of finding the right jargon in which to frame hypotheses in the first place."[3] The force of "right" here is just the practical one insisted on by Quine and Feyerabend. Yet what Rorty also denies, unlike the others just mentioned, is that there is any interesting way to determine which view is right even in this limited sense.

[2]Richard Rorty, "A Reply to Dreyfus and Taylor," *Review of Metaphysics* 34 (September 1980):55.

[3]Richard Rorty, "Method, Social Science, and Social Hope," in *Consequences of Pragmatism (Essays: 1972–1980)* (Minneapolis: University of Minnesota Press, 1982), p. 193.

Exactly how do Rorty's views diverge from those examined in the previous chapter? The basic epistemological contrast Rorty urges is that between commensurable (or normal or epistemological) discourse and hermeneutic (or abnormal or edifying) discourse. Simply put, the search for commensurable discourse is the search for a neutral framework in which all meaningful questions may be asked and rational answers provided (p. 316). The critical difference between the Quine-Feyerabend position defended in Chapter 3 and Rorty's emerges in the latter's discussion of the alternatives to a universal framework for rational discourse. This is where he parts company with the position I am elaborating and defending.

Rorty imagines, in fact, two responses to the demise of traditional epistemology, and he endorses both. I argue that the two positions are not self-consistent. Rorty asserts that he endorses both epistemological behaviorism and what he terms, as noted above, hermeneutic or edifying philosophy. His epistemological behaviorism is fully in the spirit of the position I defend; what puzzles me, at least, is the harsh contrast on which Rorty insists between edifying philosophy and epistemology. The contrast is so stark that it rules out even that epistemological doctrine Rorty is otherwise willing to endorse.

To philosophize in the hermeneutic or edifying mode is to consciously eschew the adoption of any method of inquiry. Even more, it is to oppose, as best one can, proposals to adopt a particular model of research. As Rorty understands the alternative to traditional epistemology, the issue is not how to balance experimentation and constraint but what to do to oppose constraints altogether:

> In the interpretation I shall be offering, "hermeneutics" is not the name for a discipline, nor a method of achieving the sort of results which epistemology failed to achieve, nor a program of research. On the contrary, hermeneutics is an expression of hope that the cultural space left by the demise of epistemology will not be filled—that our culture should become one in which the demand for constraint and confrontation is no longer felt. . . . Epistemology proceeds on the assumption that all contributions to a given discourse are commensurable. Hermeneutics is largely a struggle against this assumption. [pp. 315–316]

This hermeneutic approach, together with the Quinean precepts Rorty accepts, in turn engenders Rorty's account of rationality:

> For hermeneutics, to be rational is to be willing to refrain from epistemology—from thinking that there is a special set of terms in which all contributions to the conversation should be put—and to be willing to pick up the jargon of the interlocutor rather than translating it into one's own. For epistemology, to be rational is to find the proper set of terms into which all contributions should be translated if agreement is to become possible. For epistemology, conversation is routine inquiry. For hermeneutics, inquiry is routine conversation. [p. 318]

The tension infecting Rorty's position is revealed in his distinction between conversation and inquiry. In the above-cited quote he speaks both of being "willing to refrain" from epistemology and of inquiry as "routine conversation." Conversation qua routine inquiry is, in other words, said to be different in kind from routine conversation.

Clearly "routine conversation" *cannot*, for Rorty, be epistemology—conversation constrained by a set of fixed standards. Epistemology, in his pejorative sense of that term, inhibits conversation by "freezing" or "fixing" according to some prescribed routine the direction conversation can take. Routine conversation, then, rules out epistemology because epistemological routinization is incompatible with letting conversation go its own way (which is what is routine *for conversation* in Rorty's sense). The sort of conversation Rorty believes ought to be encouraged is not constrained in advance by any admonitions about what may or may not be challenged or subject to revision.

But, one might think, this certainly leaves as an option the much more open and speculative account of rationality and scientific method offered by, for example, Feyerabend. And, in fact, Rorty himself proposes, or so it seems, just such a vision of what epistemology ought to be. He calls it epistemological behaviorism. "To be a behaviorist in epistemology, on the contrary, is to look at the normal scientific discourse of our day bifocally, both as patterns adopted for various historical reasons and as the achievement of objective truth, where "objective truth" is no more and no less than the best idea we currently have about how to explain what is going on (p. 385; see also pp. 173–182). Rorty qua epistemological behaviorist does not worry about maintaining a rearguard reaction against systematic philosophy. One avoids philosophical sin by being epistemologically self-conscious.

The question, then, is whether or why a Rortian hermeneuticist must also refrain from being an epistemological behaviorist? Insofar as hermeneutic philosophy is a "struggle against the assumption" that all discourse is commensurable, the positive contribution to this struggle is what makes hermeneutic philosophy edifying (again, in Rorty's sense). As Rorty puts it,

> I shall use 'edification' to stand for this project of finding new, better, more interesting, more fruitful ways of speaking. . . . The activity is . . . edifying without being constructive—at least if "constructive" means the sort of cooperation in the accomplishment of research programs which takes place in normal discourse. For edifying discourse is *supposed* to be abnormal, to take us out of our old selves by the power of strangeness, to aid us in becoming new beings. [p. 360]

Here lies the problem. On this view, epistemological behaviorism obviously cannot be edifying. The epistemological behaviorist, as characterized above, is constructive. Yet treating truth as immanent and rational standards as subject to change is just not sufficient to ward off the adverse effects of philosophizing. Such an intellectual position remains constructive, in the sense Rorty condemns above. In order to achieve the appropriate revolution in thought, the revolution must be ongoing; Rorty has, it seems, adopted an Maoist stance toward intellectual stability.

One of the more striking features of Rorty's post-empiricist philosophy is its profound and somber pessimism. Rorty is explicitly fearful that a belief in the existence of One True Method would put an end to philosophical (and, one assumes, scientific) development. There would be, in Rorty's terms, no room for conversation, no hope of yet another Kuhnian revolution. So the model for the Rortian facing an audience is not Socrates of the *Apology* but a Nietzsche or Sartre accusing intellectual slackers of varying degrees of bad faith:

> Great edifying philosophers are reactive and offer satires, parodies, aphorisms. They know their work loses its point when the period they were reacting against is over. They are *intentionally* peripheral. . . . Great edifying philosophers destroy for the sake of their own generation. . . . Edifying philosophers want to keep space open for the sense of wonder which poets can sometimes cause—wonder that there is something new under the sun, something which is *not* an accurate representation of what was already there, something which (at least for the moment) cannot be explained and can barely be described. [pp. 369–370]
>
> The danger which edifying discourse tries to avert is that some given vocabulary, some way in which people might come to think of themselves, will deceive

them into thinking that from now on all discourse could be, or should be, normal discourse. The resulting freezing-over of culture would be, in the eyes of edifying philosophers, the dehumanization of human beings. [p. 377]

There are clear echoes here of the point made in Chapter 4 on the relation between liberty and rationality. But, unlike Feyerabend or the philosophers and social scientists who urge Feyerabendian research strategies, Rorty insists on assuming a purely reactive stance, a defensive position from which to protect people from an encroaching science.

The threat of dehumanization arises, however, even if one, following Rorty, declares for epistemological behaviorism. In order to see how this develops, I examine further Rorty's views on physicalism, edification, and epistemological behaviorism.

One line of reply to Rorty's position might seem simply to claim that we have much to learn by conducting research as if there were a neutral matrix for inquiry. Even Feyerabend and Quine, recall, recommend tenacity as an important element in learning from any scientific theory. Rorty, for his part, argues from the fact that we currently possess no such neutral framework to the conclusion that it would be a mistaken research strategy to assume that we could have one:

We have not got a language which will serve as a permanent neutral matrix for formulating all good explanatory hypotheses, and we have not the foggiest notion of how to get one. (This is compatible with saying that we do have a neutral, if unhelpful, observation language.) So epistemology—as the attempt to render all discourses commensurable by translating them into a preferred set of terms—is unlikely to be a useful strategy. The reason is . . . the Whiggish assumption that we have got such a language blocks the road of inquiry. [pp. 348–349]

It is invalid to infer from the fact that we now have no permanent neutral matrix of investigation to the conclusion that a research strategy based on an assumption counter to this fact is unlikely to be useful. It is invalid even if one adds as a premise the belief that no such matrix will ever exist. Rorty himself cites the reason this inference is invalid. What the success of contemporary science has taught is precisely the *usefulness* of relentlessly pursuing such a counterfactual belief. As Rorty himself observes, "physicalism is probably right in saying that we shall someday be able, 'in principle,' to predict every movement of a person's body . . . by reference to microstructures within his body" (p.

354; see also pp. 347, 387). But if Rorty believes that this sort of predictive success is obtainable by unceasing application of scientific method on experience, then he has no grounds for inferring that a search for a commensurable framework is not a useful research strategy. We can expect this strategy to go awry for other reasons, and relative to other questions that might be raised, but the fact is that such a strategy has been (and probably will remain) very fruitful for all that.

In Rorty's very willingness to concede the success of physicalistically oriented discourse we glimpse why, in the end, he cannot reconcile his epistemological behaviorism and his hermeneutic, edifying approach. The dehumanization about which he worries has, as one of its faces, the *reduction* of humans to an intellectual (and so moral?) status that would allow no special consideration for humans' place in rational deliberations. It is the very success of this epistemological assumption as a research strategy (whatever its philosophical shortcomings) which, he believes, threatens to crowd out other voices from the conversation of mankind.

Inquiry in Rorty's sense leads to research results; his ideal of conversation leads to seeing things in new ways. "One way to see edifying philosophy *as* the love of wisdom is to see it as the attempt to prevent conversation from degenerating into inquiry, into an exchange of views. Edifying philosophers can never end philosophy, but they can help prevent it from attaining the secure path of a science" (p. 372). The shortcoming, then, of being *just* an epistemological behaviorist is, on this view, that it might still permit conversation to degenerate into inquiry and so help foster, in Quine's words, the illusion of there being just one solution to the riddle of the universe.

> I shall be claiming that the difference between conversation and inquiry parallels Sartre's distinction between thinking of oneself *pour-soi* and as *en-soi*, and thus that the cultural role of the edifying philosopher is to help us avoid the self-deception which comes from believing that we know ourselves by knowing a set of objective facts. [p. 373]

> From this point of view, to look for commensuration rather than simply continued conversation—to look for a way of making further redescription unnecessary by finding a way of reducing all *possible* descriptions to one—is to attempt escape from humanity. To abandon the notion that philosophy must show all possible discourse naturally converging to a consensus, just as normal inquiry does, would be to abandon the hope of being anything more than merely human. [p. 377]

So even if one surrenders a belief in One True Method and in truth as correspondence to reality, the danger of dehumanization remains. Dehumanization, in this respect, is inseparably linked with just the sort of freedom to question which Mill emphasizes as being a key component for insuring human liberty. We become like automatons—which is surely one key sense of dehumanization—not only when we follow rules unquestioningly, but also when the rules we create are left unchallenged. Indeed, one contributes to this process by not seeking to edify as well as to inquire. To recall an old slogan, if you are not part of the solution, you are part of the problem.

Not everything Rorty says may appear consistent with the interpretation I offer. He sometime writes as if there need be no tension between epistemology and hermeneutics: "If we draw the line between epistemology and hermeneutics as I have been drawing it—as a contrast between discourse about normal and about abnormal discourse —then it seems clear that the two do not compete, but rather help each other out" (p. 346). But this suggestion, as Rorty develops it (pp. 346–347), comes to no more than the claim that neither people nor things have essences, and that not all questions we ask can be answered in some single theoretical vocabulary. This is just the view characteristic of epistemological behaviorism, and that, as noted above, is not consistent with Rorty's account of the edifying endeavors of hermeneutic philosophy. The tension generated for someone who tries to satisfy both of Rorty's alternatives to epistemology is that one must undo, in one's edifying moments, whatever one does qua epistemological behaviorist.

Note here that the problem for the edifying philosopher is not the Socratic paradox; the issue is *not* how to cause people to rethink their account of justification; rather, it is an insistence that the philosopher acts in good faith only in the role of intellectual gadfly. And this characterization points to an even deeper difference between Rorty and the Quine-Feyerabend view outlined earlier. For Quine and Feyerabend surrender any belief in truth as correspondence and yet retain an interest in perpetuating inquiry. Rorty, for his part, believes that if you give up truth as correspondence, then it is simply a case of bad faith to insist that "success" and "method" are still worth pondering about. One can, like Socrates or Galileo, simply luck out and stumble on a vocabulary that, eventually, people are convinced to adopt. But one has accomplished no more than a selling of a particular way of talking; there is no progress because there is nothing to progress toward:

> Let me sum up by offering a third and final characterization of pragmatism: it is the doctrine that there are no constraints on inquiry save conversational ones—no wholesale constraints derived from the nature of the objects, or of the mind, or of language, but only those retail constraints provided by the remarks of our fellow-inquirers. . . . The only sense in which we are constrained to truth is that, as Peirce suggested, we can make no sense of the notion that the view which can survive all objections might be false. But objections—conversational constraints—cannot be anticipated.[4]

> For the traditional, Platonic or Kantian philosopher, on the other hand, the possibility of *grounding* the European form of life . . . seems the central task of philosophy. He wants to show that sinning against Socrates is sinning against our nature, not just against our community. So he sees the pragmatist as an irrationalist. . . . If the traditional philosopher gets beyond such epithets, however, he raises a question which the pragmatist must face up to: the *practical* question of whether the notion of "conversation" *can* substitute for that of "reason."[5]

Rorty admits he is unsure how to answer the "question of whether the notion of 'conversation' can substitute for that of 'reason.'" The issue cuts deep, however, for it is a question "about whether we can be pragmatists without betraying Socrates, without falling into irrationalism."[6] In short, Rorty presents us with the following problem: either continue to believe in truth as correspondence, glassy essences, and so forth *or* accept the substitution of conversation for a clear-cut account of reasoning. Faith must be blind or it is not faith at all.

This Rortian Either-Or, however, is based on a false dichotomy. In order to appreciate why, one need only consider just why Rorty, who shares so many of Feyerabend's political and intellectual concerns vis-à-vis the negative intellectual effects of a misguided belief in scientific method, comes to such different conclusions about the efficacy of inquiry.[7] Feyerabend's answer to those who would constrain the meaning of "rational" to some fixed list of rules is to insist that this

[4]Richard Rorty, "Pragmatism, Relativism, and Irrationalism," in *Consequences of Pragmatism*, p. 165.

[5]Ibid., p. 172.

[6]Ibid., p. 174; ibid., p. 169.

[7]Rorty does not say much about the place or role of constraint in his concept of conversation. Paul Feyerabend has a much sharper, more interesting, and, I suggest, more sensible account of the sort of constraints which affect inquiry; see, in particular, Feyerabend's remarks in *Against Method: Outline of an Anarchist Theory of Knowledge* (London: New Left Books, 1975), p. 187 n. 15, 196–198, 221–222, 309.

view badly misrepresents the fundamental nature of scientific thought. This is the key to the difference between Feyerabend and Rorty. Rorty takes Kuhn's account of science to heart and so is impressed by normal science, by the view that within a given paradigm most of what goes on is "hack science."[8] Feyerabend, true to his Popperian origins, strongly denies that science proceeds even normally in this way.[9] In short, Feyerabend does not worry about inquiry having the degenerative effects on humanity that Rorty does, provided, of course, that good scientific thinking is understood in Feyerabend's way.

Put another way, the dilemma Rorty poses is based on certain assumptions about the nature of scientific reasoning. He confuses, I suggest, certain metaphysical positions held by some philosophers with empirical questions regarding how scientific reasoning proceeds. What one learns, if nothing else, from the sociologists of science is that the facts favor Feyerabend; what goes on in a laboratory (as opposed, say, to what is written for publication) is quite different from what any idealized account of scientific method would have one believe. This is not, moreover, to simply ignore the hoary distinction between discovery and justification; this distinction goes by the way on a Feyerabendian account, since it presupposes that the logic of justification remains static and that the logic of discovery may vary. The point is, of course, that new discoveries may alter what counts as justification. (This point was also affirmed by those social scientists cited in Chapter 3.)

Rorty believes that some special effort must be made in order to insure that abnormal discourse be heard. Feyerabend's response is just that if we understood how most innovative reasoning does proceed, in and out of the laboratory, then this is sufficient to establish that abnormal discourse is a pervasive and integral part of the research process. Feyerabend would claim, to put the matter in a Rortian way, that Rorty has drawn an invidious distinction between inquiry and conversation; there is, in fact, no such distinction to be drawn.[10]

[8]J. W. N. Watkins, "Against 'Normal Science,'" in *Criticism and the Growth of Knowledge*, ed. I. Lakatos and A. Musgrave (Cambridge: Cambridge University Press, 1970), p. 27.

[9]See Paul Feyerabend, "Consolations for the Specialist," in *Criticism and the Growth of Knowledge*, ed. Lakatos and Musgrave, pp. 197–230, especially sec. 6, "Does Normal Science Exist?"

[10]It is interesting to note that a parallel criticism to what I develop here, but applied to Rorty's treatment of the history of philosophy, is offered by Alasdair MacIntyre in "Philosophy, the 'Other' Disciplines, and Their Histories: A Rejoinder to Richard Rorty," *Soundings* 65 (Summer 1982).

Hearkening back to the criticisms I developed of Rorty's account of Quine's indeterminacy thesis in Chapter 2, my general complaint is that Rorty has generated a pseudoproblem for philosophy based on a pair of false dichotomies. The first dichotomy, the one discussed in Chapter 2, is that between mirroring and convention. In that context, Rorty asserts that the language of science either expresses Nature's Own Vocabulary or is all a matter of conventions. (The assumption that these alternatives are exclusive and exhaustive is one that guides Rorty's analysis; pp. 170–171). Against these alternatives I argued that Quine's account of language learning and its relation to his holist doctrine preserves a tie between our theories of the world and matters not of our making and does so without recourse to sensory givens or any other discredited notions.

Rorty's second problematic dichotomy, that between inquiry and conversation, presupposes the correctness of Kuhn's account of normal science. Yet there is strong evidence, based on the philosophical work of Feyerabend and the Popperians, on the one hand, and in the sociological investigations to be discussed in later chapters, on the other, that the methodological monolith Rorty presupposes does not, in fact, exist.[11]

In stressing what I take to be an important *difference* between Rorty and Feyerabend, at least with regard to what they accept from Kuhn, the fundamental *similarities* between the positions at issue must also be kept in mind. For my goal is, finally, to explain away Rorty's deviant conclusion given the assumptions he shares with Quine and Feyerabend. If what I have said is correct, then the conflict Rorty perceives between edification and inquiry can be dismissed. Inquiry is, on the Feyerabendian line incorporated as a part of methodological pluralism, appropriately edifying (provided it is properly understood) and already linked to practice (as discussion in Chapter 3 indicated). What Rorty does contribute to the purge of epistemology is his analysis of what is mistaken about the pervasive distinction between *Geisteswissenschaften* and *Naturwissenschaften*. He argues that assuming this distinction in the study of human behavior presupposes just the sort of

[11]For a reading of Kuhn's position that indicates that what sustains Kuhn's account is not so much presumptions about method as about problems, see Gerald Doppelt, "Kuhn's Epistemological Relativism: An Interpretation and Defense," originally printed in *Inquiry* 21 (1978); reprinted in *Relativism: Cognitive and Moral*, ed. M. Krausz and J. W. Meiland (Notre Dame, Ind.: University of Notre Dame Press, 1982).

essentialism which the efforts of Quine and others have shown to be untenable. This methodological point about the natural versus the human sciences does not involve the presuppositions regarding normal science which vitiate Rorty's discussion of inquiry. His considerations here depend only on the holist and antiessentialist assumptions he shares with Quine and Feyerabend (p. 355). It is, moreover, of particular significance for the position I develop that, in his essay devoted to applying his views to the social sciences, "Method, Social Science, and Social Hope," Rorty likens his projects to John Dewey's attempt to synthesize Hegel and Mill.[12] And, of course, it is just such a synthesis of Hegel and Mill which Feyerabend claims to be attempting in his methodological reflections.[13]

Rorty characterizes the humanist versus scientist dispute in the social sciences in the following way: "The traditional quarrel about the 'philosophy of the social sciences' has proceeded generally as follows. One side has said that 'explanation' (subsumption under predictive laws, roughly) presupposes, and cannot replace, 'understanding.' The other side has said that understanding simply *is* the ability to explain, that what their opponents call 'understanding' is merely the primitive stage of groping around for some explanatory hypotheses" (p. 347). Although this is a standard fashion in which to frame the problem, Rorty's response to the seemingly disparate alternatives is "both sides are right" (p. 347).

It is, of course, the tradition to hold that both sides cannot be right, since the methods of verification basic to each are fundamentally incompatible. The friends of understanding insist that a hallmark (that is, a necessary condition) of correct explanation of human behavior is that the action be comprehensible as that of a human. This is the basic point of Weber's *Verstehen*. When explaining human behavior, the idea is not to recreate a subjective state of mind but to provide an explanation in which the behavior described is distinctively and recognizably human. Those who fancy themselves hard-nosed about such matters insist that explanations need meet only whatever standards must be met by any good scientific explanation; if the *Verstehen*

[12]In *Consequences of Pragmatism*, pp. 209–210 n. 16.

[13]See "Against Method," *Minnesota Studies in the Philosophy of Science*, vol. 4 (1970), pp. 27–36; reprinted in Feyerabend's *Collected Papers*, vol. 2 (Cambridge: Cambridge University Press, 1981), as chap. 4.

condition is not necessary for physicists, it is not necessary for social scientists either.

Rorty complains, primarily against the champions of *Verstehen*, that their assumption "leads us back into the bad old metaphysical notion that the universe is made up of two kinds of things" (p. 350). But this is not the end of the matter. Rorty's point, following the methodological pluralist line but explicitly developed for the social sciences, is to insist that *no* methodological conditions are necessary. Whether or not to seek understanding in the Weberian sense is neither mandated nor foreclosed by considerations of some abstract ideal of rational inquiry. What, then, does determine whether or not *Verstehen* is taken to be a methodological prerogative? Rorty provides, I suggest, the only good answer in light of what has been said about the constraints on inquiry, namely that the apparent

> need to look for *internal* explanations of people or cultures or texts takes civility as a methodological strategy. But civility is not a method, it is simply a virtue. . . . What we hope from the social sciences is that they will act as interpreters for those with whom we have difficulty talking. This is the same thing we hope from our poets and dramatists and novelists. Thus, for example, the contrast which Hirschman draws between good and bad political science, like Rabinow's contrast between anthropology in the manner of Geertz and in the manner of Boas, seems to me a contrast between fellow feeling and moralizing condescension—between treating men as moral equals and as moral inferiors.[14]

The choice between methods, in other words, is a moral decision—a question of how one chooses to view one's fellow humans, or a question of the purpose for which one is studying them. The method is a function of the interests of the researcher and not of the essences of the objects studied.

> In this sense, "method" and "rationality" are names for a suitable balance between respect for the opinions of one's fellows and respect for the stubbornness of sensation. But epistemologically-centered philosophy has wanted notions of "method" and "rationality" which signify more than good epistemic manners, notions which describe the way in which the mind is naturally fitted to learn Nature's Own Language.

[14]Richard Rorty, "Method and Morality," in *Social Science as Moral Inquiry*, ed. N. Haan et al. (New York: Columbia University Press, 1983), pp. 169–170.

If one believes, as I do, that the traditional ideas of "an absolute ("objective") conception of reality" and of "scientific method" are neither clear nor useful, then one will see the interlocked questions "What should be the method of the social sciences?" and "What are the criteria of an objective moral theory?" as badly posed.[15]

We shall not think either style particularly appropriate or inappropriate to the study of man. For we shall not think that "the study of man" or "the human sciences" have a nature, any more than we think that man does. When the notion of knowledge as representation goes, then the notion of inquiry as split into discrete sectors with discrete subject matters goes. The lines between novels, newspaper articles, and sociological research get blurred. The lines between subject matters are drawn by reference to current practical concerns, rather than putative ontological status.[16]

With respect, then, to the study of human behavior, Rorty arrives at the conclusion endorsed in the previous chapter—that the criterion of success is a practical one; in Rorty's words, "hermeneutics is not 'another way of knowing'—'understanding' as opposed to (predictive) 'explanation.' It is better seen as another way of coping" (p. 356).[17]

In a world without essences, the old methodological disputes do not matter because the presumptions on which they are based are no longer tenable. Rorty's remarks simply serve to drive home the larger point implicit in the epistemological position I develop in Chapters 1 and 2 and scout further in Chapter 6. The conclusion I finally urge is that there is no mystery, or, better, no more a mystery, to investigating meaning than to investigating any other phenomenon. Neither the method nor the subject matter of such research is importantly different from garden-variety forms of empirical inquiry.

But we must not be gulled into thinking that there is an essence to rationality. I have asked why, on Quinean grounds, we should be skeptical of traditional epistemology and what, in any case, this skepticism implies for a more general notion of rational inquiry and scientific method. I then traced Feyerabend's account of the notion of rational inquiry given the Quinean assumptions I endorse and Feyerabend exploits. This exploration, in turn, led to the articulation of methodological pluralism as a response and reaction to the unity-of-method

[15]Rorty, "Method, Social Science, and Social Hope," p. 195.

[16]Ibid., p. 203.

[17]See also *Consequences of Pragmatism*, p. 199.

thesis of positivism. Further, I have explored why Rorty, someone with many of the same assumptions, reaches such a different conclusion on the issue of strategies of inquiry.

The nihilistic consequences Rorty draws from premises shared with Quine and Feyerabend are, I have shown, unwarranted. They are based on a pair of false dichotomies, one concerning problems of objectivity arising in a holistic context, the other concerning the actual nature of scientific research. But this still leaves it open to us to appreciate the lessons to be learned from the Mill-inspired notion of rationality with which we are left once we have learned what Quine has to teach us. There is no compulsion, in the absence of an absolutist epistemology, to advocate "anything goes," just as there is no logical requirement to believe that "everything is permitted" in the absence of a dogmatic moral theory. There is, on this view, no "problem" about rationality in general or about social scientific method in particular. The belief that there is is grounded on mistaken or untenable assumptions about the nature of human knowledge. The "problem" simply becomes a practical question of means and ends; it ceases to be an abstract philosophical question of finding the final list of rules which delimit rationality as such. Quine, Feyerabend, and Rorty, to be sure, do not present a unified front on the question of how inquiry into standards should proceed. But this matter does not affect my general conclusion about defining rationality as a dynamic balancing of experimentation and constraint.

A friend of mine began each of his classes on critical reasoning by warning his students against what he termed the "warm tummy" standard for evaluating arguments. By this he meant the tendency of some students (and not just students, to be sure) to judge the logical acceptability of an argument by their emotional response to the claim being made. If the claim was to their liking (left them with a comfortable, warm tummy glow), the argument was judged valid. Like the Athenians on Socrates' jury, people are apt to be swayed by what "sounds" right or "feels" right. Socrates is rightly celebrated for seeing the dawn of a new intellectual day, a day of better—more effective—ways of arriving at conclusions. Some, like Stove, see the acceptance of a Quine-Feyerabend stance as the return of a long night, an incomprehensible drive to renounce all that has been learned about logic and science in the course of some 2500 years. My own suggestion is that the "warm tummy" or fixed-list view of rationality is itself just another false dichotomy.

What I have sought to establish is that there are important connections, and connections previously unappreciated, between what to count as rational and how to live one's life. There is no one way to live, but that is hardly to say that any one way is as satisfactory and as likely to allow for pleasure and development as any other. My attempt has been to distill and synthesize Quine, Feyerabend, and Rorty (suitably corrected, anyway) in order to provide an account of rational inquiry as a balancing of constraint and experimentation.

When one reads Goody and Watt's magnificent discussion of the implications of the intellectual changes implicit in the transition from a preliterate to a literate society, a fundamental irony is discernible. As noted earlier, once arguments are present in written form, they are open to preservation and so to critical scrutiny. In an oral tradition, contradictions either go unnoticed or are, perhaps, obliterated by selective amnesia. More important, cultural authority resides in what can be recalled to memory; a social standard has an indispensable role in the settling of argument. Thus, although literacy helps to foster the rise of objective standards for evaluating arguments, it also fragments and disperses the sources of authority.

> Literate society leaves more to its members; less homogeneous in its cultural tradition, it gives more free play to the individual, and particularly to the intellectual, the literate specialist himself; it does so by sacrificing a single, ready-made orientation to life. And, insofar as an individual participates in the literate, as distinct from the oral, culture, such coherence as a person achieves is very largely the result of his personal selection, adjustment and elimination of items from a highly differentiated cultural repertoire; he is of course influenced by all the various social pressures, but they are so numerous that the pattern finally comes out as an individual one.[18]

In this perspective, MacIntyre's quip that Feyerabend makes "every man his own Galileo" takes on greater significance. The fragmentation of any consensus on standards of rationality now appears to be the ineluctable outcome of the revolution wrought by the rise of literacy among the ancient Greeks. The irony to which I alluded above is, in short, that the very process that promotes the creation of objective standards is a process that leads to cultural fragmentation, and so to the breakdown and rejection of common standards.

[18]Jack Goody and Ian Watt, "The Consequences of Literacy," *Comparative Studies in History and Society* 5 (1962– 63):340.

This situation engenders an additional irony, an irony that brings my discussion of rationality and method to a full Kuhnian circle. The movement from preliteracy to literacy charted in Chapter 3 is, on my account, mirrored in the movement from Socrates to Feyerabend. This latter development is readily describable, given what has been said about cultural transitions, as the rise and degeneration of some grand paradigm of "normal rationality." Debates over logic since Aristotle, on this account, can be read as attempts to work out recurrent anomalies in each era's version of logical analysis. There have been, to be sure, "revolutions" along the way; the dramas in the development of reason are exemplified by the trials of Socrates and of Galileo. Our current historical position is, to continue my account, one confronting the questions now being raised by Kuhn, Feyerabend, and Rorty. The debate is aggravated, moreover, because, as Kuhn has taught us, there is no clear criterion for telling just when an old paradigm is so overwhelmed by anomalies that it is worth abandoning.

I have tried to indicate why this reading of our condition is plausible. The irony, then, is Hegelian; it seems that the human condition is that humans can tell a story about how they have reasoned but are fated never to achieve complete Reason. The history of reason becoming self-conscious is one that suggests, on this Kuhn-like view, that there can be no end to the process of attempting to understand what good reasoning is. But if the relation of rationality and liberty are also as I have suggested, then this is an edifying conclusion.

CHAPTER 5

# Who Needs Paradigms?

In this chapter and those that follow I explore the implications for the philosophy of the social sciences of the epistemological issues examined so far. The consequence of methodological pluralism of interest in this chapter is its denial of the unity-of-method thesis. This thesis is critical for the characteristic attempts to underwrite the scientific status of the social sciences offered in this century. I examine the import of denying the unity-of-method thesis for such rationalizations. I proceed by analyzing certain uses of the philosophy of science to justify ascribing scientific status to the social sciences. I argue that, ironically, it is due only to uncritical acceptance of the unity-of-method thesis and the attendant notion of explanation that doubts are raised about the scientific status of the social sciences. In the absence of the thesis, the doubts cease to have a focus or a point.

At least since Weber, social scientists have asked the question, Are the social sciences really sciences? Their answers, by and large, have been affirmative. The fact that social scientists persist in asking this question, however, may be reason to doubt that they are convinced by their affirmative answers. As I understand them, the doubts to which social scientists give voice could be expressed as follows:

(i) All "real" (i.e., the natural) sciences yield causal laws and instrumental control of the environment;

(ii) The social sciences have not produced distinctively social causal laws nor have they provided their practitioners with means for instrumental control; therefore,

(iii) The social sciences are not (yet, anyway) genuine sciences.

Even worse, there is a tendency in these disciplines to assume that knowledge properly called is to be identified with accepted scientific results. This, in conjunction with the argument just cited, suggests that social scientists worry about the nature of their contribution to knowledge.

In order to forestall the unwanted conclusion that their disciplines are not sciences, social scientists are apt to stress a formal definition of what it is to be a science. It is then open to them to argue that the social sciences satisfy, in principle, the formal criteria. One problem here, however, is that the articulated formal criteria for what it is to be a science are provided by philosophers of science, and the philosophy of science has not held steady of late to any one formal account. What I examine in this chapter is how social scientists have attempted to dress up their claim to scientific status according to the dictates of philosophical fashion. I argue that the fashions do not fit. More generally, I suggest that, while the social sciences have rejected an image rooted in logical positivism, they have retained a fundamentally positivistic conception of knowledge, a conception that identifies knowledge with the results of natural science. What methodologically self-conscious social scientists have overlooked, in other words, is how changes in the philosophy of science relate to changes in the concept of knowledge.

Once again, Kuhn's *Structure of Scientific Revolutions*[1] has profoundly shaped the course of debate. Social scientists have attempted to use Kuhn to fill the methodological void left by the demise of positivism. In Section I, I indicate how social scientists employ a positivist vocabulary when framing their claim to scientific status. In Section II I show how Kuhn's critique of positivism undercuts a key facet of this rationale. In the third and final section I argue that the attempts to reconstruct this rationale in a Kuhnian vocabulary prove futile.

## I

The spirit of the positivist enterprise is neatly captured by the aphorism "Philosophy of science is philosophy enough."[2] By "science" the

[1]Thomas Kuhn, *The Structure of Scientific Revolutions*, 2d ed., enlarged (Chicago: University of Chicago Press, 1970). Page references to Kuhn in the following discussion are to this work. Kuhn's book is Volume II, No. 2, in the *International Encyclopedia of Unified Science*. Its companion volume in the series, Volume II, No. 1, is Otto Neurath's *Foundations of the Social Sciences* (Chicago: University of Chicago Press, 1944). The irony of this situation is quite marvelous.

[2]The aphorism is, of course, Quine's.

logical positivists mean natural science, with a special view to physics. By "logical" they mean the formal methods of deduction propounded by Russell and Whitehead in *Principia Mathematica*. A tenet of positivism is that every meaningful statement is either logically true or empirically testable. Since the most sophisticated methods of empirical verification and analysis belong to the natural sciences, the question of the truth value of any contingent statement becomes answerable by the methods of the natural scientist.

A corollary of the positivist view of science is the claim that there is a unity of method between the natural and the social sciences. In practice, this corollary implies that the social sciences must conform to the canons of inquiry established by the natural sciences. The position is strongly endorsed by Otto Neurath, a social scientist and charter member of the Vienna Circle. What may be taken as the definitive positivist statement on the social sciences is found in Neurath's *Foundations of the Social Sciences*. Neurath there vilifies Weber's claim that *Verstehen* is a necessary condition for sociological explanation. The reason for Neurath's opposition is that *Verstehen* supposedly distinguishes social scientific and natural scientific methods. *Verstehen* is to capture how the study of humans differs from that of nonhumans. In opposition to the claim that there is such a difference, Neurath insists that the vocabulary of the social scientist does not (or should not) differ from the vocabulary of the natural scientist. If Weber were right, there would not be a unified language of scientific analysis. But it is just such a unity to which positivists are committed, be the object of study human or not: "Social scientists, therefore, are interested in a language which enables them to speak of animals, plants, and crystals in the same way, as far as possible, without anticipatively creating distinctions. Not only the unification of the sociological language is at stake, but a much more comprehensive unification and orchestration, which leads us to a lingua franca of unified science."[3]

In a similar vein, Carl Hempel, in his classic studies of the logic of scientific explanation, explicitly denies that Weber's "adequacy at the level of meaning" is a necessary condition of sociological explanation:

In the natural sciences a particular event is explained by showing that its occurrence can be inferred by means of laws or theoretical principles from other, usually antecedent or simultaneous, particular circumstances. As Max

[3]Neurath, *Foundations of the Social Sciences*, p. 2.

> Weber's writings make clear, an adequate explanation of a particular event in sociology or historiography has to be of essentially the same character. . . . Weber's limitation of the explanatory principles of sociology to "meaningful" rules of intelligible behavior, on the other hand, is untenable; . . . and, indeed, the more recent development of psychological and social theory indicates that it is possible to formulate explanatory principles for purposive action in purely behavioristic, non-introspective terms.[4]

In short, Hempel endorses Neurath's claim that the social sciences can be sciences.[5]

Even though the original positivists were sanguine about the prospects of a science of society, Neurath, from his vantage point in 1944, acknowledged that there was little by way of actual scientific achievement in this area. Neurath suggested that the historical situation of the social sciences is the best explanation for the paucity of results. "In sociology we have, up to now, no clear trend of hypotheses, as we had no such trend in the hypotheses on electricity in a period in which undulation and emission theories of light already existed. Perhaps at the moment our sociological studies are in their youth."[6] Neurath's reference to the youth of the discipline is revealing, for it reflects a basic positivist view of the process by which science advances. Scientific progress, on this account, is the result of collecting more and more truths over time. If scientific advancement is a product of cumulative inquiry, then the youth of the discipline constitutes a ready explanation for the lack of results in the social sciences.

A quarter century after Neurath, however, this apologia is again employed by another prominent social scientist to explain to the members of his discipline why scientific progress has eluded them. Robert Merton, in his classic essay "Sociological Theories of the Middle Range," states: "Some sociologists still write as though they expect, here and now, formulation of *the* general sociological theory broad enough to encompass the vast ranges or precisely observed details of social behavior . . . and fruitful enough to direct the attention of research workers to a flow of problems for empirical research. This I take to be a premature and apocalyptic belief. We are not ready. Not

[4]Carl Hempel, *Aspects of Scientific Explanation* (New York: The Free Press, 1965), pp. 163–164.

[5]Ibid., p. 171.

[6]Neurath, *Foundations of the Social Sciences*, p. 42.

enough preparatory work has been done."[7] In other words, the intellectual immaturity of the social sciences makes it inappropriate to compare the natural and the social sciences. Such comparisons, Merton maintains, only induce theory envy. Having observed and admired the mature intellectual apparatus of the natural sciences, according to Merton, social scientists have become painfully self-conscious about their lack of scientific development:

> Looking about them, many sociologists take the achievements of physics as the standard for self-appraisal. They want to compare biceps with their bigger brothers. They, too, want to *count*. And when it becomes evident that they neither have the rugged physique nor pack the murderous wallop of their big brothers, some sociologists despair. They begin to ask: is a science of society really possible unless we institute a total system of sociology? But this perspective ignores the fact that between twentieth-century physics and twentieth-century sociology stands billions of man-hours of sustained, disciplined, and cumulative research. Perhaps sociology is not yet ready for its Einstein because it has not yet found its Kepler—to say nothing of its Newton, Laplace, Gibbs, Maxwell, or Planck.[8]

Merton, like Neurath, conceives of scientific knowledge as a cumulative matter. And once again, social scientists are counseled that only time separates social science from the other sciences. Merton's rationale for taking the social sciences to be sciences is fundamentally the positivist one. In particular, it relies on a positivist view of the history of science. And it is precisely this view—that scientific knowledge is fundamentally cumulative—that Kuhn's work makes problematic.

## II

In order to appreciate how Kuhn's work has undercut the Neurath-Merton explanation for the current state of the social sciences, it is necessary to briefly review the impact of Kuhn's views on the philosophy of science. Once this is done, we can examine both why the positivist account is unsatisfactory and how social scientists have gone about creating a Kuhnian rationale for their claim of scientific status.

[7]Robert Merton, in *On Theoretical Sociology* (New York: The Free Press, 1967), p. 45.

[8]Ibid., p. 47.

For our purposes, the impact of *The Structure of Scientific Revolutions* on the philosophy of science is best understood by seeing Kuhn's target as the positivist view of the history of science. Successive scientific theories provide, on this positivist account, *reforms* of earlier views. The key claim is that there exists, through reforms, a fundamental continuity in the growth of scientific knowledge. Against this view, Kuhn emphasizes the discontinuities, the *absence*, of a single, unbroken skein of scientific truths connecting disparate theories. Major scientific changes, argues Kuhn, result from complete breaks with established scientific outlooks. One important aspect of such breaks is that notions that play key explanatory roles in earlier theories disappear after the break has been effected. Entities indigenous to older theories (e.g., phlogiston and entelechies) simply cease to be; these notions are discarded, not refined. The important point here is that there exists no privileged subset of notions that is, as science progresses, constantly improved or reformed. Hence the appropriateness of the term "revolution" in the title of Kuhn's book.

A shift in scientific worldview, that is, a shift that alters both the scientific perception and the inventory of existent entities, is what Kuhn calls a change of paradigm. Paradigms delimit the working concerns of scientists between revolutions—the periods of "normal science." Radical breaks in the scientific tradition, on the other hand, involve paradigm shifts. Kuhn has often been taken to task for his multiple and vague use of "paradigm," but we need not worry about the necessary and sufficient conditions (if such there be) for the term. What is of concern for my analysis are the consequences, and not the details, of these shifts. What is important is that Kuhn's view undercuts the cumulative account of scientific knowledge. It does so by showing that key episodes in the history of science involve, not the addition of new laws to old, but the incommensurability of the successor theory and its predecessors. The process of scientific change is not one of gradual accumulation; it is better understood as one of destruction and recreation. In the pre-Kuhnian story line, One Science is gradually shaped over time to better fit Reality. With Kuhn, we can no longer speak of One Science and its history nor, for that matter, of a Reality approached as a limit by this science.

An equally important implication of Kuhn's view is his attack on the identification of knowledge with scientific results. One reason for favoring this identification has been that it seems to enable one to distinguish eternal truth from the ephemeral, the culture-free from the culture-bound. Positivism promised an escape from relativism (if not from skepticism). If Kuhn is right, however, whatever it is that distinguishes the scientifically endorsed knowledge claims from other statements people are likely to affirm, it is *not* that scientific statements reflect reality while nonscientific statements do not: "We may . . . have to relinquish the notion, explicit or implicit, that changes of paradigm carry scientists and those who learn from them closer and closer to the truth" (p. 170). Again, Kuhn says of science that "nothing that has been or will be said makes it a process of evolution *toward* anything" (pp. 170–171). The Kuhnian picture is dynamic in disturbing ways; we cannot be assured that we are progressing over time to a more accurate picture of the world. I return later to the broader implications of this Kuhnian account of the nature of knowledge.

Neurath and Merton are examples of social scientists who explain the problem in their disciplines by appeal to a certain view of the history of science. If it were not for this view, they would be hard pressed to explain why the social sciences lack the predictive capacities and the instrumental knowledge that characterize other sciences. Hence the positivist history of science is a key element in their account of the nature of the social sciences. If, however, we follow Kuhn and reject this cumulative view of scientific knowledge, then the Neurath-Merton rationale appears quite unsatisfactory. What I now want to examine is how social scientists have responded to the Kuhnian revolution in the philosophy of science.

## III

I mentioned at the outset that social scientists have turned to the philosophy of science to determine the formal criteria for deciding what is a science. It is not surprising, then, that social scientists understand Kuhn's work as *redefining* science itself. This is a mistake, because Kuhn's concern is *not* to challenge the "logic of scientific inquiry," the logic internal to a theory and so the method of "normal science." What Kuhn attacks is the idea that there is some ahistorical, rational algorithm governing scientific choice between competing theories. The fact that choice between theories does not hinge on objective or purely rational considerations is an important part of Kuhn's rejection of the epistemological presuppositions built into the positivist history of science.[9] Kuhn wants ultimately to dispel the temptation to believe in the existence of special value-free notions of "scientific objectivity," "scientific progress," and "science as the representation of reality."

Talk of paradigms provides a focus for Kuhn's discussion of the radical shift that occurs when a scientific community switches allegiance from one theory to another. Kuhn, however, does not, and his remarks indicate that he never intended to, make the possession of a *shared* paradigm—the existence of a theoretical *consensus*—a necessary condition of scientific inquiry. When speaking of paradigms and normal science, he states that "both these related concepts will be clarified by noting that there can be a sort of scientific research without paradigms" (p. 11). The existence or nonexistence of a theoretical consensus *does*, Kuhn believes, separate mature from immature sciences. Kuhn does not have much to say about what precisely differentiates a mature science from the others. In his "Postscript" to the second edition of *The Structure of Scientific Revolutions*, however, he notes (including in the purview of his remarks here the social sciences), "The members of all scientific communities, including the schools of the 'pre-paradigm' period, share the sorts of elements which I have collectively labelled 'a paradigm.' What changes with the transition to maturity is not the presence of a paradigm but rather its nature" (p. 179). Theoretical consensus marks the mature phase of a science; it is not what is needed to transform a discipline into science as such.[10]

Kuhn does distinguish, as the positivist tradition most explicitly does not, between the natural and social sciences. The distinction is marked by the theoretical consensus—the shared paradigms—of the natural science and the absence of such consensus in the social sciences (p. viii). The important point, however, is that this distinction does not make

[9]This point is not always made clear in the literature. One could consistently hold, for example, to a Hempelian hypothetico-deductive model of explanation for normal science and to a Kuhnian view of the history of science. One traditional problem in the philosophy of science about which Kuhn has little to say is that of how to characterize the reasoning used during periods of "normal science."

[10]See also Kuhn's essay "The Essential Tension," in *The Essential Tension: Selected Studies in Scientific Tradition and Change* (Chicago: University of Chicago Press, 1977), p. 232, and "Second Thoughts on Paradigms," in *The Structure of Scientific Theories*, 2d ed., ed. P. Suppes (Urbana: University of Illinois Press, 1977), p. 460, 460–461 n. 4.

one form of inquiry genuinely scientific and the other not.[11] Rather, Kuhn takes the theoretical consensus within the natural sciences as a fact itself in need of historical explanation.

Social scientists, however, read Kuhn's disclaimer of the existence of paradigms in the social sciences as indicating a failure on the part of their discipline to satisfy some defining criteria for science. Specifically, certain social scientists use the lack of a paradigm (in the sense of a consensus or governing model) to explain the poor state of the social sciences. For example, Robert I. Watson, in his 1966 Presidential Address to the Division of the History of Psychology of the APA, asked, "What are the consequences in those sciences that lack a defining paradigm?" and answered that "foremost is a noticeable lack of unity within a science. . . . That psychology lacks this universal agreement about the nature of our contentual model that is a paradigm, in my opinion, is all to readily documented. In psychology there is still debate over fundamentals."[12] Watson here sounded a theme that is constantly replayed in the social scientific literature today. Now it is the lack of agreement among workers in the field, and not, as before, the lack of time, which is said to constitute the major obstacle to scientific progress in the social sciences.

Representative of the use made of the notion of a paradigm is Robert W. Friedrichs' *A Sociology of Sociology*. Friedrichs claims that a science is defined or constituted by the presence of a paradigm.[13] The success of the natural sciences is a function, on this account, of their possession of a shared paradigm: "With the paradigmatic base thus secured, the group or community turns its attention to what is essentially mop-up work. . . . Such science progresses rapidly because it is not distracted by alternate frames. It narrows the range of meaningful

[11]Kuhn elsewhere suggests that, although paradigms are not a necessary condition for scientific activity, they are necessary if one is to identify a discipline as having a "normal" scientific practice. And without normal science, there cannot be the paradigm shifts that crises in the physical sciences frequently prefigure. Without paradigm shifts there are no "scientific solutions" in Kuhn's sense in the social sciences; see his remarks in "The Function of Measurement in Modern Physical Science," in *The Essential Tension*, p. 222. Thus the absence of a governing paradigm (and so changes in paradigm) excludes the social sciences from the type of analysis of the history of science Kuhn develops.

[12]Robert I. Watson, "Psychology: A Prescriptive Science," *American Psychologist* 22 (June 1967):436.

[13]Robert W. Friedrichs, *A Sociology of Sociology* (New York: Free Press, 1970), p. 324.

problems sufficiently so that only the limited ingenuity of the particular scientist involved should inhibit their solution."[14] Friedrichs' view, first published in 1970, has strongly influenced the social scientific literature. It is a view now found, for example, in undergraduate texts in sociology.[15] For Kuhn, the notion of a paradigm is part of his method for structuring the history of science. Social scientists have made the notion part of the definition of what it is to be a science, which is not what Kuhn intended.

Friedrichs also inaugurated a second tradition in the social scientific view of paradigms. He identifies several competing paradigms in his chosen field of sociology and, taking a lead from Kuhn, stresses that conflicts between individuals who subscribe to these different paradigms tend to be irrational: "Advocates of alternative models talk past one another, for there is . . . no fully institutionalized framework of substantive assumptions that both accept. Personal factors, aesthetic predilections, the age, role and private interests of individuals, and subspecializations all are involved. Persuasion rather than proof is king."[16] For Friedrichs, the existence of multiple paradigms precludes consensus, and consensus is a necessary condition for productive science.

The significance of the lack of consensus in the social sciences is further developed in George Ritzer's *Sociology: A Multiple Paradigm Science*. Ritzer here states that a multiple paradigm science is

> [one] in which there are several paradigms vying for hegenomy within the field as a whole. One of the defining characteristics of a multiple paradigm science is that supporters of one paradigm are constantly questioning the basic assumptions of those who accept other paradigms. Thus, scientists have a difficult time conducting 'normal science' because they are constantly defending their flanks against attacks from those who support other paradigms. It is in the category of a multiple paradigm science that I would place sociology, as well as the other social sciences.[17]

[14]Ibid., p. 5.

[15]Janet S. Chafetz, *A Primer on the Construction and Testing of Theories in Sociology* (Itasca, Ill.: F. E. Peacock, 1978), characterizes Kuhn as having established that a paradigm delimits and defines what it is to be a science.

[16]Friedrichs, *A Sociology of Sociology*, p. 2.

[17]George Ritzer, *Sociology: A Multiple Paradigm Science* (Boston: Allyn & Bacon, 1975), p. 12.

Since there is no consensus as to the discipline's paradigm, there is no normal science (this is, of course, the point made by Watson). "Because there is no dominant paradigm in sociology, sociologists find it difficult to do the highly specialized work needed for the cumulation of knowledge." Even worse, since major intellectual advances are a result of revolutions—paradigm shifts—and not normal science (although the revolutions grow out of normal science), "the inability to practice normal science also acts as an impediment to revolutionary advances."[18] Thus the absence of consensus explains both the absence of normal science in the social sciences and the lack of revolutionary breakthroughs.

A second feature of Ritzer's analysis is his emphasis on the irrational nature of paradigm disputes. Ritzer states that "sociologists often completely forget the question of knowledge advancement in their efforts to politically advance the cause of their paradigms." He accuses sociologists of purposely distorting their opponent's position in order to better attack them; calling such power struggles "political," he declares that, "in the social sciences, and in sociology in particular, political factors are preeminent." According to Ritzer, then ideologically inspired warfare explains the anemic state of the sociological art.[19]

What requires close scrutiny in Ritzer's explanation of sociology's current state is the extent to which the consensual model does, in fact, account for the absence of instrumental knowledge. In Ritzer's argument, the absence of consensus assumes just the role played earlier by the claim that the social sciences are still in their youth. Ritzer cites a study, which, he contends, supports the view that theoretical fragmentation is primarily what separates sociology from physics:

> More generally, Lodahl and Gordon have provided some empirical support for the entire base upon which this book is built. They have tended to confirm Kuhn's idea that there is variation among fields in terms of paradigmatic development. More specifically, they have shown that the social sciences are less developed paradigmatically than the natural sciences. Sociology is at, or near, the bottom of paradigmatic development in terms of those fields studied. . . . It is my thesis that this lowly status is attributable to the

[18]Ibid., pp. 201–202.

[19]Ibid., pp. 202–203; see Ritzer's remarks on the "straw man" fallacy.

fact that paradigms within sociology have not been able to maintain preeminence. . . . Each paradigm is contested by those who accept the other paradigms. In my opinion, the finding that sociology is a low paradigm science results from this fact.[20]

Even critics of Friedrichs and Ritzer tend to agree with the assumption that every science exists and develops by virtue of a shared paradigm. Thus all we find in the recent literature is a philosophical updating of the problems discussed by Merton and Neurath. Time, however, is no longer the key problem. Now social scientists are told that sociology is an intellectual Sleeping Beauty awaiting the theoretician's kiss to bring her to life. In the words of two typical exponents of this view,

> those who state so emphatically that there are paradigms in sociology must support their assertions by showing that there is at least one area of research that is guided by concrete examples of scholarship, which serve to generate and to solve puzzles. What we often actually find is research modeled upon no other research at all, upon a short, soon-extinguished line of research or upon a single theorist's speculation. . . . We find constant arguing, bickering, and debate, but very little agreement. This lack of agreement affects operationalization and manipulation of concepts, such that different research requires different, often incommensurable data. The concepts themselves seem to change from study to study.[21]

In answer to the question, Are the social sciences really sciences? we are given a promissory note. We are assured that, given the mode of defining science provided by philosophers of science, there is no reason to think that sociology cannot be shaped to fit.

One worry arising from this analysis is that it might be used to underwrite a type of intellectual totalitarianism in the social sciences;[22] if the absence of a paradigm-inspired consensus is the central

[20] Ibid., p. 19.

[21] D. L. Eckberg and L. Hill, Jr., "The Paradigm Concept and Sociology: A Critical Review," *American Sociological Review* 44 (1979):925–937; reprinted in *Paradigms and Revolutions*, ed. G. Gutting (Notre Dame, Ind.: University of Notre Dame Press, 1980), p. 131 (page reference to Gutting).

[22] See, for example, Herminio Martins, "The Kuhnian 'Revolution' and Its Implications for Sociology," in *Imagination and Precision in the Social Sciences*, ed. T. J. Nossiter, A. H. Hanson, and S. Rokkan (London: Faber & Faber, 1972), pp. 52–53.

obstacle to normal science, and normal science is the royal road to scientific achievement, then there is a rationale for insisting that one method predominate "for the good of the field."

More to the philosophical point, however, are the concerns suggested by Richard Bernstein in *The Restructuring of Social and Political Theory*. Chief among Bernstein's explanations for the failure of the Kuhnian model to provide the sort of rationale sought by Friedrichs et al. is that Kuhn does not distinguish some special defining characteristic of a *scientific* consensus: "Kuhn's theses are most ambiguous and unsatisfactory precisely where one most needs illumination. Kuhn does not help to distinguish scientific paradigms from ideological paradigms—a fundamental point ignored by those who are eager to see Kuhn's relevance to social and political studies."[23] To insist that consensus is a necessary condition of, say, political science, is, I argue below, to misidentify an *effect* of the type of achievement that marks a science's maturity as the cause of scientific achievement.

Do the social sciences suffer, in any case, as a result of a failure of ideological consensus? Perhaps there is low consensus just as the aforementioned social scientists maintain. Still, at least with regard to accounting for the dearth of scientific results, the consensual model provides no better an explanation than the appeal to the discipline's youth. If we look again at Kuhn, we see that what Ritzer et al. take as differentiating the social sciences and the physical sciences is, in fact, shared by both. One cannot use the multiple-paradigm thesis to explain the social sciences' current state, for this feature does not account for the difference between the social and the natural sciences. As Kuhn points out, the questioning, sniping, and political infighting that supposedly constitute obstacles to normal science in the social sciences has historical parallels in various natural scientific disciplines. The multiple-paradigm view leaves social scientists no worse off than, for example, workers in the field of electrical research in the late eighteenth century.[24] In early work on the Leyden jar (a rudimentary electrical condenser), "there was no single paradigm for electrical research. Instead, a number of theories, all derived from relatively

[23]Richard J. Bernstein, *The Restructuring of Social and Political Theory* (Philadelphia: University of Pennsylvania Press, 1978), p. 105.

[24]And just as important, where multiple paradigms do exist, as in psychology, each goes merrily on its way. I owe this point to Dick Ketchum.

accessible phenomena, were in competition" (p. 61). The Leyden jar is significant because it presented a puzzle all workers in the field sought to explain. One way of understanding paradigms is as providing an exemplary case of problem solving. In our example, the solution (explanation) to the question of how the Leyden jar works established a paradigm where previously there had been none. This suggests that the obstacles to science in the social sciences are not primarily political, as Ritzer and others insist. Sociologists of this ilk have, I argue, gotten the intellectual connections backward, for they contend that consensus permits normal science, and that normal science makes scientific achievements possible. On Kuhn's analysis, on the other hand, what make normal scientific activity possible are actual achievements. A discipline coalesces—and accepts a governing model or paradigm—because of some concrete achievement, some solution, that serves to define work for others in this area of research. The ideological commitment results from the achievement in concrete problem solving. It is a misreading of Kuhn and of the nature of scientific inquiry to derive from either the view that instrumental control of nature is gained by ideological cohesion. This emphasis on ideology as the key to instrumental control and scientific success is only a case of yearning for the "triumph of the will."

The attempts to explain the state of the social sciences by an appeal to Kuhn's works are, then, unsatisfactory. Certainly our image of what constitutes a science is plastic, as philosophical speculation from Aristotle on indicates. The positivists offer a clear reason for thinking that the social sciences are sciences, but this reason turns out to be untenable. Kuhnian philosophy of science suggests to many social scientists an explanation for the lowly states of their disciplines, but the Kuhnian perspective does not explain why there continues to be a lack of appropriately scientific results in the social sciences. This unhappy state of affairs leaves us unable to answer the question, Are the social sciences really sciences?

By way of ameliorating this glum position, I want to return to a point made earlier, namely, the identification within the positivist tradition of genuine knowledge and achieved scientific results. I suggested that what many philosophers have found challenging about Kuhn's work is the implication for our view of scientific knowledge. Seen through the perspective of Kuhn's historical analyses, there are no timeless, context-free truths of nature that the laws of science might capture.

To paraphrase Wittgenstein's famous caution to philosophers,[25] a picture (of what it is to be a science) has held social scientists captive. The appropriate therapy, Wittgenstein suggests, is one that breaks the hold these pictures or problems have. With respect to the question, Are the social sciences really sciences? my discussion is meant to be therapeutic.

[25]Ludwig L. Wittgenstein, *Philosophical Investigations*, 3d ed. (New York: Macmillan, 1958), §115.

CHAPTER 6

# Pseudoproblems in Social Science: The Myth of Meaning Realism

Chapter 5 chided those unduly concerned to show by definition that the social sciences are true sciences. This chapter examines attempts to establish that the social sciences *cannot* be sciences. I term such arguments "impossibility arguments." This is, of course, what generates the *Methodenstreit.*[1] A characteristic reason cited by impossibility arguments is the nature of the phenomena the social sciences investigate. Social sciences cannot be sciences, go the impossibility arguments, because the proper study of human social behavior only promotes understanding. Understanding does not permit the formulation of laws and predictions. Hence the social sciences cannot be sciences in the usual sense of that term.

Classic impossibility arguments are found in the writings of Peter Winch.[2] The particular dispute he initiated has been perpetuated, expounded, and expanded in at least two volumes devoted to various responses to his views.[3] The principals in the debate divide between those, such as Winch, who deny that one standard of evaluation is

[1]See "Introduction" to this volume, pp. 2–3.

[2]Peter Winch, *The Idea of a Social Science* (London: Routledge & Kegan Paul, 1958). "Understanding a Primitive Society," *American Philosophical Quarterly* 1 (1964): 307–324; reprinted in *Understanding and Social Inquiry*, ed. F. Dallmayr and T. McCarthy (Notre Dame, Ind.: University of Notre Dame Press, 1977); page references are to the Dallmayr and McCarthy volume. Page references in the following discussion are to *The Idea of a Social Science*.

[3]The important initial responses to Winch are collected in B. Wilson, ed., *Rationality* (New York: Harper Torchbooks, 1970). A recent collection that includes essays by many of the principals of the original controversy is M. Hollis and S. Lukes, eds., *Rationality and Relativism* (Cambridge, Mass.: M.I.T. Press, 1982).

appropriate for all people, and those, such as Martin Hollis, who champion a belief in "the epistemological unity of mankind."[4]

An unnoticed common denominator to both sides in this dispute, I argue in this chapter, is the assumed existence of either universal meanings or incontrovertible logical standards. These semantic or logical universals are the standard against which attempts at understanding are measured. I dub this view "meaning realism" and discuss it at length below. All forms of meaning realism engender a commitment to methodological exclusivism since the realist assumptions on each side entail that there is a fact of the matter to the interpretation of beliefs. What divides Winch and his critics, on my analysis, is a metaphysical dispute regarding what the underlying semantic or logical facts are. But this common and unquestioned metaphysical commitment to meaning realism is inconsistent with what is established by the argument for the indeterminacy of translation. Hence meaning realism is to be rejected. Once rejected, however, the controversies arising from the debate relying on this issue become mere pseudoproblems. My critique of meaning realism in this chapter, in conjunction with the analysis presented in Chapter 9, undercuts the basis for the *Rationalitätstreit*.

In Section I of this chapter I develop Winch's thesis. I then criticize two recent attempts to use Quine's work to show Winch's meaning realism to be implausible. I offer, in turn, an interpretation of the argument for the indeterminacy thesis which does render Winch's view untenable.

In Section II I defend a claim made, surprisingly, by both Winch and Quine against certain critics who, for reasons other than those surveyed in Section I, assume that translation must be determinate. My conclusion sketches the implications of a thoroughgoing Quinean style antirealism with regard to both translation and standards of rationality for the practice of social science.

## I

Prominent among the pseudoproblems alluded to in the title of this chapter is the debate fostered by the assumption that meaning realism

[4] Martin Hollis, "The Epistemological Unity of Mankind," in *Philosophical Disputes in the Social Sciences*, ed. S. C. Brown (Atlantic Highlands, N.J.: Humanities Press, 1979), p. 230; see also the articles by Hollis in the volumes cited in n. 3.

is a necessary condition to the understanding of socially significant action. Meaning realism, as I use the term, is of a piece with the view Quine terms "the myth of the museum." At issue between meaning realists and those who accept the indeterminacy thesis is whether or not there exists some "fact of the matter" that provides a truth value for statements about meanings.

I argue that there is good reason to reject the claim that social inquiry must concern itself necessarily or exclusively with adequacy at the level of meaning. Winch, for example, presumes that the sole or central task of social science is to specify those rules, implicit or explicit, conscious or unconscious, that members of a society share and that give meaning or significance to their behavior. Similar views are to be found, on the philosophical side, in the writings of Alfred Schutz and in those in the phenomenological philosophical tradition;[5] in the social sciences, work by ethnomethologists reflect the view I am describing.

Two claims developed by Winch concern me in regard to the issue of meaning realism. The first claim is that the primary purpose of the social sciences is to understand how members of a society understand their socially significant relations. Winch claims that such understanding is possible only if each member of the society has knowledge of a particular set of rules. The second claim, a subject of much criticism, is that the canons of justification—what counts as being rational—are also internal to the beliefs of a given culture. Put another way, the claim is that standards of rationality are local and not universal.

Winch's first claim holds that shared rules are a necessary condition for communication; the rules in question are semantic, not syntactic, and are held to be required for the appropriate conceptualization of social behavior. Social relations are, on Winch's view, relations of ideas. This is to say that social events owe their existence to whatever shared accounts members of the society are prepared to give them.

> An event's character as an act of obedience is *intrinsic* to it in a way which is not true of an event's character as a clap of thunder; and this is in general true of human acts as opposed to natural events. In the case of the latter, although

[5]See, for example, H. Garfinkle, *Studies in Ethnomethodology* (Cambridge: Polity Press, 1984); p. 31; Alfred Schutz, *Collected Papers, Volume I: The Problem of Social Reality* (The Hague: Martinus Nijhoff, 1971), pp. 58–66; Dan Sperber, *On Anthropological Knowledge* (Cambridge: Cambridge University Press, 1982), pp. 29–34.

human beings can think of the occurrences in question only in terms of the concepts they do in fact have of them, yet the events themselves have an existence independent of those concept. . . . But it does not make sense to suppose that human beings might have been issuing commands and obeying them before they came to form the concept of command and obedience. For their performance of such acts is itself the chief manifestation of their possession of those concepts an act of obedience itself contains, as an essential element, a recognition of what went before as an order. [p. 125; see also pp. 23, 123, 133]

Different societies, of course, have different ideas. Hence there is no understanding of the social realities without a prior understanding of the local rules governing linguistic behavior. A fundamental problem of the social sciences, then, is to uncover and translate such rules, for without them there is no possibility of understanding what counts as socially significant action.

Most important, at least with respect to the methodological import of Winch's account, is that the translation of these rules is an activity both prior to and different in kind from the type of investigation conducted by natural scientists: "For whereas in the case of the natural scientist we have to deal with only one set of rules, namely those governing the scientist's investigation itself, here *what the sociologist is studying*, as well as his study of it, is a human activity and is therefore carried on according to rules" (p. 87). In other words, the goal of social inquiry is to attain the type of understanding whose hallmark is fluid translation and *not* the type of explanation marked by successful prediction.[6] Indeed, Winch maintains that the former type of understanding—knowledge of the rules—is a necessary condition for the latter—formulating generalizations: "People do not first make generalizations and then embody them in concepts; it is only by virtue of their possession of concepts that they are able to make generalizations at all" (p. 44). We do not have a reality to investigate until we have the appropriate set of rules by which to discern it: "Our idea of what belongs to the realm of reality is given for us in the language that we use. The concepts we have settle for us the form of the experience we have of the world. . . . The world *is* for us what is presented through

[6]For recent reflections on why social science explanations are like the latter, see Alasdair MacIntyre, *After Virtue* (Notre Dame, Ind.: University of Notre Dame Press, 1981), chap. 8.

those concepts. That is not to say that our concepts may not change; but when they do, that means that our concept of the world has changed too" (p. 15). It is this suggestion that all members of a society possess a certain set of concepts which, I argue below, runs afoul of the argument for the indeterminacy of translation.

I am not imputing to Winch some simpleminded view that people have some set of rules clearly in mind or that the rules are somehow intrinsic to each person's mind. His mistake is subtle, and its very subtlety makes it appear innocuous. But closer examination shows how insidious an error it really is. The error is Winch's assumption that there are or must be *shared rules* that function as a necessary condition of language use. Winch frequently writes as follows: "the two concepts of reality involved"; "the point which following those rules has in a society"; "The conception of reality is indeed indispensable to any understanding of the point of a way of life"; "The specific forms which these concepts take . . . vary considerably from one society to another; but their central position within a society's institutions is and must be a constant factor."[7] The use of the definite article in all such remarks is no mere stylistic tic. It represents an important misapplication (or so I argue)[8] of Wittgenstein's vexed remarks on "criteria." In particular, Winch writes that where it makes sense to say that someone did something correctly or incorrectly, "then it must also make sense to say that he is applying a criterion in what he does even though he does not, and perhaps cannot, formulate that criterion" (p. 58). Again, Winch speaks of "the appropriate criteria for deciding whether the actions" (p. 87) of two people are the same as if there were such rules, clear or fuzzy, that all participants in a form of life must share. Such criteria are assumed by Winch to be social, but this does not alter their "realist" determinateness: "It is only by reference to the criteria governing that system of ideas or mode of life that they [social institutions, etc.] have an existence as intellectual or social events" (p. 108). In short, Winch hypostasizes social rules and talks of them (and their "criteria of application") as if there were an independent object of study.[9]

[7]Winch, "Understanding a Primitive Society," p. 170; p. 172; p. 172; p. 183.

[8]I am greatly influenced here (i.e., in thinking that the error is primarily Winch's and not Wittgenstein's) by Saul Kripke's discussion in *Wittgenstein: On Rules and Private Language* (Cambridge, Mass.: Harvard University Press, 1982), esp. pp. 55–57.

[9]Basically the same problem permeates Charles Taylor's much cited essay, "Interpretation and the Sciences of Man," *Review of Metaphysics* 25 (September 1971);

Of the prominent criticisms of Winch's first thesis—his claim that we share, by virtue of sharing a language and a certain cultural background, knowledge of a specific set of rules of behavior—the one that interests me here asks whether the goal Winch has set for social science is reasonable. This line of criticism is inspired by Quine's discussion of the indeterminacy of translation. Quine's claim, as I understand it, is that one fundamentally errs by taking a realist attitude toward the existence of semantic rules; that is, that a view that holds that there is a uniquely correct way to interpret what another, or even ourselves, has to say is mistaken:

> When someone asks the linguist 'What did the native say?', he thinks the question has a right English answer which is unique up to equivalence transformation of English sentences. He expects this even when the native's remarks were far from the category of observation sentences. He expects this insofar as we agree, with him, to neglect the omnipresent underdetermination of natural knowledge generally. But in this expectation, even as hedged by this last proviso, he is mistaken.
>
> A conviction persists, often unacknowledged, that our sentences express ideas, and express these ideas rather than those, even when behavioral criteria can never say which. There is the stubborn notion that we can tell intuitively which idea someone's sentence expresses, our sentence anyway, even when the intuition is irreducible to behavioral criteria. This is why one thinks that one's question 'What did the native say?' has a right answer independent of choices among mutually incompatible manuals of translation.[10]

The mistake made in asking "What did the native say?" is in the expectation that there is some one right answer. The problem is not (as is sometimes thought) that one is unable to choose among a variety of possible answers. In other words, the problem is not one of the methodology of translation.[11] Rather, Quine's claim is that there is no one

---

reprinted in *Interpretive Social Science*, ed. P. Rabinow and W. Sullivan (Berkeley: University of California Press, 1979); page references are to the latter work. Taylor seems to think that good translations approach, if only asymptotically, the "real" meaning. "A successful interpretation is one which makes clear the meaning originally present in a confused, fragmentary, cloudy form" (p. 27); see also pp. 34–35, p. 38. Both Taylor and Winch stress the holistic constraint on interpretation and the social origins of meanings. In this they are in accord with Quine.

[10]W. V. O. Quine, in *Words and Objections*, ed. D. Davidson and J. Hintikka (Dordrecht: Reidel, 1969), pp. 303–304.

[11]For an expanded analysis and defense of this line of Quine interpretations, see Chapter 1.

right answer. There is no right answer because there is no determinate meaning relative to which a translation is right or wrong. The problem posed by the question is a pseudoproblem.[12]

Central to Winch's account is the view that communication is grounded on a shared, internalized set of semantic rules for a given society. Quine rejects precisely the assumption that we can make sense of there being common or shared rules for determining meaning. He rejects the very question that Winch argues is *the* relevant question of understanding human social behavior. The dispute is not methodological but ontological. The problem is, not that Winch's proposed goal lies beyond the grasp of current techniques in the social sciences, but rather that Winch's proposal presupposes a set of concepts that have no application. Any problem arising exclusively from Winch's conception of translation as a quest for such a set of concepts is, then, a pseudoproblem that disappears once Quine's view of translation is accepted in place of Winch's.

Two reasons that the meaning realist is mistaken are as follows. First, we have no empirical support for the claim that people, in learning a language, learn anything more than coordination of behavior given certain stimulus cues. Briefly, we learn to speak under varying conditions (the conditions may vary greatly or not much, but they vary nonetheless). Since we all start from a different evidential basis, and since we are unable to reconstruct deductively the connections between our way of talking about the world and the stimulus conditions to which we are exposed, the only empirical support we have is for the claim that we have acquired outward conformity in language use. An explanation of behavioral similarities need not appeal to any Winchian-style rules. What an examination of learning situations suggests, in other words, is that, for any two speakers of even the same language, they "may attain to an identical command of English through very dissimilar processes of tentative association and

[12] Another line of criticism rejects both Winch's contention that discerning the rules governing behavior is the sole purpose of social scientific explanations and the corollary view that the study of these rules somehow precludes a scientific study of society. Although I think both aspects of these criticisms of Winch are correct, they do not challenge the plausibility of meaning realism. I examine aspects of this criticism of Winch in Chapter 9. A typical example here is the treatment offered by Richard Rudner, *The Philosophy of Social Science* (Englewood Cliffs, N.J.: Prentice-Hall, 1966), chap. 4, esp. pp. 81–83.

adjustment. . . . The identical elephantine form may . . . overlie very unlike configurations of twigs and branches."[13] We can successfully coordinate our behavior with others, and so communication goes forward.

The issue, however, is whether the coordinated behavior is, as Winch suggests, only possible while learning, along the way, the "same rules." To merely point out these differences in language learning does not deter a meaning realist like Winch. He claims that the possession of such rules is a necessary condition for having (using) a language. One might argue, on Winch's behalf, the position that using a language like ours requires that we all possess the *sort* of rules to which Winch alludes.

Now it is clear that Quine opposes this view as well; but it is at just this point—the point where the objection to meaning realism is extended beyond the alleged inability to choose among competing interpretations, that even sympathetic Quinean critics have difficulty. I examine two recent attempts, one by Robert Feleppa and the other by Christopher Hookway, to interpret Quine's argument for the indeterminacy in a way that provides a reply to Winch's view on meaning. In appreciating why these reconstructions are unsatisfactory, I indicate why Winch's position must be attacked from a rather different angle and how Quine's argument, at least on my reading of it, provides such an attack.

As noted above, Quineans have long puzzled over just how, above and beyond underdetermination (where we simply possess rival empirically equivalent but logically incompatible theories), one is to distinguish in kind between truth relativized to a scientific theory and meaning relativized to a manual of translation. Feleppa expresses the puzzlement well when he writes: "What empirical sense do we make of the claim that the translator *might* thus be wrong, given that other steps in the argument show us that there can be no empirical basis to any claim to the effect that the translator *is* wrong in choosing from among a set of alternatives that are underdetermined in Quine's strong sense?" (pp. 6–7, see also p. 6 for similar remark).[14]

[13]W. V. O. Quine, *Word and Object* (Cambridge, Mass.: M.I.T. Press, 1960), p. 94. See also Roth, "Paradox and Indeterminacy," and "Reconstructing Quine."

[14]Robert Feleppa, "Translation as Rule-Governed Behavior," *Philosophy of the Social Sciences* 12 (1982):1–31. Page references in the following discussion are to this essay.

In order to answer this question, Feleppa suggests an ingenious solution (but one, he admits, that is not Quine's). Feleppa's solution is this: translation is a problem of rule coordination—specifically, coordination of the language of the person doing the translating and that of the person or group whose language is being translated. The translator, on this view of the matter, seeks to create a metalanguage within which to express meaning equivalences of expressions from each of the other languages. What is suggestive and novel about Feleppa's account, as I understand it, is that translation thus understood is prescriptive rather than descriptive. It prescribes, that is, a method of coordinating two languages via a third. Since translation is never meant to be a descriptive activity, the equivalences provided by the manual of translation are justified pragmatically and not by claiming that they are true: "The mark of a good translation manual will be that it will contain rules which, if adhered to by target-culture users. . . , will enable them to conform to rule-governed regularities of speech behavior operative in the source-language community" (p. 21). This suggestion is, I believe, very close to Quine's actual view of communication. Nonetheless, although this account of communication is in accord with Quine, it is inadequate as an explication of what is at issue in claiming that translation is indeterminate. That Feleppa's analysis is lacking here can be seen by examining what he has to say in response to anthropologists who do believe that there is a uniquely correct translation (the touchstone of the accuracy of such translation is some internalized set of rules and concepts).

Against those who believe that there exist conceptual models lurking in mental space awaiting discovery by a sufficiently sensitive translator, Feleppa offers the following argument:

> if one considers carefully, as does Quine, the very purposes of the manual and ethnography, which, by their nature, are in part conditioned by the needs of the target language speakers, and by the somewhat different needs of the linguistic metalanguage speakers, one will see that manuals of translation and other ethnographical semantic analyses cannot possibly achieve the task of intercultural coordination, while at the same time revealing what is going on 'inside' the source culture, in isolation from other cultures. So much of the manual of translation is determined by the explicit codifications of usage among speakers of the target language . . . that it *makes no sense* [emphasis added] to ask that the manual come to capture the native's 'inner meanings' as well. [pp. 26–27]

The claim, in other words, is that it is a mistake to think of translation manuals as reproducing, possibly, the mental model held by speakers of the source language, and the reason this belief is mistaken is that it misconstrues the purpose of translation manuals: "The rules one learns from the translation manual are *not* the rules of the society, but rules that enable an outsider (or a bilingual) to get along. Ideally, these rules will enable one to get on *as well* as if one understood the native's rules" (p. 28). Translation manuals never had, in the first place, the recovery of such mental models as a goal; the goal was coordination of linguistic behavior between two distinct language communities.

Yet Feleppa's argument leaves untouched the key issue to which Quine addresses himself: the reasonableness of believing that there exists a mental model that a propitious translation might mirror. The key problem comes out in Feleppa's assertion that it makes no sense to ask if the translation manual describes the native's mental model. This might appear to conflict with Winch's view, an impression Feleppa strengthens when he states that since the manual "is directed to the coordination of linguistic activity . . . [it] cannot serve to 'reflect' the 'inner' character of just one [of the linguistic communities]" (p. 28). Why? For what reason does it make no sense; why is it that the manual cannot serve to represent the conceptual model of the source community? The only reason Feleppa gives is that that was not the purpose of the manual. But surely this is not sufficient to rule out as meaningless the question of whether or not we have found the uniquely correct translation.

Feleppa gives a more modest statement of the upshot of his argument at another point in his paper: "I believe my reconstruction provides . . . a clearer basis for arguing that successful translational correlations *need not* involve the social inquirer with recovery of the 'real' belief of subjects or cause him to worry as to whether their cognitive structures have been accurately 'captured' or 'reproduced'" (p. 30, emphasis added; see a related remark on page 29 to the effect that the manual "need involve no 'penetrations' into what is demonstrably the source—society's mental or cognitive realm.") Here Feleppa's analysis of translation as a method of codification and coordination does sustain the claim that the purpose of translation "need not" be Winchian; but surely that claim does not move the dispute between Quine and Winch off center. At most Feleppa provides an interesting interpretation of why a Quinean might say that there is no warrant for asserting that translational hypotheses are true or false; but there is nothing is his argument supporting the claim that it makes no sense to view translation as representing the actual rules speakers use. For anyone who believes that translation either is or should be a descriptive enterprise, Feleppa has said nothing to show that he or she is wrong. Feleppa, unable to see how to justify Quine's strong views on the indeterminacy of translation, provides a reconstruction that, while essentially Quinean in spirit, nonetheless fails to undercut a meaning realist view of translation.

Christopher Hookway is another philosopher sympathetic to Quine's views who attempts to plumb the significance of the indeterminacy thesis for social science. Like Feleppa, Hookway reconstructs the argument for the indeterminacy thesis by appeal to the methodology of translation. But it can be quickly seen that, however interesting in other regards Hookway's analysis of indeterminacy is, his reconstruction is totally unconvincing as an argument against meaning realism.

Like Feleppa, Hookway takes Quine's argument to proceed from the method of translation: "The indeterminacy thesis is justified by the use of a highly abstract argument based on methodological features of the translation situation: it can only be refuted by a demonstration that the abstract argument is ineffective" (p. 19).[15] I show below that this account is unsatisfactory both as a response to Winch (for he gives no reason that precludes the correctness of Winch's view) and as a reconstruction of the argument for indeterminacy of translation (for Hookway relies on at least one premise that we have, at present, no reason to believe true).

Hookway notes that the heart of Quinean objections to Winch is that

> [Winch] seems to hold that the social context renders the rule formulations determinate, and concludes that there are difficulties facing one who attempts to interpret the behavior of a society from the outside. . . . [We] may object that he does not justify this theory of meaning, and that there is reason to think that the notion of rule cannot be made to do this kind of work. If we acknowledge that meaning is indeterminate, the problem he envisages disappears. [p. 40]

[15]Christopher Hookway, "Indeterminacy and Interpretation," in *Action and Interpretation*, ed. C. Hookway and P. Pettit (Cambridge: Cambridge University Press, 1978), pp. 17–41. Page references in the following discussion are to this essay.

Hookway is modest, moreover, in his assessment of the import of the indeterminacy thesis; he concludes only that "while the indeterminacy thesis does not itself provide answers to the central questions of the philosophy of anthropology, it does enforce a certain perspective upon them which rules out some otherwise fruitful lines of approach" (p. 41). (As I indicate in the next section, the lesson to be learned is much more radical than this.)

Hookway identifies Quine's underdetermination thesis as constituting a key premise in his argument for the indeterminacy of translation. As Hookway recognizes, however, there is a telling objection to any reconstruction of Quine's indeterminacy thesis which relies exclusively on the claim that theories are underdetermined. Specifically, "a number of critics of Quine's views have protested that Quine has done nothing to justify his view that underdetermination by evidence impugns the objectivity of translation but not of (say) physics. Both are empirically underdetermined, yet only translation displays indeterminacy" (p. 28). In order to fill out the argument and so answer Quine's critics, Hookway suggests that, although truth on the Quinean account is relativized to theories in the natural sciences, Quine also takes the view that we should not be casual about our account of truth, theory-dependent though it may be. "The point seems to be that we now hold a non-relativist attitude towards theories, and there is no reason to abandon it" (p. 31). This supposedly contrasts with our stance toward translation, for there is "no act by which we commit ourselves to absolute synonymy relations. Consequently, there is no obstacle to relativizing reports of translation or synonymy relations explicitly to a particular translation theory" (p. 31). In relativizing our account of synonymy to a manual of translation, Hookway also assumes that more than one manual will be available, that is, that manuals of translation are underdetermined. We can, in this case, speak of meaning relative to one or another theory. There is no reason, however, or so Hookway claims, to think that we can speak of meaning apart from relativizing it to one or another manual: "There are no objective truths about what expressions mean *tout court*. There is no absolute notion of meaning to which these relativized notions approximate. This . . . hypothesis makes the claim that translation is indeterminate" (p. 32). Since we do not have competing theories to choose among with respect to our commonsense theory of the world, we treat our account of truth as if it were absolute. Hookway also concedes that "if one translation theory was ever empirically adequate, then there is no reason not to treat that as capturing the absolute notion of meaning. It is the only meaning notion, after all" (p. 32).

This reconstruction of Quine's argument will just not do. First, we are not any the less committed to a commonsense view of translation than we are to commonsense beliefs about the world. Second, and more important for Hookway's argument, the suggestion that alternative theories of meaning are or could be available is no more than that—a suggestion. We would do better to conclude, on Hookway's reconstruction, that at present we ought to view meaning as determinate until such time as genuinely underdetermined manuals of translation are available. In short, Hookway's account actually sustains the claim that translation is, at present, determinate until proven otherwise.

Against Winch's view of determinacy, then, Hookway does no more than assert that the account of following a rule is underdetermined (pp. 39–40). How does this argument function as a reply to Winch? Hookway's contention here is that, since rules can be underdetermined, there is an "epistemological gap" between the possible rule that might apply to a given situation and our ability to rationally choose among rules (p. 39). But, again, this argument does not itself disprove meaning realism, or, at least, it gives no reason to take seriously Quine's denial that there is a right answer to the question "What did the native say?"

A further weakness in Hookway's reconstruction is his reliance on the claim that manuals of translation are underdetermined.[16] We have, he acknowledges, no examples of genuinely underdetermined theories—theories that are empirically equivalent and yet which we are unable to make compatible by some reconstrual or predicates. Whether there exist underdetermined theories, Quine concludes, is simply an empirical question: "The thesis of underdetermination, even in my latest tempered version, asserts that our system of the world is bound to have empirically equivalent alternative that are not reconcilable by reconstrual of predicates however devious. This, for me, is an open question."[17] The most telling point Hookway has to make against Winch's notion of rule-governed behavior is that there could be more than one system of rules adequate to the task, and the reason for saying

[16]See especially W. V. O. Quine, "Empirically Equivalent Systems of the World," *Erkenntnis* 9 (1975):313–328.

[17]Ibid., p. 327.

this is a general claim about underdetermination. We have seen that Hookway's argument is suspect even if this premise is true; however, we have no guarantee that the premise is true.[18]

What is significant about both Hookway's and Feleppa's attempts to reconstruct Quine is that their respective accounts of indeterminacy by appeal to methodological considerations prove ineffectual in refuting meaning realism. The alleged epistemological gap between meaning and truth—translation and natural science—is not established in this way. What we need to show is that the very assumption that people necessarily share semantic theory by virtue of sharing a "form of life" is, in fact, unreasonable.

On the interpretaion developed in the previous chapters, Quine's claim that translation is indeterminate is to be understood as the claim that we cannot show, as we can for our belief in a shared environment, that the existence of a semantic model is a necessary condition for language learning. Lacking any argument for taking the semantic model as necessary for the language we speak, and having good empirical reasons not to think that there exists such a model, we may conclude that there is no basis for saying that some translation is really the correct one. We *lack* an argument to show that we must assume that there are objectively determinable conditions that make analytical hypotheses—proposed equivalences of meaning—true or false. There are no facts of meaning parallel to the facts of nature. The paradox of language learning, or the need to resolve it, warrants the claim that there are objectively determinable stimulus conditions for observation sentences. We have no similar warrant for an assumption about a shared semantic model, and so we "misjudge the parallel" if we think we can reasonably assert that there is a fact of the matter to meaning.

Understood in the sense developed in the previous chapters, the argument for the indeterminacy of translation does undercut the plausibility of the Winchian proposal for the social sciences. If we have no reason for assuming that there exist some unique set of rules by which individuals jointly make sense of their social environment, then it can

[18]Quine is admittedly unclear with regard to just how the underdetermination thesis affects indeterminacy. His remarks (ibid., p. 322) suggest, on the one hand, that there is no change, but, on the other hand, he notes that the "principle of charity" might well decide the issue, that is, might provide basis for choice in this case. But if there is a basis for choice, then indeterminacy—in the sense crucial for Hookway—does not obtain.

hardly be maintained that the sole purpose of social analysis is to uncover such rules.

## II

The interpretation of indeterminacy offers as well an answer to criticism of both Quine and Winch by Martin Hollis and by Steven Lukes. What links Quine and Winch, according to Hollis, is their shared view that all beliefs are revisable (or, put in a more Winchian way, that our standards for rationally evaluating beliefs are context-dependent).[19]

According to Winch, we cannot say whether or not someone is rational until we know what that person counts as rational, and determining what is rational, in this case, is not a job for the scientist but a matter of correct translation, of mastering the rules of a person's language: "Criteria of logic are not a direct gift of God, but arise out of, and are only intelligible in the context of, ways of living or modes of social life. It follows that one cannot apply criteria of logic to modes of social life as such. . . . Science is one such mode and religion is another; and each has criteria of intelligibility peculiar to itself (*The Idea of a Social Science*, p. 100). Knowledge of the shared rules is necessary for knowledge of the truth conditions for a particular statement. Hence proper translation is a prerequisite of the logical and scientific evaluation of beliefs.

In opposing this variability even of the rules that count as warranting a belief to be rational, Hollis appeals to something like a Quinean notion of an observation sentence—he calls them "bridgehead" utterances. The existence of bridgehead statements is part of the explanation of how translation is possible. Hollis agues that a native must both

[19]Martin Hollis, "Reason and Ritual," reprinted in *Rationality*, ed. Wilson, pp. 227–228, esp. n. 1, p. 228; page references in the following discussion are to this work; see also Steven Lukes, "Some Problems about Rationality," in ibid., pp. 194–213. A confusion persists in the secondary literature insofar as some believe that Quine holds that the translation of logical connectives is immune to indeterminacy. This "immunity view" is propounded by Barry Stroud in "Conventionalism and the Indeterminacy of Translation," in *Words and Objections*, ed. Davidson and Hintikka, and is rejected by Quine in his "Reply to Stroud" therein. For further elaboration on this point, see Roth, "Theories and Nature and the Nature of Theories," *Mind* 89 (July 1980), and "Logic and Translation: A Reply to Alan Berger" *Journal of Philosophy* 79 (March 1982).

share our concept of rationality and, more or less, perceive the world as we do:

> This paper stands or falls with the claim that a theorist of social anthropology must budget for a priori elements which are not optional. . . . The a priori elements are those notions which the natives must be assumed to have, if any identification of their ritual beliefs is to be known to be correct. . . . To establish a bridgehead, by which I mean a set of utterances definitive of the standard meanings of words, he has to assume at least that he and the native share the same perceptions and make the same empirical judgments in simple situations. This involves assumptions about empirical truth and reference. [p. 238]

> The class of utterances which form the bridgehead for [the anthropologist's] advance must be one for which his specification and his informants coincide. [p. 214]

> Some overlap in concepts and precepts is a necessary condition of successful translation. The *sine qua non* is a bridgehead of true assertions about a shared reality. [p. 216]

> If anthropology is to be possible, I have argued, the natives must share our concepts of truth, coherence and rational interdependence of beliefs. [p. 218]

We share not just stimulations but perceptions; these shared perceptions, in turn, form a shared basis for common beliefs about what there is. On Hollis's account, the failing common to the otherwise dissimilar views of Winch and Quine is that both accept the claim that the standards of rational evaluation and of evidence are determined, more or less, by norms internal to a society. It is Quine's willingness to admit that even logical truths and observation sentences might be revisable which leads Hollis, an otherwise professed admirer of Quine, to accuse Quine of "sailing too close to the idealist wind." Yet both Winch and Hollis make the necessary conditions for communication and language use too strong. The important difference between them is that Hollis imagines the standards of observation and deductive inference to be universal, whereas Winch allows that conditions governing both might vary from culture to culture. Hollis is, in this respect, a rigid Kantian about the necessary conditions of rational thought; Winch takes a relaxed, somewhat Hegelian attitude in allowing the categories of understanding to vary. Hollis's claim about what is necessary for rationality is based on his case for what is necessary for communication (translation). I argue that translation can proceed on weaker assumptions and that we can thus discount Hollis's claims about the univocal nature of reality and rationality.

Imagine the situation Quine calls "radical translation"—the case in which the only available guide to communication happens to be the correlation of expressions and observations. The issue here is whether, at this minimal level of communication (a level where we can assume no more than joint exposure to similar stimulus conditions), we need to assume, following Hollis, that those involved *must* share both "concepts and percepts." The problem here for Hollis is how to determine that another's response to particular stimulation, for example, uttering "Gavagai" as a rabbit scurries past, entails that what is perceived is a rabbit (and not, to follow out the Quinean example, undetached rabbit parts). In short, Hollis's notion of a percept has ontological implications; Quine, for his part, argues that the notion of stimulus meaning is causal and anontological.[20]

It seems that the other's referent cannot be determined without knowing more than we already do, ex hypothesi, about the native language. As Quine notes, reference "cannot be mastered without mastering its principle of individuation; where one rabbit leaves off and another begins. And this cannot be mastered by pure ostension, however persistent."[21] Translational (analytical) hypotheses that differ from the one that straightforwardly equates "gavagai" and "rabbit," such as those under which "gavagai" refers to undetached rabbit parts or is said only when the native perceives rabbit flies (Donald Davidson's example), are also supported by the available evidence. Whichever of these (or other) hypotheses one finds plausible in turn determines how additional analytical hypotheses are formulated and, ultimately, how the overall manual of translation is shaped.[22] This approach leads an English-speaking linguist to dismiss certain hypotheses as perverse:

[20]W. V. O. Quine, "Grades of Theoreticity," in *Experience and Theory*, ed. L. Foster and J. Swanson (Amherst: University of Massachusetts Press, 1970), p. 16.

[21]W. V. O. Quine, *Ontological Relativity and Other Essays* (New York: Columbia University Press, 1969), p. 31.

[22]Ibid., p. 32.

The implicit maxim guiding his choice of 'rabbit', and similar choices for other native words, is that an enduring and relatively homogeneous object, moving as a whole against a contrasting background, is a likely reference for a short expression. If he were to become conscious of this maxim, he might celebrate it as one of the linguistic universals, or traits of all languages, and he would have no trouble pointing out its psychological plausibility. But he would be wrong; the maxim is his own imposition, toward settling what is objectively indeterminate. It is a very sensible imposition, and I would recommend no other. But I am making a philosophical point.[23]

The perceptual evidence is not sufficient to determine the concept—the intended reference. In short, Quine concludes, the "indeterminacy of translation now confronting us . . . cuts across extension and intension alike. . . . Reference itself proves behaviorally inscrutable."[24] With regard, then, to Hollis's proposed list of necessary conditions for translation, I take it that the thought experiment of radical translation indicates that translation could (and probably does) proceed from a much more parsimonious basis than Hollis contends, that is, without universal and objectively valid ontological assumptions. Although Hollis would reject Winch's view that there need be a shared, determinate theory of meaning common to a given group of language users, he would insist that the world must appear more or less the same to all. What we need posit in order to explain how communication is possible, however, turns out to be less than Hollis requires. (I criticize Hollis's position in further detail in Chapter 9.)

One final position I would like to consider in the context of this debate is a recent proposal by Michael Luntley.[25] Luntley suggests that attention to the assertability conditions for a given statement provide an argument to support Hollis's claim that there is more to be said about rationality than Winch (and Quine) allow. Assertability conditions, in turn, can themselves be specified by appeal to those logical rules recognized as warranting beliefs. The rationality of a society's judgments can then be evaluated, he claims, in some nonrelativistic

[23]Ibid., p. 34.

[24]Ibid., p. 35.

[25]"Understanding Anthropologists," *Inquiry* 25 (1982):199–216. Page references to Luntley are to this essay.

sense according to how carefully and completely the canons of rational inquiry are themselves examined in a given society. We would, on this account, have a basis for saying that Western science is a more rational system than, for example, that of the Azande, just because Western science is self-conscious about its methods of justification and has critically reflected on these whereas the Azande have done neither. Thus Luntley appears to offer a criterion for judging the rationality of beliefs which does not involve the assumptions of Hollis or Winch.

> Local norms of justification are not criteria of rationality, but of taking something as true. . . . But rationality should be a question of one's methods in assessing one's beliefs irrespective of their truth or falsity. The Azande do justify their beliefs in a logical and rational manner. . . . They are rational in so far as they do just this. At most we might accept the idea of degrees of rationality, primitives are less rational than ourselves because of the preponderance of dogmatic faith in their thinking. This only means that they uncritically accept beliefs at an earlier stage than we do, rationality is only an ideal. [p. 214; see also pp. 202, 206]

Luntley's interesting suggestion, however, is marred by an ambiguity in his use of "degrees of rationality." On the one hand, Luntley sometimes uses this phrase to point to a sociological or anthropological issue, one of why a given society has not been self-reflective about their norms: "The argument serves to suggest a philosophical underpinning for an intellectualist interpretation of ritual that has no need to think of primitive cosmologies as the creation of necessarily inferior intellects. There may be all sorts of explanations why such societies have not reached the necessary division of labor that would enable them to develop the skills and interest for critically assessing their beliefs about ritual" (p. 214). On the other hand, Luntley also uses the notion of "degrees of rationality" in an evaluative sense, specifically, in a sense implying that any society that is self-critical about its criteria of rationality is ipso facto more rational than one that is not so reflective. Hence the Azande are less rational than we are, not because their beliefs do not accord well with the world seen by the lights of Western science, but because they have been intellectually "lazy": "In bringing to our attention the dogmatic refusal of primitive peoples to justify their beliefs beyond a certain limit, it enables us to see how to justify the assertion that their beliefs are false" (p. 213). Since their standards are not self-reflective, we have warrant for saying that our beliefs, when they conflict with theirs, are true because better warranted.

By taking note of the ambiguity discussed above, we see that the notion of "degrees of rationality" is used to support two very different claims. One suggestion is that the fact that certain cultures reflect on their standards of justification but others do not is important in helping to explain why scientific thought arises in some areas but not in others. Another claim is that such reflection is an important part of what it is to be rational. Why is self-reflection a sufficient condition for making one set of beliefs more rational than another? I am reminded here of the cosmologist who asserts that the world rests on the back of the turtle. He is asked on what the turtle in turn rest "Why," he responds, "It's turtles all the way down." Analogously, suppose a native tribe reasons in accord with the accepted rules of first-order logic but does so without ever wondering why these rules are good rules or ever attempting to prove consistency and completeness of their system. Suppose that another group (a Copi cult?) also reasons in this way but happens to have in its possession a sacred text that prescribes, as luck would have it, just these rules. Moreover, this society has a metarule that says, "Only count as acceptable rules of inference those mentioned in the sacred text." Would we say that the latter society, because it has an effective method for justifying its first-order rules, is more rational than the former group? The mere fact that a group reflects on its standards of justification is not a sufficient reason for saying that the group is more rational than one that does not.

Can we even say that such reflection is necessary to our understanding of what it is to be rational? What could such reflection possibly add to our notion of rationality as such? What sort of gain is achieved in rationality by reflecting on standards? Consider, in this regard, the debate early in this century concerning how to clarify the epistemological status of logical truths. In his classic contribution to this debate, Quine observes that the various proposals to "ground" or account for the status of logical truths are, ultimately, circular: "The difficulty is that if logic is to proceed immediately from conventions, logic is needed for inferring logic from the conventions."[26] And although Quine does

[26] "Truth by Convention," reprinted in W. V. O. Quine, *The Ways of Paradox* (New York: Random House 1966), p. 97.

not say, in a Winchian voice, that logic is tied to a particular way of life, his counsel with regard to the status of logic is easily seen in this light: "We may wonder what one adds to the bare statement that the truths of logic and mathematics are a priori, or to the still barer behavioristic statement that they are firmly accepted, when he characterizes them as true by convention."[27] Since Quine does not see, in the end, that we can progress beyond the "barer behavioristic statement," his analysis offers no support for Luntley's suggestion. In short, Luntley wants to restrict the notion of levels of rationality to how well-defined or explicated the inference patterns happen to be. But since what counts as a logically adequate explication must (and this is the core of what troubles Quine) be in some respect antecedently known, it is hard to credit the suggestion that the explication provides a universal standard of rationality.[28] Hence Luntley offers no clear account of what it means for one culture to be more rational than another.

I have critically examined two claims made by Winch: first, that our understanding of social relations in particular and the world in general is rule-governed (in the sense that all speakers need to possess the same semantic rules) and second, that these rules alone provide the norms of justification and understanding of beliefs within a given culture. With respect to the first claim, I have argued, on the one hand, that Winch's view of rules is based on an untenable theory of meaning. Hence his proposal that the purpose of social science be the translation or uncovering of such rules is misguided. On the other hand, however, I have argued, against critics of Winch such as Feleppa and Hookway, that one cannot show why Winch's account of rules is unacceptable merely by appeal to the *methodology* of translation. I have defended Winch's second claim, that the norms of justification are internal, at least against those critics such as Hollis who would also see translation as more determinate than it is reasonable to assume. In short, I have

[27]Ibid., p. 99.

[28]Quine is clearly willing to entertain the notion that the whole of current logic, and the science of which it is a part, might be replaced by something radically different: "Our success in predicting observation might fall off sharply, and concomitantly with this we might begin to be somewhat successful in basing predictions upon dreams and reveries. At that point we might reasonably doubt our theory of nature in even fairly broad outline"; W. V. Quine, *Theories and Things* (Cambridge, Mass.: Belknap Press of Harvard University Press, 1981), p. 22.

espoused, in regard to ongoing controversies in the philosophy of social science, Quine's claim that the indeterminacy of translation "cuts across extension and intension alike." My concern has been to attack epistemological assumptions that assert, in one form or another, that the meaning of words is fixed by virtue of some special relation, whether this special relation be, as with Winch, to rules or concepts, or, as to Hollis, to objects in the world.

What constitutes a pseudoproblem in social science, or so I have argued, is any purported problem that makes realist assumptions with regard to meaning or a priori standards of rationality. There is just less to know than Winch or Hollis happens to believe there is. The implications of indeterminacy are however, even more radical than this. In my concluding chapter, I sketch what I take some of these additional implications to be.

CHAPTER 7

# Voodoo Epistemology: The Strong Programme in the Sociology of Science

> Reflection on the method of science has become increasingly thinner since Kant. If there's any upshot of that part of modern philosophy, it's that the scientists didn't have a secret. There isn't something there that's either effable or ineffable. To understand how they do what they do is pretty much like understanding how any other bunch of skilled craftsmen do what they do. Kuhn's reduction of philosophy of science to sociology doesn't point to an *ineffable* secret of success; it leaves us without the notion of the secret of success.
>
> Richard Rorty
> "A Reply to Dreyfus and Taylor"

Discussion so far has focused on traditional methodological disputes in the philosophy of the social sciences. My concern in Chapters 7 and 8 is to forestall the conclusion that the proper *successor* to the collapse of traditional epistemology is the sociology of knowledge. This suggestion is explicit in an outpouring of books and articles by those championing what is known as the "strong programme" in the sociology of knowledge. The term "strong programme" was coined and much of the substance of the program itself shaped by a trio of scholars, Barry Barnes, David Bloor, and Steve Shapin. Their theoretical writings and case studies constitute the core of this movement. What follows is a detailed reconstruction of the main tenets of the strong programme (Section I); a discussion of how its philosophical assumptions are related to the Quinean themes discussed in previous chapters (Section II); and an analysis of the strong programme views of philosophy of science and epistemology (Section III). Chapter 8 is devoted to a critical discussion of these views.

## I

Central to the philosophical concerns of the strong programme are the implications of the underdetermination thesis for tradititional philosophy of science and epistemology. The underdetermination thesis maintains that it is always possible to formulate logically incompatible but empirically equivalent theories. Put another way, underdetermination claims that competing theories may always be available to account for the available experiential data. The underdetermination thesis, as interpreted by the aforementioned sociologists of science, raises two critical questions, neither of which, they contend, can be adequately answered by traditional epistemology:

(i) When competing theories are, in fact, available, what factors determine which theory prevails? One cannot, in such cases, appeal to the evidence as determinative, since, given underdetermination, the theories are equally well supported.

(ii) How is scientific change (especially of the sort of cases Kuhn discusses) to be explained? In such cases, characteristically, none of the particular theories in competition receives conclusive empirical support (and, in fact, in such cases the very issue of "empirical support" may be clouded).

In response to each of these questions, advocates of the strong programme insist that *social* factors are determinative of which *scientific* theory triumphs; even more, social factors dictate the very content of particular scientific theories. Strong programmers detailed analyses of scientific disputes (which range from relatively recent cases such as the rise of quantum mechanics to more distantly historical cases such as the reception of phrenology by the scientific community in the seventeenth and eighteenth centuries) are meant to persuade us that sociological factors play a deciding role in putatively scientific or rational disputes.

If there were a "pure" or sociologically undetermined account of scientific reasoning, then traditional philosophy of science could explain theory change and the overcoming of underdetermination simply by appeal to the logic of scientific inquiry. Neither theory change nor the resolution of choice between underdetermined theories, however, can be explained in this way. There is no account of scientific reasoning, or so the strong programmers conclude, which can ignore the determining role of extrascientific, and specifically sociological, causes in scientific debates. The logic of scientific justification is therefore to be understood as a special case in the study of ideological rationalizations. In his *Wittgenstein: A Social Theory of Knowledge*, Bloor titles his last chapter (intentionally alluding to a well-known remark by Wittgenstein in the *Blue and Brown Books*) "The Heirs to the Subject That Used to be Called Philosophy." Here Bloor provides a blunt and provocative statement of the relation between the sociology of knowledge (as he understands it) and philosophy (again, as he understands it): "My whole thesis could be summed up as the claim to have revealed the true identity of these heirs: they belong to the family of activities called the sociology of knowledge."[1]

Exactly what is the strong programme in the sociology of science? Those sociologists who subscribe to this view take as their primary area of concern the natural sciences; indeed, some of their most challenging work consists of sociological case studies of controversies in mathematics and physics.[2] On the strong programme account, the form and content of what passes as scientific knowledge is determined by social influences on and political brokering by various groups within and without particular disciplines in the natural sciences.

Taking their philosophical cues from Kuhn's account of scientific revolutions[3] (in particular, the claim that paradigm changes are more akin to conversions than to reasoned judgments), Wittgenstein's insistence on the thoroughly social and conventional determinations of language use, and Quine's and Duhem's claims that theories can always be revised to accommodate seemingly adverse evidence, advocates of the strong programme conclude that neither reason nor fact (both of which they view as conventionally determined anyway) serve to explain the choice of one scientific theory over another:

We need to know how the field has been narrowed down. These are questions about the cultural inheritance of those who are conducting the crucial experi-

[1]David Bloor, *Wittgenstein: A Social Theory of Knowledge* (New York: Columbia University Press, 1983), p. 183.

[2]Bloor's analysis of mathematical reasoning may be found, among other places, in his book *Knowledge and Social Imagery* (London: Routledge & Kegan Paul, 1976). The favorite case study of the sociological determination of physics is Paul Forman's "Weimar Culture, Causality, and Quantum Theory, 1918–1927: Adaptation by German Physicists and Mathematicians to a Hostile Intellectual Environment," in *Historical Studies in the Physical Sciences*, vol. 3, ed. R. McCormmach (Philadelphia: University of Pennsylvania Press, 1971). I discuss Forman's paper in Chapter 8.

[3]Thomas Kuhn, *The Structure of Scientific Revolutions*, 2d ed., enlarged (Chicago: University of Chicago Press, 1970).

ment. It is no use trying to invoke previous experimental results or the constraints of reality as a sufficient ground for this narrowing process, because this just raises all the same problems over again. We need to invoke some further processes to work in conjunction with experiment and observation. It is necessary to introduce some process such as socialization into a tradition of normal science in order to explain the constraints which limit the acceptable interpretations which can be put on the facts of experience. And if this applies to the circumstances which lead up to a crucial experiment, it applies equally to the decisions that are made about its outcome.[4]

Neither the world nor the methodological canons of a scientific discipline impose the constraints that determine the outcome of scientific inquiry; ideological interests, in fact, play the *determining* role. (The social interests in question, however, may range from narrow concerns arising from competition between specialized subdisciplines to those of a more explicitly political or social nature.)

The question of the kind or scope of the social factors at work in a system of knowledge is entirely contingent and can only be established by empirical study. The important point, however, is that where broad social factors are not involved, narrow ones take over. The sociology of knowledge is still relevant. As well as an *external* sociology of knowledge there is also an *internal* sociology of knowledge. . . . To see what this amounts to we may turn to the literature that deals with professional vested interests in science. . . . Much that goes on in science can be plausibly seen as a result of the desire to maintain or increase the importance, status and scope of the methods and techniques which are the special property of a group.[5]

The successes of science, both in the laboratory and in the prevailing textbook account, are to be explained by citing those social factors that cause, in a given historical context, a particular scientific theory to triumph (be judged correct) in place of its competitors. More specifically, the considerations determining which scientific theory will prevail, including the standards by which any such theory is deemed better than its alternatives, are tied to perceptions of which theory best rationalizes the interests of the dominant social group. This view differentiates the strong programmers from those in the sociology of

[4]David Bloor, "The Strengths of the Strong Programme," *Philosophy of the Social Sciences* 11 (1981):202.

[5]Ibid., p. 203.

knowledge (most prominently Karl Mannheim and Robert Merton) who hold that the process of scientific justification is not a form of ideological rationalization and so not to be explained by sociological inquiry.[6] The strong programmers strive to avoid what I term "Mannheim's mistake"—the view that natural scientific knowledge (including mathematics) is a product of a *disinterested* contemplation of experience. Science, if one makes Mannheim's mistake, is thought to serve no rationalizing function; it is viewed as different in kind from other sociocultural products.

What, then, is the strong programme alternative to the epistemological and sociological traditions it rejects? Against the sociological tradition, it insists that science is to be explained in the way any other social phenomenon is, by reference to social factors. Against the philosophical tradition, it claims to offer a more accurate account of the processes and procedures underlying scientific reasoning. Knowledge claims are to be treated in a purely relativized manner: "The sociologist is concerned with knowledge, including scientific knowledge, purely as a natural phenomenon." By "natural" is meant knowledge claims in any given society taken at face value; the question is not, What is knowledge? but, rather, What does a given group call knowledge?[7] A sociologist is expected to "bracket" his or her own views of what to count as knowledge.

Although they deny that some single standard is appropriate for evaluating all knowledge claims, Barnes et al.'s view of explanation is not so laissez faire. Indeed, they insist that the study of scientific knowledge is to be carried out scientifically:

> The sociology of knowledge focuses on the distribution of belief and the various factors which influence it. . . . For the sociologist these topics call for investigation and explanation and he will try to characterize knowledge in a way which accords with this perspective. His ideas therefore will be in the same causal idiom as any other scientist. His concern will be to locate the regularities and general principles or processes which appear to be at work

[6]Bloor puts the point by saying that Mannheim's nerve failed him when it came to natural science. Bloor has no lack of nerve for such an undertaking; see, for example, *Knowledge and Social Imagery*, p. 8.

[7]Ibid., pp. 2–3. See also the article by Barry Barnes and David Bloor, "Relativism, Rationalism and the Sociology of Knowledge," in *Rationality and Relativism*, ed. M. Hollis and S. Lukes (Cambridge, Mass.: M.I.T. Press, 1982), p. 22.

> within the field of his data. His aim will be to build theories to explain these regularities. If these theories are to satisfy the requirement of maximum generality they will have to apply to both true and false beliefs, and as far as possible the same type of explanation will have to apply in both cases. The aim of physiology is to explain the organism in health and disease; the aim of mechanics is to understand machines which work and machines which fail, bridges which stand as well as those which fall. Similarly the sociologist seeks theories which explain the beliefs which are in fact found, regardless of how the investigator evaluates them.[8]

> In the main science is causal, theoretical, value-neutral, often reductionist, to an extent empiricist, and ultimately materialistic like common sense. This means that it is opposed to teleology, anthropomorphism and what is transcendent. The overall strategy has been to link the social sciences as closely as possible with the methods of other empirical sciences. In a very orthodox way I have said; only proceed as the other sciences proceed and all will be well.[9]

Sociology is to explain the scientific results that the scientific method is unable, on this view, to appropriately justify. The sociologist achieves this end by judicious application of this self-same scientific method in search of the sociological determinants of knowledge. (Why scientific method is presumed to yield an analysis of knowledge claims with respect to sociological factors is an issue to which I return in Chapter 8.)

The explanation of beliefs, for the strong programme, is achieved not by citing the *reasons* that warrant this belief but by citing the *causes* of this belief. (A person may have any number of reasons to, e.g., justify a belief in God. The cause of this belief, however, might be traced to a religiously oriented upbringing, a fear of death, etc.) The view that all beliefs are to be explained causally, and not by reference to their truth, falsity, or rational warrant, is what those in the strong programme call their "symmetry" principle. It is their claim that all beliefs are to be explained in this way, and not just those that are false or held intransigently, that has excited much of the philosophical opposition to this view. For the symmetry principle asserts, in effect, that rational justification is not justification enough. Let me first sketch the core principles that define, for its advocates, the methodological credo of the strong

[8]Bloor, *Knowledge and Social Imagery*, p. 3.
[9]Ibid., p. 141.

programme. I then return to discuss in more detail the symmetry principle and its significance.

The strong programme is defined by its advocates in terms of four basic tenets. First, the sociology of scientific knowledge should provide causal explanations, that is, explanations "concerned with the conditions which bring about belief or states of knowledge."[10] Bloor provides the following gloss of such causal explanation: "general laws relating beliefs to conditions which are necessary and sufficient to determine them."[11] The basic assumption here is that it is possible to specify a network of *social* causes.[12] It must be noted, however, that the strong programmers are quite explicit that not all causal conditions are social.[13]

Second, the credo of the strong programme insists that the investigation be "impartial." The impartiality appealed to here is meant to dispel any bias in favor of what is believed true; all beliefs, in other words, must be considered subject to investigation and explanation. This requirement is motivated by the desire to avoid Mannheim's mistake, that of assuming that any knowledge claim is interest-free.[14] A third, and related, requirement is that the sociology of knowledge be reflexive. This means that sociologists' beliefs are to be subject to the same sort of analysis and investigation as are scientists' beliefs. Yet, if challenged on the point of *their* interests, Bloor or his colleagues reply that they are only interested in the natural sciences. If someone wishes to pursue a sociology of sociology, they may. Moreover, the retort continues, the strong programme theorists cannot reasonably be condemned for failing to do everything.[15]

[10]Ibid., p. 4.

[11]David Bloor, "Wittgenstein and Mannheim on the Sociology of Mathematics," *Studies in the History and Philosophy of Science*, 4 (1973):173.

[12]Barry Barnes, *T. S. Kuhn and Social Science* (New York: Columbia University Press, 1982), p. xi.

[13]Nevertheless, the status of the seeming concession to facts is quite unclear. The "facts" are, it turns out, never sufficient to determine theory choice. A question arising in Chapter 8 is whether facts are, on the strong programme account, even necessary. See Steven Shapin's discussion in "The History of Science and Its Sociological Reconstruction," *History of Science* 20 (1982):196–197.

[14]The strong programmers also claim that their project is morally neutral, although that is not the sort of impartiality at issue here; see Bloor, *Knowledge and Social Imagery*, p. 10.

[15]Again, the issue of whether, given their general epistemological position, the advocates of the strong programme can afford to be so sanguine with respect to their reflexivity principle awaits discussion in the next section.

The fourth and final principle, one that has received much critical attention,[16] is the symmetry principle. It says, in effect, that even *rationally justified* claims are still in need of explanation. Put another way, according to the symmetry principle "the same sort of causes must generate both classes [i.e., true and false] of belief."[17] The claim that rationality and truth are neither necessary nor sufficient conditions of explanation must be understood as simply applying to agents' rationales of their actions. The symmetry principle, moreover, is part of the strategy by which to avoid the Mannheim mistake; social causes must be located for all beliefs. Unlike Mannheim, those of the strong programme are not going to be deterred from establishing the sociological causes of even well-justified scientific explanations. Strong programmers are apt to complain that, without the symmetry rule, sociologists are consigned to be the garbagemen of epistemology—having in their purview only false or nonrational beliefs and the task of explaining them.[18]

Why is a rational explanation not explanation enough? In order to answer this, we must examine the conceptions of knowledge and rationality to which Bloor et al. appeal. This is necessary in order to appreciate their stance with regard to philosophy of science (or, at least, their somewhat narrowed view of what constitutes the philosophy of science.) These considerations, in addition, help to bring into relief the parallels sketched in the next section between key claims in the strong programme and some of the Quinean theses I have already discussed.

Knowledge is taken to be, in the strong programme, whatever a group under study calls knowledge: "The sociologist is concerned with the naturalistic understanding of what people take to be knowledge, and not with the evaluative assessment of what deserves so to be taken; his orientation is normally distinct from that of the philosopher or

[16]Typical examples are found in Larry Laudan, *Progress and Its Problems* (Berkeley: University of California Press, 1977), chap. 7, and W. H. Newton-Smith, *The Rationality of Science* (London: Routledge & Kegan Paul, 1981), chap. 10. Both focus their attack on the symmetry principle.

[17]Bloor, "Wittgenstein and Mannheim," p. 174; see also *Knowledge and Social Imagery*, p. 5.

[18]For further elaborations on the importance of the symmetry principle, see Barry Barnes, *Interests and the Growth of Knowledge* (London: Routledge & Kegan Paul, 1977), p. viii, and H. M. Collins, "What Is TRASP? The Radical Programme as a Methodological Imperative," *Philosophy of the Social Sciences* 11 (1981):217, 218.

epistemologist."[19] Again, "All knowledge is made by men from existing cultural resources; old knowledge is part of the raw material involved in the manufacture of the new; hence, whatever the interests which guide knowledge generation, socially sustained consensus and a modification of existing meanings will always be involved in the process."[20] The emphasis on the social context of knowledge is meant to legitimate the symmetry principle in the following way. If one denies that the standards of rational evaluation are themselves theory-neutral (and the strong programme advocates most emphatically do deny this), then to say that an explanation is rationally acceptable is only to indicate which "theory of evaluation" a group accepts. Given the prevailing "standard of rational taste," the question remains, on the sociological view, why *this* standard of rational taste and not some other.[21]

In addition, the claim that knowledge is simply whatever society wants to make it is taken by the members of the Edinburgh school to itself be an empirical (testable) hypothesis that is, moreover, well confirmed by many case studies in the history of science. As Bloor puts it, "the central themes of this book, that ideas of knowledge are based on social images, that logical necessity is a species of moral obligation, and that objectivity is a social phenomenon, have all the characteristics of straightforward scientific hypotheses."[22]

Strong programmers prefer to call their method of study "naturalistic"; in the case where the object of study concerns knowledge claims, they speak of themselves as studying the "natural rationality" of humans (the term "natural rationality," Barnes's coinage, functions as a technical term in the writings of this group of sociologists). Natural rationality, as it is used in the writings of the Edinburgh school, is taken to be a *descriptive* account of human reasoning. Rationality *simpliciter* is an *evaluative* notion, one used to designate reasoning as good or bad. Natural rationality, on the other hand, connotes nothing about the success or failure of the inference-drawing process; rather, it is claimed

[19]Barnes, *Interests and the Growth of Knowledge*, p. 1.

[20]Ibid., p. 18.

[21]Ibid., pp. 18–19.

[22]Bloor, *Knowledge and Social Imagery*, p. 141. For a particularly detailed but polemical statement of the general position on knowledge, and an enthusiastic embrace of the relativistic implications of the position, see Barnes and Bloor, "Relativism, Rationalism and the Sociology of Knowledge."

to be simply descriptive of that process as observed in humans: "In order to cope with this problem [the problem of the descriptive vs. the evaluative senses of rationality] I suggest we distinguish between what may be called 'natural' and 'normative' rationality. Natural rationality refers to typical human reasoning propensities; normative rationality refers to patterns of inference that are esteemed or sanctioned. The one has reference to matters of psychological fact; the other to shared standards or norms."[23] The force of the term "natural" here (and in related remarks on this topic) is twofold: First, a natural account is one depicting what people are observed doing; second, however, it connotes a deeper, noncultural (i.e., biological) human propensity.

The suggestion that an account of natural rationality is to be taken as descriptive is underlined by Barnes's reference (following Mary Hesse) to humans as "inductive learning machines."[24] This type of characterization of rationality carries in its wake, moreover, two notions of irrationality. One may be irrational, in an evaluative sense, by virtue of a failure to adhere to accepted norms of reasons. One may also, however, be irrational in a descriptive sense; the inductive learning machine may not function in the usual way. In this regard, one might ask, without revealing any evaluative prejudices, whether "institutionalized beliefs [are] ever produced and sustained *in spite of* the tendencies of the learning machine, i.e., irrationally."[25] One way of understanding the strong programme is to see its account of natural rationality as an explicit competitor to the evaluative notions of rationality, and the corresponding method for studying the history of science, found in Laudan and Lakatos.[26] The suggestion, in short, is that the study of natural rationality yields both a more accurate history of science and, as a consequence, a better basis for evaluating just how humans reason (as distinct from what philosophers have said about how scientists and others should reason).

Closely related to this naturalistic nonevaluative notion of rationality is the view of all inference as inductively grounded. The ability to learn from particular experiences is part of the mechanism of humans

[23]Bloor, "The Strengths of the Strong Programme," p. 207.

[24]Barry Barnes, "Natural Rationality: A Neglected Concept in the Social Sciences," *Philosophy of the Social Sciences* 6 (1976):116.

[25]Ibid., p. 117.

[26]See Barnes's essay "Vicissitudes of Belief," *Social Studies of Science* 9 (1979):247–263, for explicit criticisms of Laudan and others along the lines mentioned here.

qua inductive learning machines; it is what is "natural" with regard to our reasoning propensities: "General associative tendencies underlie simple, unconscious, non-verbal learning, such as we continually automatically engage in as organisms moving through a physical environment." And, relatedly, Barnes asserts that "it is difficult to argue that basic inductive propensities are learned, or conventional or optional in character. Induction is a propensity we possess prior to learning, which is necessary for learning. Even the most heavily socialized kinds of learning depend upon prior inductive propensities."[27] Indeed, the fact that all learning presupposes these inductive tendencies on the part of the human intellect is taken to support, in turn, the claim that *stable* linguistic conventions are a product of cultural nurturing and not unadorned reasoning.[28]

Put another way, the evaluative notion of reasoning has a built-in bias in favor of explicit rules and algorithms. If, however, we see learning as based on socially reinforced, inductively confirmed, and largely unarticulated habits, then attempts to deductively formalize reasoning seem a distortion of natural processes:

> The student of the piano may not be abe to *say* what features are unique to the playing of his teacher, but he can certainly attempt to emulate them. In the same way we acquire habits of thought through exposure to current examples of scientific practice and transfer them to other areas. Indeed some thinkers such as Kuhn and Hesse believe that this is exactly how science itself grows. Thought moves inductively from case to case.
>
> My suggestion is simply that we transfer the instincts we have acquired in the laboratory to the study of knowledge itself. Those . . . who reject the symmetry postulate are trying to stop our inductive intuitions moving from case to case.[29]

The account of natural rationality and the concomitant stress on actual strategies of problem solving should lead research away from abstract questions concerning the "logic of science" and should stress, instead, work by psychologists on actual strategies of problem solving people employ.[30]

[27]Barry Barnes, "On the Conventional Character of Knowledge and Cognition," *Philosophy of the Social Sciences* 11 (1981):319–320.

[28]See David Bloor, "Durkheim and Mauss Revisited," *Studies in the History and Philosophy of Science* 13 (1982):296–297.

[29]Bloor, "The Strengths of the Strong Programme," pp. 206–207.

[30]Ibid., p. 208.

## II

The advantage of indicating the parallels, both real and apparent, of the strong programme to Quine's thought is that it clarifies the philosophical force of the former's critique of foundationalist epistemology. A tendency to polemicize and an equally unfortunate proclivity to argue by appeal to their favorite authorities (e.g., Wittgenstein, Kuhn, and Hesse) often obscures the force of the criticisms entered by Bloor, Barnes, Shapin, and the rest. In addition, once the parallels between the strong programme more recognizably philosophical criticisms of epistemology are appreciated, the confusions and differences between the project advocated by the Edinburgh school and the Quinean views as I interpret them can be made plain.

The strong programme parallels Quine's thought on at least four basic epistemological theses. First, it endorses Quine's holism (which, following Hesse, is sometimes referred to as the Duhem-Quine thesis). The noteworthy consequences drawn from this in the strong programme account are the context-dependence of meaning and the revisability of theories in the face of adverse evidence. Second, it accepts the underdetermination of theories by the data.[31] Third, indeterminacy of translation is also part of the general philosophical position of the strong programme. Fourth, and of particular significance for the controversies surrounding the symmetry rule, the rationale for the symmetry rule bears more than a passing resemblance to Quine's call to naturalize epistemology by using science to help explain the development of science. Indeed, Quine has been criticized in just the same vein as the strong programme theorists—for ignoring the alleged role of truth in explaining belief formation.[32]

The Edinburgh school strongly embraces holism and, by and large, takes it to imply just what Quine does: the claim is that the evidence for

[31]Advocates of the strong programme do not always, as we observe below, keep in mind the fact that holism and underdetermination are distinct theses and that the former does not imply the latter. Quine has been concerned to stress this distinction; see W. V. O. Quine, "On Empirically Equivalent Systems of the World" and "On Popper's Negative Methodology," in *The Philosophy of Karl Popper*, ed. P. A. Schilpp (La Salle, Ill.: Open Court Press, 1974). I argue elsewhere that Quine himself has not always been careful to distinguish the two; see Roth, "Semantics without Foundations," in *The Philosophy of W. V. Quine*, ed. L. Hahn (La Salle, Ill.: Open Court, 1987), pp. 433–458.

[32]See Roth, "Siegel on Naturalized Epistemology and Natural Science," *Philosophy of Science* 50 (1983):482–493.

a statement is found only by considering the theory of which it is a part. This is, moreover, not some easily avoidable feature of our language, or a feature of only certain special languages; rather, holism is understood as a consequence of the way language is learned and as a feature of every language, natural or otherwise, with which we are acquainted.

The knowledge associated with any part of a conceptual fabric is only fully acquired when the whole fabric has been acquired. Conceptual fabrics, including those in the natural sciences, have the character of hermeneutic systems; all that has been written of such systems and how they must be understood applies in the context of science.

Parallel conclusions can be drawn concerning the use and the evaluation of knowledge. As well as being learned as a whole, knowledge is related to experience as a whole. To use a concept is to appraise an instance in terms of an entire fabric. To evaluate a generalisation is to evaluate the over-all pattern of generalisations within the fabric. No statement or concept can be isolated so that its truth or appropriateness can be studied in isolation.[33]

The knowledge of a society designates not so much the sensory experience of its individual members, or the sum of what may be called their animal knowledge. It is rather, their collective vision or visions of Reality. Thus knowledge of our culture, as it is represented in our science, is not knowledge of a reality that any individual can experience or learn about for himself. It is what our best attested theories, and our most informed thoughts tell us is the case, despite what the appearances may say. It is a story woven out of the hints and glimpses that we believe our experiments offer us. Knowledge, then, is better equated with Culture than experience.[34]

Bloor, in his discussion (and endorsement) of Hesse's "network model," remarks that "the network model breaks down the distinction between the observation language and the theoretical language." This, in turn, is thought to follow from the fact that "none of the conditioned connections of symbols and situations has a privileged epistemological status over any other. Any of them may be sacrificed for the sake of harmony. All the symbols which function in the language of science do so in interconnection with other symbols and so none is anchored to the world of fact alone." The conventionality of facts and standards of reasoning, Bloor wants to argue, flow naturally "from seeing language

[33]Barnes, *T. S. Kuhn and Social Science*, p. 73; see also p. 78.
[34]Bloor, *Knowledge and Social Imagery*, p. 12.

and experience as an organic whole or system of interacting associations."[35]

The consequences drawn from holism include, not just the revisability noted above, but also a notion of truth as immanent and a (roughly) instrumental view of theory acceptance:

> It is now possible to see why the relation of correspondence between a theory and reality is vague. At no stage is this correspondence ever perceived, known or, consequently, put to any use. We never have the independent access to reality that would be necessary if it were to be matched up against our theories. All that we have, and all that we need, are our theories and our experience of the world. . . . The processes of scientific thought can all proceed, and have to proceed, on the basis of internal principles of assessment.[36]

Finally, Bloor insists that "there is no Archimedean point."[37] This image repeats Quine's and to the same effect; it denies that there is a "point of cosmic exile" from which to judge our theories of the world.[38]

Underdetermination, to recall, is the claim that two (or more) theories can be logically incompatible but empirically equivalent. There is a question, however, regarding whether any theories are genuinely underdetermined, that is, that both satisfy the prima facie requirements for being underdetermined and cannot be made compatible (with their ostensible competitor) by any reconstrual of predicates.[39] In adapting the notion of underdetermination to the strong programme, Barnes and Bloor tend to regard the existence of genuinely underdetermined theories as not only unproblematic but also readily available. Again, their discussion is couched in terms of the implication of "Hesse nets," the network model of language scouted above:

[35]David Bloor, "Epistemology or Psychology?" *Studies in the History and Philosophy of Science* 5 (1975):384. Bloor develops what he takes to be an account of the Hesse net in his book on Wittgenstein; see *Wittgenstein*, esp. chaps. 2–4. Also, like Quine, the strong programmers imagine language learning to be an inductive, bootstrap operation; see Barnes, *T. S. Kuhn*, p. 24, 39; "On the Conventional Character," p. 311; Bloor, "Durkheim and Mauss Revisited," pp. 270–271.

[36]Bloor, *Knowledge and Social Imagery*, p. 34; see also p. 35.

[37]Ibid., p. 38.

[38]*Ontological Relativity and Other Essays* (New York: Columbia University Press, 1969), p. 6.

[39]Quine, "On Empirically Equivalent Systems of the World."

More generally, I have conjectured that *all* systems of verbal culture can be modeled as Hesse nets. . . . There are two crucially significant ways in which different Hesse nets are always equivalent. Consider first the different tensions in any two nets. These represent different ways of clustering particulars together. But the clustering is something which we do to the particulars, not something which is already done in 'reality.' 'Reality' does not mind how we cluster it; 'reality' is simply the massively complex array of unverbalized information which we cluster. This suggests that *different nets stand equivalently in relation to 'reality' or to the physical environment*. . . . This strongly suggests that *different nets stand equivalently as far as the possibility of 'rational justification' is concerned.* All systems of verbal culture are equally rationally-held: any sociological enquiry into the rationality of communities sustaining different, even conflicting, networks should result in the same outcome in every case.[40]

By way of example, Barnes takes a much discussed case from the anthropological literature on the taxonomic classification of certain animals (in particular, the cassowary) made by the Karam tribe of New Guinea. The Karam, although known for their highly sophisticated and exact taxonomic system, do not classify the cassowary as a bird.[41] Barnes's suggestion is that

[the different taxonomies] can be modeled as alternative Hesse nets. Both nets can be satisfactorily read onto reality (in the sense of the physical environment). It is not that one net distorts reality more or less than the other. . . . And as for reality, so too for logic. The equivalence of the alternative nets indicates a lack of any formal differences in the two related patterns of cognition, theirs and ours. Again the alternatives stand equivalently. There are no differences in logical consistency to be found.[42]

Likewise, Bloor asserts that a theory "is not given along with the experience it explains, nor is it uniquely supported by it."[43]

Indeed, what is clear is that the underdetermination of theories by the data *defines* a central problem for the strong programme. Underdetermination, on the Edinburgh understanding of it, legitimates talk of alternative schemes of the world: "To describe the specific characteristic of our representations of natural kinds, in contrast say to those

[40]Barnes, "On the Conventional Character," pp. 315–316.
[41]Ibid., pp. 316–318.
[42]Ibid., p. 318.
[43]Bloor, *Knowledge and Social Imagery*, p. 13.

of the Karam, is to describe alternative institutions. The explanatory problem is one standard throughout sociology, 'why this institution, in this context?' "[44] But this conflates holism, and so the contextual dependence of the meaning of terms, and underdetermination, and so the existence of alternative, empirically equivalent schemes of the world. Both are assumed to legitimate the claim that what leads scientists to prefer one theory to another is not evidence but socially determined interests. The notion of objective evidence is cavalierly assumed to play no significant role—despite the fact that some such notion of evidence is crucial to maintain a nonparadoxical form of holism (as noted in Chapters 1 and 2) and despite, as well, that the very posing of the problem of underdetermination assumes comparable bodies of facts.

> The indeterminacy of scientific criteria, the inconclusive character of the general knowledge claims of science, the dependence of such claims on the available symbolic resources all indicate that [a] the physical world could be analyzed perfectly adequately by means of a language and presuppositions quite different from those employed in the modern scientific community. *There is, therefore, nothing in the physical world which uniquely determines the conclusions of that community.* It is, of course, self-evident that the external world exerts constraints on the conclusions of science. [b] But this constraint operates through the meanings created by scientists in their attempts to interpret the world. These meanings, as we have seen, are inherently inconclusive, continually revised and partly dependent on the social context in which interpretation occurs. If this view, central to the new philosophy of science, is accepted, there is no alternative but to regard the products of science as social constructions like all other cultural products.[45]

Claim [a] is a statement of underdetermination, [b] of holism. If we seek the reasons cited for [a] above, we find the following:

(i) the indeterminacy of scientific criteria;

(ii) the inconclusive character of the general knowledge claims of science;

(iii) the dependence of such claims on the available symbolic resources.

[44]Barnes, "On the Conventional Character," p. 324.

[45]Michael Mulkay, *Science and the Sociology of Knowledge* (London: George Allen & Unwin, 1979), pp. 60–61 (my lettering); for related claims and references to case studies, see p. 114.

Without worrying at this point just how to specify what is implied by each of these premises, let us look at the explication of [b]. Again, citing from the above quote:

(iv) meanings . . . are inherently inconclusive;
(v) [meanings are] continually revised;
(vi) [meanings are] partly dependent on the social context in which interpretation occurs.

It is plain that (iii) and (vi) simply assert the context-dependence of the meaning of statements; (ii) and (v) assert that all statements are only contingently accepted; (i) and (iv) both state that there are always ambiguous and unclear cases concerning the proper application of, for example, terms or laws. So from the quoted material, one might infer that [a] and [b] are logically equivalent. But, as noted before, holism and underdetermination are not equivalent theses. Thus holism and underdetermination are improperly conflated. This conflation of holism and underdetermination suggests that the strong programme advocates have underestimated the philosophical and empirical task before them. Since underdetermination does not follow from the Duhem-Quine thesis, it is not obvious that one must impute a determining role to covert social interests harbored by the scientists in question. Moreover, when one examines the case studies of those critical historical junctures at which competing theories do appear underdetermined, one finds that the role of social interests in such cases is not shown to be determinative (see Chapter 8).

While it is not always clear just what they take the supporting arguments to be, it is the case that advocates of the strong programme share Quine's animus toward meanings as entities. Bloor, for example, urges reading Wittgenstein's critique of private languages and inner states as basically a Skinnerian view of language learning.[46] Barnes, for his part, explicitly rejects the myth of the museum: "Concepts do not come with labels attached, carrying instructions which tell us how they are to be used. We ourselves determine usage, taking previous usage as precedent. Moreover, such precedent is corrigible, since it is itself the product of judgments. It can always be said that previous usage was wrong, that it weighed similarity and difference incorrectly, and that it must be revised."[47] Indeed, the strong programme advocates see inde-

[46]Bloor, *Wittgenstein*, pp. 54–64.
[47]Barnes, "On the Conventional Character," p. 313.

terminacy as a consequence of finitism—the view that all learning involves inductive procedures. Questions of likeness and difference are socially determined and controlled; there are no natural kinds or mental determinants of meaning:

> All attempts to achieve a perfect translation of a concept seek to match the inherent properties of the concept with the inherent properties of concepts in the second language. Correspondences are sought between the extensions and intensions of two concepts, or their references and senses, or their denotations and connotations. But finitism calls the existence of such properties into question. Not only does it thereby undermine standard methods of matching the concepts of two languages, it also indicates difficulties in equating the meaning of a single term to one point of use with its meaning at the next, when the similarity relation will have changed. . . . All the problems of translation encountered where two cultures, and two languages, are involved have analogues in the case of the temporal development of a single system of culture.[48]

Indeterminacy extends (as for Quine) even to the case of "homophonic" translation; there is no exempting one's colinguists or oneself from the problem of indeterminacy.[49] Moreover, Barnes's and Bloor's criticisms[50] of Hollis's view on bridgehead assertions are based on the foregoing view of meaning; they deny that there are, or that one need postulate, any a priori constraints on translations.

The fourth and final point of comparison between the strong programme and Quine's views concerns the use of science to explain science. Given that there is no Archimedean point, Quine concludes that science self-applied is the best that we can use in analyzing knowledge claims. In the strong programme, however, the first three theses discussed above are taken to be sufficient reasons for giving up on the natural sciences as a source of self-explanation. The reason for this has already been indicated. Neither the available evidence nor theory-free standards of rationality determine what the theory choice should be. Assuming that the evidence might have been made to fit some other theoretical framework, then their question is what social interests determined the choices that were, in fact, made. Epistemology natu-

[48]Barnes, *T. S. Kuhn and Social Science*, p. 34.

[49]See Quine, *Ontological Relativity*, p. 46.

[50]Barnes and Bloor, "Relativity, Rationalism and the Sociology of Knowledge," pp. 37–40.

ralized, on this account, merely obfuscates the social causal factors actually at work.

The members of the Edinburgh school are *not* suggesting that causal explanations are nonrational. Their opposition is to distinguishing certain explanations in the natural sciences as "rational" and assuming that no other sort of explanation is necessary. To think this way is to commit Mannheim's mistake. Barnes, Bloor et al. do not want to dichotomize the realm of explanation into two mutually incompatible types—rational and causal. They prefer to speak of one type of explanation—the causal—and then add that what is desired is an explanation of maximal generality.[51]

This consideration leads us back to the previous discussion of the notion of natural rationality. To recall, members of the strong programme characterize the views of Popper, Laudan, and Lakatos as ones that advocate an "artificial" rationality; the complaint is that normative, as opposed to "natural" (descriptive), conceptions constitutes bad history because they fail to depict how people do, in fact, reason. Even worse, normative accounts are just attempts to enshrine historically contingent standards in the mantle of timeless principles, and so are profoundly misleading.[52]

Ultimately, the strong programmers see themselves as *recovering* the notion of rationality from philosophers, who have mistakenly torn in from its proper (i.e., social) context of study. They are returning it to those who understand that what is rational is a question requiring empirical investigation:

> To make the example more realistic let me go back to the procedures of experimental psychologists. This is the science of natural rationality because it develops models of our typical cognitive processes. . . . They offer single models which under appropriate conditions produce the various observed outcomes. . . . In fact such models which focus on means-end calculations *have* been explored in great and fascinating detail but not, of course, by philosophers. The real home of these models is learning theory and its great

[51]Bloor, "Wittgenstein and Mannheim," p. 180 n. 15.

[52]There is a recurrent suggestion in the literature of the strong programme that, since knowledge is power, standards of knowledge are best seen as formed with an overall political process; see John Law, "Is Epistemology Redundant? A Sociological View," *Philosophy of the Social Sciences* 5 (1975):331, 334; see also S. Shapin, "Social Uses of Science," in *The Ferment of Knowledge*, ed. G. Rousseau and R. Porter (Cambridge: Cambridge University Press, 1980).

exponents are, in their different ways, Hull and Tolman. It would be pleasant to see rationalists acknowledging psychologists as the true leaders in their field and reading their works with the appreciation they deserve.[53]

Indeed, Bloor accuses those who oppose the symmetry principle of trying to mystify knowledge. He suggests that only those who wish to view science as sacred will oppose the sort of sociological analysis of science he and his fellow workers advocate.[54]

The strong programme call to study sociologically the creation of scientific knowledge differs radically from Quine's proposal because, in the end, it understands a scientific theory as a social product, as much a part of the social world as the other cultural artifacts of human civilization:

The mere assertion that scientific knowledge "has to do" with the social order or that it is "not autonomous" is no longer interesting. We must now specify how, precisely, to treat scientific culture as social product. We need to ascertain the exact nature of the links between accounts of natural reality and social order. In short, we need to provide a social epistemology appropriate for the history of science.[55]

The process whereby knowledge is evaluated, changed and re-evaluated involves continuing reference to shared goals and interests. But among such goals are specific, socially situated, predictive and technical requirements: it is not that agents operate by reference to goals and interests instead of to considerations of technical and empirical adequacy; rather it is that their sense of technical and empirical adequacy is itself intelligible only in terms of contingent goals and interests.[56]

The examples I have given from science, and the network model, both show that it is perfectly possible for systems of knowledge to reflect society and be addressed to the natural world at the same time. Put simply, the answer to the problem is that the social message comprises one of the coherence conditions, whilst the negotiability of the network provides the resources for reconciling

[53]Bloor, "The Strengths of the Strong Programme," p. 208.

[54]See, for example, Bloor, *Knowledge and Social Imagery*, p. 68, and "Durkheim and Mauss Revisited."

[55]Steven Shapin, "Homo Phrenologicus: Anthropological Perspectives on an Historical Problem," in *Natural Order*, ed. B. Barnes and S. Shapin (London: Sage, 1979), p. 42.

[56]Barnes, "On the Conventional Character," p. 325.

those demands with the input of experience. The idea that knowledge is a channel which can convey two signals at once requires us to drop the assumption that nature and society are polar opposites. It also requires us to become less complacent about what it is to 'fit the physical world.'[57]

The last quoted remark, which challenges us to be less complacent about what is involved in deciding that a theory in the natural sciences "fits the facts," represents the main challenge of the strong programme to the philosophy of science. The claim is that the strong programme gives a *better* theory of scientific activity (better than the aforementioned philosophers and historians of science, anyway), one that both fits the known cases and helps to explain what is currently involved in scientific controversies.

Parallels with Quine suggest that the strong programme theorists have understood at least part of what is important in Quine's critique of traditional epistemology. Moreover, they have come to apparently Quinean conclusions about at least some of the implications of these antifoundationalist theses. The crucial question to be addressed, then, is whether the advocates of the strong programme have, in their analysis of scientific rationality, a more satisfactory account of knowledge than that supplied in the philosophy of science they seek to replace. It is to their conception of the philosophy of science which I now turn.

## III

Two conceptions of the philosophy of science should be reviewed in order to appreciate the strong programme view of the subject: the orthodox philosophy of science and the new philosophy of science.[58]

[57]Bloor, "Durkheim and Mauss Revisited," p. 293.

[58]One might just as well speak, in this connection, of an omitted philosophy of science. The strong programmers fail to ever discuss that branch of philosophy of science which poses the most formidable challenge to their view. In particular, those philosophers of science who seek to reconstruct scientific reasoning on statistical or decision-theory models provide an account of scientific reasoning in accord with the finitist epistemological premises insisted on by the strong programmers. Nonetheless, such accounts analyze scientific reasoning in terms of reasoning from evidence. Two thinkers representative of this line of research within the philosophy of science are Bas van Fraassen, author of *The Scientific Image* (Oxford: Clarendon Press, 1980), and

What I term the "orthodox philosophy of science," the account on which the strong programme focuses, includes the Hempelian hypothetico-deductive model and the views of Lakatos or Laudan, that is, those who attempt to focus on the rational reconstruction of the history of science. The "new philosophy of science" embraced by the strong programme originates in a reading of Kuhn. Indeed, those in the strong programme believe that all history of science is a footnote to Kuhn (this despite the fact that Barnes and Bloor argue that Kuhn did not even appreciate his own best insights).

As the earlier discussion of Mannheim's mistake suggests, orthodox sociology of science simply adopts the conventional wisdom of positivist-oriented philosophers of science. The orthodoxy concerns the tenet that scientific method, properly formulated, provides context-independent standards of justification. The orthodoxy, both philosophical and sociological, is nicely summarized by sociologist Michael Mulkay:

> From the orthodox perspective, it is assumed that sociologists can identify that set of general normative principles which in practice guides most activities in science and, indeed, which *has* to be institutionalized within the research community in order to guarantee that the great majority of accepted knowledge-claims will be faithful to the real physical world. These general principles

---

Clark Glymour, author of *Theory and Evidence* (Princeton: Princeton University Press, 1980). The strong programmers apparently take it for granted that, if scientific reasoning has a finitist (that is, inductive) nature, then belief formation is amenable to explanation only by reference to social control. But if one checks under "belief" in the index of van Fraassen's book, for example, the cross-reference is to "theory acceptance," and theory acceptance, in turn, is cashed out in terms of a number of different parameters, including both a pragmatic dimension and an account of statistical testing. Barnes's insistence that "what a community finds inductively reasonable is invariably a matter of convention" (*T. S. Kuhn*, p. 110) appears empty.

Glymour's work accommodates both the holist and finitist proclivities of the strong programme. Glymour argues that "there is nothing in Quine's writings that tells us how our beliefs are, or ought to be, linked with one another, or how the net is constructed, or whether the linkages really generate a kind of holism" (p. 6). Glymour's bold strategy cannot be answered by glibly asserting that statistical laws and so forth are themselves conventional. The force of such an answer is undercut immediately by the reflexivity thesis; that is, it can hardly count against Glymour's account that what he presumes is, itself, a matter of convention, for all investigation, including that of the strong programme, must make some presupposition.

The works by these philosophers of science challenge the strong programme conclusions about how science is to be studied. In short, whatever "gaps" are evident in orthodox explanations of scientific behavior, the strong programmers have been far too sanguine in their conclusion that only sociology remains to fill the breach.

are conceived as providing clear prescriptions for virtually all social action involved in the production and certification of scientific knowledge. Their application by participants to particular acts is taken to be quite straightforward. Specific acts are regarded as either conforming to a given rule or not, in a fairly unambiguous manner.[59]

Strong programmers tend to offer a somewhat more polemical assessment of traditional philosophy of science. In this spirit, Barnes speaks of the "Manichean view of knowledge" harbored by traditional philosophers, a view that attempts to portray the "scientific light of reason" as struggling to shine undimmed by mundane social and political considerations.[60]

The objections to the standard view are easily discerned in the earlier discussions of natural rationality and the strong programme view of knowledge. The standard philosophy of science is rejected for reasons nicely summarized by John Law: "The above account has suggested the following major difficulties in the writings of the philosophers discussed. (1) The logics of science proposed vary greatly and (2) having an ambiguous relationship with the history of science, they may be expected to continue changing. (3) They have a tendency to become emptied of content, and (4) they can be seen as disguised versions of the judgments passed by later groups of scientists."[61]

At the philosophical center of the strong programme is Kuhn's *The Structure of Scientific Revolutions*. It is to this work that those in the strong programme appeal by way of justifying their ascription to the sociology of science the explanatory powers previously thought to be the provenance of the philosophy of science. Barnes, in his book dedicated to propagating the Kuhnian gospel according to the strong programme, asserts that "Kuhn has made one of the few fundamental contributions to the sociology of knowledge";[62] Barnes's concern, two

[59]Mulkay, *Science and the Sociology of Knowledge*, p. 93.

[60]Barnes, *T. S. Kuhn and Social Science*, p. 22.

[61]Law, "Is Epistemology Redundant?" p. 328. For specific comments on Laudan, see Barnes, "On the Conventional Character." Popper, who is much discussed and ambivalently viewed by strong programmers, is taken to task in representative ways in *Knowledge and Social Imagery* and in Law's essay cited in n. 52. Many of the criticisms of the two philosophers of science just mentioned are taken to apply, a fortiori, to Lakatos. A direct but not very enlightening confrontation between Laudan and Bloor may be found in Bloor, "The Strengths of the Strong Programme" and a piece by Laudan in the same issue entitled "The Pseudo-Science of Science?"

[62]Barnes, *T. S. Kuhn and Social Science*, p. x.

decades after the publication of Kuhn's work, is to bring the good word to the attention of other social scientists. (A pre-Barnesian assessment of Kuhn's impact on the social sciences is detailed in Chapter 5.)

In what follows, I am not concerned to comment on the accuracy of Barnes et al.'s exegesis of Kuhn's work. What is important at this juncture is to appreciate just which aspects of Kuhn's account of the history of science they believe can be exploited for their purposes and, conversely, which aspects of Kuhn's account they attempt to hold in abeyance. In Chapter 8 I return to their use (and abuse) of Kuhn and indicate why their selective treatment of his writings is inconsistent with some of the Quinean themes they endorse. In short, I attempt to sidestep quibbles concerning their reading of Kuhn (although the fact that I am mute on exegetical points will not, I trust, be read as an uncritical endorsement of the strong programme reading of Kuhn) and focus instead on the issue of whether the strong programme is self-consistent.

First and foremost, *The Structure of Scientific Revolutions* is read as a revolt against the tendency to write "Whiggish" history in the philosophy and history of science. The relevant feature of "Whiggish" historical writing is that "historical change was preconceived as 'progress', and accounted for as a movement closer to the present. . . . Thus Whig history read the past backwards, finding its explanations in a later period than the events explained." If one views rational standards as asocial and ahistorical, and scientific method as incarnating or approaching rational standards so conceived, then it is natural to write the history of science in a Whiggish mode. Barnes acknowledges that this tendency is strong and persistent and then enters the following caution with regard to such writings: "It is not always easy to remember that current science is our *interpretation* of reality, something which did not exist until we constructed it, and which cannot be projected back to operate as an underlying influence upon the perception of historical agents."[63] What is to Kuhn's particular credit is that his work is not just a non-Whiggish history of science; more important, it is an argument that shows why it is wrong to write the history of science from a Whiggish perspective.

The core of Kuhn's argument in *Scientific Revolutions*, as Barnes understands it, is a demonstration that there are cultural and social

[63]Ibid., pp. 4–5.

considerations intrinsic to scientific practice. Learning to be a scientist is not mastering some abstract, objective, and timeless set of methodological norms. It is, rather, a socialization process that is very much a product of particular times and places:

> These sources reflect Kuhn's recognition that to understand the way a tradition develops one has to address the basis of human behaviour; moreover, what is involved is *social* behaviour, as much a sociological as a psychological problem. It is this insight, combined with his historical sensibility, which gives Kuhn's work its originality and significance. The continuation of a form of culture implies mechanisms of socialisation and knowledge transmission, procedures for displaying the range of accepted meanings and representations, methods of ratifying acceptable innovations and giving them the stamp of legitimacy. . . . When there is a continuing form of culture there must be sources of cognitive authority and control. Kuhn was initially almost alone among historians in giving serious attention to these features of science.[64]

The fundamental point emphasized in *Scientific Revolutions*, then, is that scientists do not behave as philosophers of science imagine they ought. Rather, the fundamental norms of scientific behavior prove to be culturally and historically contingent.

> It is not just problems, techniques and existing findings which are culturally specific; so, too, are the modes of perceiving and conceptualising reality, the forms of inference and analogy, and the standards and precedents for judgment and evaluation which are actually employed in the course of research. Science is not a set of universal standards, sustaining true descriptions and valid inferences in different specific cultural contexts; authority and control in science do not operate simply to guarantee an unimpeded interaction between 'reason' and experience. Scientific standards themselves are part of a specific form of culture; authority and control are essential to maintain a sense of the reasonableness of that specific form. Thus, if Kuhn is correct, science should be amenable to sociological study in fundamentally the same way as any other form of knowledge or culture.[65]

In short, by dint of his efforts, Kuhn established that a Whiggish approach to the history of science simply did not fit the facts. And if a Whiggish history of science cannot be sustained, then doubt is cast on

[64]Ibid., p. 9.
[65]Ibid., p. 10.

the presupposition, as well, that there is something epistemologically privileged about scientific method and the scientific image of the world. Undermining a particular history of science effectively scotches one argument for the existence and persistence of a theory-free notion of scientific method.

Indeed, the specific conclusion strong programmers draw from *Scientific Revolutions* is that science now stands within, and not above, the purview of those who study other social and cultural institutions:

> By introducing a social dimension, and relating the status of scientific knowledge to the contingent judgments of specific communities of people, Kuhn undermined a whole range of philosophical arguments designed to secure a privileged epistemological or ontological status for science. Like any thoroughgoing sociological account of scientific judgment, Kuhn's involved a form of relativism—something which always seems to inspire revulsion among philosophers.[66]

> Recent philosophies, coming to terms with Duhem, Quine, and Lakatos, admit to the potential revisability of theoretical and even observation claims. The same message can be read from historical studies such as Kuhn's. . . . Taken as a whole this new philosophy, history and sociology could be said to have introduced the dimension of *time* into discovery. It seems that the *best* that can be said of scientists' judgments of the scientific value of their claims is that a consensus (sometimes a temporary one) is formed after a period of time in many disputes.[67]

Put another way, Kuhn's brief against the Whiggish reading of the history of science (which is certainly a central thrust of his work) is read as endorsing the view that matters of scientific method and of evidence are, at any given moment, a product of contingent circumstances and so open to change. It is not just that science is evolving in no particular direction;[68] rather, the claim is that what changes are found are products of social interests and not a result of the dynamics of theory testing. This claim is critical, since it marks a major break with the usual understanding of Kuhn's position. Kuhn most characteristically views scientific change as a function of the internal dynamics of scien-

[66]Ibid., p. 12.
[67]Collins, "What Is TRASP?", p. 220.
[68]Bloor, *Knowledge and Social Imagery*, p. 143.

tific theories; although he eschews the project of attempting to specify just when a given paradigm is going to be overwhelmed by anomalies, he nonetheless perceives the motivation for change as arising within the context of the testing of a theory against experience and in the face of competitors. And although Kuhn explicitly recognizes that scientific theories are underdetermined, he also maintains that there must be some motivation—some dissatisfaction with the existing paradigm—for seeking an alternative explanation.[69]

The reasons for this view are, first, Kuhn's belief that scientists achieve the greatest amount of technical success—problem solving—by working within a given model of inquiry, and second, that the more mature a science, the more difficult it is to find an alternative. In any event, Kuhn's emphasis, as Barnes's remarks on Whiggish history make clear, is on the topic of reconstructing scientific change. The claim for which Kuhn is famous is that no "rational reconstruction" of such changes is to be found if one is faithful to the details of scientific history. The strong programmers, however, are apt to read Kuhn's attack on the traditional *history* of science as constituting ipso facto a refutation of the view that the *method* of even *normal science* permits of rational reconstruction. It is, of course, the thesis of holism—the Quine-Duhem view of theories—that poses problems for the classical positivist attempts to explicate scientific method. That story has been told often enough.[70] Those who subscribe to the strong programme, however, emphasize Kuhn's remarks regarding the dogmatic and authoritative nature of *normal* science. For philosophers, what is of epistemological moment is Kuhn's attack on the view of science as cumulative (and so rational over the long run). But what is significant for sociologists of science is that they take Kuhn's account to imply that there is nothing epistemologically special about scientific activity as currently perceived:

> In my judgment the general significance of Kuhn's work lies neither in its specific historical narrative of the development of science, nor in the concepts invented for that narrative, but simply in its explicit discussions of general problems concerning cognition, semantics and culture. Kuhn is important

[69]Kuhn, *The Structure of Scientific Revolutions*, pp. 76–77.

[70]For Quine's account, see "Epistemology Naturalized," in *Ontological Relativity and Other Essays*. I comment on these matters in "On Missing Neurath's Boat," *Synthese* 61 (1984):205–231.

where he examines similarity relations, concrete problem-solutions, and the development of usage and procedure by analogy and direct modeling. Here, our understanding of the conventional nature of knowledge is advanced, as is our understanding of the nature of convention itself. This is material which no one in the social sciences should pass over, even if Kuhn himself has not advertised its general importance.[71]

In short, what will come as news to many philosophers of science is that Kuhn's work is read, not so much for its attack on the account of theory *change*, but rather for what it is taken to say about *intratheoretical* functioning. (Insofar as Barnes views Kuhn as imperfectly prefiguring what the strong programmers have in mind, he has written, I suggest, a Whiggish history of Kuhnian thought.)

Put another way, Kuhn is taken as undercutting Hempel's hypothetico-deductive account of scientific reasoning; that is, the analysis of scientific change explicit in *Scientific Revolutions* is extended by sociologists to become a critique of theories of scientific explanation as well. The strong programme conclusion is, not only that scientific reasoning is not cumulative, but also that the form of scientific explanation—the logic of science—varies with changes in paradigms:

By postulating the existence of a basic mathematical structure of a theory, set above the clusters of application in Kuhn's account, Stegmuller envisages something which is too close in form to the traditional deductivist view of science. . . . In contrast, Kuhn's account permits the role of deduction to be called into question. . . .

Scientific inference, like empirical inference generally, is not deductive. It proceeds from particular to particular on the basis of resemblance and analogy. Knowledge is built up and extended a bit at a time by the revisable clusterings of instances and applications. . . . Any 'deduction' about empirical phenomena involves a hidden analogical step.[72]

Kuhn's work does not indicate occasional points where their notion of 'objectivity' is inapplicable; it demonstrates the total irrelevance of the notion. All the problems of evaluation which disturb philosophers because they imply the presence of a 'social' dimension and thus the insufficiency of autonomous 'reasons' are found throughout normal science. The maintenance and development of routine usage is every bit as much a social phenomenon as the radically

[71]Barnes, *T. S. Kuhn and Social Science*, p. 120.
[72]Ibid., p. 122.

innovative changes of usage which Kuhn cites in his account of revolutions. . . . Normal scientists are not rational automata, using words according to their inherent meanings or extensions. Existing usage always leaves future usage to be developed by users themselves. It is precisely because of this that the *continuing* role of authority and social control is of ineradicable significance in normal science. . . . This is the profound sense in which normal science is a social activity. And this is why Kuhn's matter-of-fact account of routine scientific activity threatens epistemological orthodoxy more radically even than his explicitly philosophical discussion of revolutionary states of affairs.[73]

Social determinants of knowledge exert their influence, not only in cases of scientific change, but also in the workaday world of normal science. Neither revolutionary nor normal science, on the strong programme, conforms to an idealized, abstract logic of justification and of scientific method. The resulting view of scientific activity is remarkably akin to Rorty's vision noted at the very outset of this chapter. Science is explicitly likened to a craft that has as its particular objective the manipulation and control of experience.[74] Underdetermination tells us that the available evidence does not force our choice of theory, and Kuhn tells us that the theory we have is maintained by institutional authority. From this, the sociologically minded inquirer concludes that, for enlightenment on how science functions, what needs attention is the fashion in which the prevailing institutions are formed and maintained. Mannheim's mistake, fostered as it was by the myth of scientific disinterestedness and impartiality, is one that no respectable social scientist now need (or should) repeat.

The sociological analysis of science, then, has previously assumed that the production of scientific knowledge can be explained by showing that general conformity is maintained to sets of formal rules (both social and technical) the strict implementation of which guarantees an undistorted revelation of the real physical world. I have argued, in contrast, that neither of these kinds of rules has a determinate meaning for participants and that implementation therefore requires a continuous process of cultural reinterpretation. By means of this process scientists construct their versions of the physical world. The broad similarity between this revised sociological position and the new philosophy of science is clearly in evidence at this point. . . . Sociologists and philosophers

[73]Ibid., p. 84.
[74]Ibid., pp. 9–10.

have converged on a conception of science as an interpretative enterprise, in the course of which the nature of the physical world is socially constructed.[75]

Experience contributes to the construction of the world science provides, but it is social interests, finally, that determine the image scientific investigators leave with us. "But what has really to be remembered here is that *all* knowledge is socially sustained, a set of agreed conventions, as well as being instrumental in character."[76] One might just as well say that scientific research comprises social interests writ small.

The position of the strong programme in the sociology of science may be summarized as follows. The fundamental premise obtained from the strong programmers' reading of Kuhn is this:

(i) How it is that one scientific theory comes to prevail over its rival(s) is not to be explained by appeal to crucial experiments or to the logic of scientific method.

The force of (i) is to rule out an explanation of scientific change by reference to the internal dynamics of theory testing.

The next two premises, the appeals made to underdetermination (iib) and to holism (iia) depend on Quinean considerations. I list them separately although, as indicated above, these points are conflated in the writings of Barnes et al.

(iia) The meanings of theoretical terms, and the evidence for their existence, are dependent on a context established by considering all the related statements of that theory.

(iib) There are empirically equivalent but logically incompatible theories between which there is no rule-guided basis for choosing.

The force of these premises is taken to be that there are no *external* criteria to determine theory choice; incompatible theories may be (indeed, on the strong programme account, often are) capable of accounting for what evidence there is. Our choice of theories is not forced by the facts or by logic.

The next premise simply summarizes the claims made for the strong programme itself:

(iii) The strong programme can provide a causal explanation, in terms of social determinants, of all beliefs an individual or a group accepts as true.

[75] Mulkay, *Science and the Sociology of Knowledge*, p. 95.
[76] Barnes, *Interests and the Growth of Knowledge*, p. 18.

The last premise, in turn, encapsulates the strong programmers' criticisms of orthodox philosophy of science:

(iv) Orthodox history and philosophy of science present a distorted account of the factors that actually determine why a scientific theory is judged rationally acceptable.

The belief that there are factors, logical or factual, that suffice to establish a rational basis for choice between theories is referred to by the strong programmers as "rationalism." Premises (i), (iia), (iib), and (iv) are taken to establish that this rationalist approach is wrong. Unstated in their argument is this assumption:

(v) Scientific change is to be explained either rationally or sociologically.

On these assumptions, it follows that

(vi) the sociology of science provides the only scientific (i.e., causal) explanation of natural scientific knowledge.

The claim, then, that the strong programme in the sociology of science is the heir to the subject that used to be called philosophy is established by "proving" that all standards of evaluation (including logical) are social products. The new theory of knowledge need then be a theory capable of identifying the social determinants of whatever is called knowledge.

CHAPTER 8

# Voodoo Epistemology: Causality and the Strong Programme

In the previous chapter I outlined the philosophical tenets of the strong programme. I now turn to the issue of whether this program, as understood by its proponents, is fully self-consistent.

In appraising the strong programme my chief concern is whether the premises I share with it commit me (or it) to the conclusion that the strong programme is the heir to the subject that used to be called epistemology. (In particular, it is taken to be the heir of that aspect of epistemology concerned with the legitimation of beliefs, and which, moreover, takes the natural sciences to provide a model method of such legitimation.)

At the conclusion of the previous chapter I rehearsed, in argument form, my reconstruction of the strong programmers' case for the "reduction" of epistemology to the sociology of knowledge. My reconstruction stressed that, if one abandons (for whatever reasons) a foundationalist approach to epistemology, and if one recognizes that the available evidence never compels the selection of some particular theory (for it is always possible, on the strong programme understanding of underdetermination, to formulate a rival account or to cling, with revisions, to the theory you have), then social forces at work in the larger (external) society determine (i.e., cause) which theory is to be preferred over another and dictate at least some of the content of that theory. The discovery of which specific interests are at work is, in turn, taken to be an empirical question. (There is, apparently, no presumption, à la Marx, for example, that the engine of social development is class conflict.) The important point is the claim that the standards of evaluation employed in the natural sciences are determined by social interests. Reason is and must remain a slave to the passions; the strong programme simply intends to make plain which master is being served.

Crucial to the strong programme in the sociology of science is the stress on the *social cause* of beliefs. The bold suggestion, in fact, is just that the sociological analysis of beliefs is a better scientific tool for analyzing knowledge than any that traditional epistemology can supply. Yet, although some account of the social conditions for belief formation and change is central to the strong programme, the strong programmers are largely silent on this point in their theoretical pronouncements and case studies. This missing account of the causes of belief is important for understanding the claim of heir to epistemology. Although the strong programmers claim that sociology has a role in formulating the necessary and sufficient conditions determining the causal genesis of a belief, no specification of such conditions is to be found in their account. It is my contention that such a causal account cannot be specified without rendering this causal claim incompatible with the philosophical position to which they otherwise adhere.

My critical discussion is divided into two general parts. In Section I I explore a series of questions arising from the strong programme's notion of causality. In Section II the focus is on the use of historical data to support the claims of the strong programme.

## I

What is the notion of causation assumed by the strong programmers? Basically, it is Humean concomitant coincidence. Any science, Bloor believes, starts with the observation of regularities and then seeks to build a theory that explains why these events are connected. What is the mechanism that explains the observed results, the occurrence of certain connections of events? "[The sociologist's] ideas therefore will be in the same causal idiom as any other scientist. His concern will be to locate the regularities and general principles or processes which appear to be at work within the field of his data. His aim will be to build theories to explain these regularities."[1] Bloor elaborates this requirement slightly by glossing the "causes of belief" in terms of "general

[1]David Bloor, *Knowledge and Social Imagery* (London: Routledge & Kegan Paul, 1976), p. 3.

laws relating beliefs to conditions which are necessary and sufficient to determine them."[2]

It is not the case that *all* the conditions are assumed to be social: "A complete study of the influences that bring about belief needs an account of the object on which the causes work. A model of man's biological nature is required to supplement the sociology of knowledge. Conversely the sociologist must not ignore the sensory input with which people must cope." What a sociologist may specifically be expected to document are the respects in which "different positions in the social structure may correlate with different beliefs."[3] Bloor has made concrete efforts in this direction, in fact, in his attempts to exploit "grid group" analysis.[4] It is also worth noting that Bloor has worried about the question, on which I insisted above, concerning the mechanism of belief formation and change. He suggests a behavioristic interpretation of Wittgenstein in general response to these concerns.[5] The extent to which this response is adequate to or appropriate for the concerns at hand is a question to which I return below.

It is not clear to what extent the notion of causality outlined above is Bloor's alone, and to what extent it is to be taken as an intrinsic part of the strong programme. For although Barnes appears to endorse the strong programme (which includes the notion of causal explanations),[6] he elsewhere demurs from offering just the sort of causal explanations championed by Bloor: "It is true that no laws or necessary connections are proposed to link knowledge and the social order, and that no abstract instructions are set out for the investigation and explanation of bodies of knowledge. But the basic claim that knowledge is a resource in activity and not a direct determinant of it makes such an approach inappropriate."[7] Steven Shapin is also more hesitant

[2]David Bloor, "Wittgenstein and Mannheim on the Sociology of Mathematics," *Studies in the History and Philosophy of Science* 4 (1973):173.

[3]Ibid., p. 174.

[4]See, for example, David Bloor, *Wittgenstein: A Social Theory of Knowledge* (New York: Columbia University Press, 1983), pp. 140–145, and Celia Bloor and David Bloor, "Twenty Industrial Scientists: A Preliminary Exercise," in *Essays in the Sociology of Perception*, ed. M. Douglas (London: Routledge & Kegan Paul, 1982).

[5]Bloor, *Wittgenstein*, pp. 52–54.

[6]See, for example, Barnes and Bloor, "Relativism, Rationalism and the Sociology of Knowledge," in *Rationality and Relativism*, ed. M. Hollis and S. Lukes (Cambridge, Mass.: M.I.T. Press, 1982).

[7]Barry Barnes, *Interests and the Growth of Knowledge* (London: Routledge & Kegan Paul, 1977), p. 85.

than is Bloor in imputing causal connections to the events described in various case studies. Remarking on a favorite series of case studies—those by Theodore Brown of changes in medical theory in the late seventeenth century in England[8]—Shapin claims only that "the relevance here of Brown's study is once more in the way in which his explanation *associates* social interests and the social use of scientific knowledge with other factors."[9]

How is the move made from temporally associating to causally relating certain social movements or changes with concomitant changes in scientific outlook?—by pointing out that the choice between competitor theories was, at the time, underdetermined. "The 'scientific context' has to be attended to in explaining the adoption of this model. . . . But the 'scientific context' is insufficient to explain the phenomenon."[10] Shapin has the acuity to perceive that merely noting that theories are underdetermined is hardly sufficient to establish that social causes must be mustered to "fill the explanatory gap." He acknowledges only that the underdetermination is what "makes room" for the operations of a sociologist of knowledge.[11]

In general, Shapin is quite cautious, in contrast to Bloor's more categorical declarations, about asserting a general causal link between social interests and scientific product: "A proper perspective of the uses of science might reveal that the sociology of knowledge and the history of technology have more in common than is usually thought."[12] These hedgings are of crucial importance, for if the sociologist of knowledge is no more in a position to lay out necessary and sufficient conditions of explanation of scientific change than philosophers are, then the strong programme is not a replacement for the account of rationality found in the sort of philosophy of science (e.g., that of Popper or Hempel) Bloor et al. criticize and reject; it stands as just an interesting approach to some of the factors at work in scientific contexts, factors that have been, as the strong programmers complain, too long neglected.

[8]See the references cited in S. Shapin, "Social Uses of Science," in *The Ferment of Knowledge*, ed. G. Rousseau and R. Porter (Cambridge: Cambridge University Press, 1980), p. 124 n. 91; see also Larry Laudan, *Progress and Its Problems* (Berkeley: University of California Press, 1977), p. 217.

[9]Shapin, "Social Uses of Science," p. 126. Emphasis added.

[10]Ibid., p. 130.

[11]Steven Shapin, "The History of Science and Its Sociological Reconstruction," *History of Science* 20 (1982):164.

[12]Ibid., p. 132.

Mary Hesse, in a highly sympathetic study of her intellectual offspring, offers the following reading of the strong programme. "The strong thesis [her term for the strong programme] as I have explicated it requires only that all aspects of social structure, including its cultural manifestations of ideas, beliefs, religions, art forms and knowledge, constitute interlocking systems of causality."[13] Hesse's characterization is at best incomplete, however, for it simply ignores the sort of confrontation the strong programmers seek to effect with epistemology as they understand it. Their claim is not that there is some architectonic uniting the various forms of cultural endeavor; the issue, rather, is the role of supposed rational justifications in the explanation or evaluation of knowledge claims in natural science. And the strong programmers' claim is that the standards of evaluation internal to a scientific theory provide only a "surface" rationalization. The "deep structure" is determined by the interplay between various class or economic interests and scientific theorizing.[14]

The question is whether what is accepted as warranted belief by scientists is to be explained primarily by appeal to a logic of justification, or whether any logic of justification is to be understood as rationalizing certain social and economic interests. Much that has gone on in the philosophy of science assumes that the logic of justification does stand aloof from such social pressures. The strong programme, for its part, is determined to show that what passes for warranted belief in science is also a product of the general fray of social forces. In this respect, traditional philosophy of science is thought of as assuming an illusory neutrality; in fact, science is the product of certain social interests rationalized by appeal to "objective" standards of evaluation. The key to being an incisive practitioner of the strong programme, in other words, is to discern how interests operate just where scientists believe them to be absent.[15]

Hesse is more insightful when commenting on the particular problem before us, the notion of causality at loose in the writings of the

[13]Mary Hesse, "The Strong Thesis of Sociology of Knowledge," in *Revolutions and Reconstructions in the Philosophy of Science* (Brighton: Harvester Press, 1980), p. 52.

[14]Laudan likewise notes that Hesse provides a reconstrual of the "Strong Thesis" which makes it acceptable at the cost of making it innocuous; "The Pseudo-Science of Science?" *Philosophy of the Social Sciences* 11 (1981):190 n. 21.

[15]See, for example, Barnes, *Interests and the Growth of Knowledge*, pp. 32–33, 94 n. 7.

strong programmers. She notes that, based on previous attempts, the project of identifying general causal laws at work in human history appears to be of dubious merit: "Historians in the extensive mode tend to make general hypotheses and to look for general correlations across societies, across periods and across sciences. Such correlations have been suggested between, for instance, social class of origin and propensities to positivism or realism. . . . Certainly such attempts have not yet been sufficiently developed for it to be possible to judge their success, but first impressions do not seem favorable."[16] She goes on to review a number of case studies produced in the style of (and, in some cases, by members of) the strong programme. Her conclusion is that sociologists are frustrated by their own reliance on the context-dependence of knowledge. It is just not open to the historical observer, she observes, to isolate which concerns "in the air" at a time may, in fact, have been determinative. The case studies suggest only "that the causality sought in such cases has more to do with the historian's perceptions of ideological relevance and irrelevance than with mere external correlations of factors in particular cases." She concludes that the "meaning of terms like 'empiricism', 'abstraction', 'conservatism', 'reformism' are too dependent on historical context to yield general laws: when they are made precise, diachronic correlations turn out false; when they are left vague, correlations become vacuous."[17]

The suggestion, then, is that the causality principle of the strong programme, although central to its claim to replace philosophy of science, is unacceptably vague. What is left obscure is how, even in principle, events are to be understood as connected and interacting. Yet even Shapin, whose doubts were canvassed above, insists that the strong programme is "to provide a social epistemology appropriate for the history of science."[18] And this epistemological enterprise, to recall, is nothing less than "a theory of how scientific culture *actually is produced*, rather than in the sense associated with some philosophy of science—of how, ideally, it *ought to be* generated."[19] Scientific

[16]Hesse, "The Strong Thesis of Sociology of Knowledge," pp. 52–53.

[17]Ibid., pp. 54–56.

[18]Steven Shapin, "Homo Phrenologicus: Anthropological Perspectives on an Historical Problem," in *Natural Order*, ed. B. Barnes and S. Shapin (London: Sage, 1979), p. 42.

[19]Ibid., p. 65 n. 1.

culture, on this view, like the orders of the Masons, is, although hierarchical and rule-governed, nonetheless purely a matter of conventional determinations. There is no higher logic manifested by scientists doing what they do than there is by Masons doing what they do.

I approach this question through a discussion of the strong programmers' account of language learning. My goal, ultimately, is to raise doubts about whether their inductive—finitistic—account of learning is consistent with the claim that it is possible to specify the necessary and sufficient conditions for the causes of beliefs.

I indicated in the previous chapter that the model of language acquisition propounded by Barnes and Bloor is, in its general scheme and many of its particulars, extremely close to the Quinean model.[20] Like Quine, they suggest that basic to the learning process is a "primitive sense of similarity."[21] They also favor a behavioral approach; indeed, even the sense of similarity, though primitive (due to evolutionary factors, Quine speculates), is itself subject to social shaping and control. A child, that is, learns "which of the possible judgments of sameness are accepted by his society as relevant to [his use of terms]. In this way the particulars of experience are ordered into clusters and patterns *specific to a culture*."[22] Although Bloor et al. are more apt to display a familiarity with Hesse's development of the Quinean program in her network model, the Quinean roots of this model are acknowledged.[23]

The strong parallels between the two accounts of language learning should alert us to the type of difficulties we may expect to find. The specific problem is the issue of how we are to determine both the stimulus conditions and the range of socially relevant responses (see Chapter 2). This is a particularly acute problem for the strong pro-

[20]Compare Barnes's "On the Conventional Character of Knowledge and Cognition," *Philosophy of the Social Sciences* 11 (1981) and Quine's "Grades of Theoreticity," in *Experience and Theory*, ed. L. Foster and J. Swanson (Amherst: University of Massachusetts Press, 1970).

[21]David Bloor, "Durkheim and Mauss Revisited," *Studies in the History and Philosophy of Science* 13 (1982):269.

[22]Barnes and Bloor, "Relativism, Rationalism and the Sociology of Knowledge," p. 38. Compare Quine, "Facts of the Matter," in *American Philosophy from Edwards to Quine*, ed. K. Merrill and R. Shahan (Norman: University of Oklahoma Press, 1977), p. 155.

[23]See, for example, Bloor, "Durkheim and Mauss Revisited," p. 269.

gramme given its advocacy of finitism. Finitism, to recall, holds that kinds are socially established categories whose elements are united by a purely conventional notion of sameness or likeness.

[Finitism] is the thesis that the established meaning of a word does not determine its future applications. The development of a language-game is not determined by its past verbal form. Meaning is created by acts of use. . . . The label 'finitism' is appropriate because we are to think of meaning extending as far as, but not further than, the finite range of circumstances in which a word is used.[24]

It is not that knowledge is a system of conventions which determines how we think and act. On the contrary it is our decisions and judgments which determine what counts as conventional, and thus which sustain and develop a conventional framework. . . .

This conception of knowledge is sometimes called *finitism*. Its core assertion is that proper usage is developed step by step, in processes involving successions of on-the-spot judgments. Every instance of use, or of proper use, of a concept must in the last analysis be accounted for separately, by reference to specific, local, contingent determinants. Finitism denies that inherent properties or meanings attach to concepts and determine their future correct applications.[25]

Finitism, then, has it that, since all classificatory schema are conventionally determined, no properties of objects dictate that they belong to one category of things and not to some other. Categories and what is placed in them are infinitely plastic. To which objects a category may be extended, or how some object is to be sorted, is a social decision.

The notion that inductively learned kind terms are open-ended or undetermined in the range of their applications is central to the epistemological rationales advanced for the strong programme, for the emphasis on the conventionality of kind terms legitimates, or so it may appear, the claim that *all* standards of evaluation are socially determined. Physical objects seem to be the obvious candidates for constituting natural kinds, and if there are no natural kinds of this sort, then nature would seem to have no intrinsic principles by which to

[24]Bloor, *Wittgenstein*, p. 25.

[25]Barry Barnes, *T. S. Kuhn and Social Science* (New York: Columbia University Press, 1982), p. 30.

guide us. "Finitism implies a thoroughgoing sociological treatment of knowledge and cognition."[26]

In this regard, the strong programmers fault Winch's reading of Wittgenstein, and so Winch's style of extending a "Wittgensteinian" analysis to social science. The source of the criticism is Winch's alleged failure to be sufficiently finitistic in his account of social rules.[27] The criticisms noted here represent an about face, at least on Bloor's part, on the acceptability of Winch. Bloor had previously praised Winch's account.[28] (To anticipate somewhat, I read Bloor's remarks on social criteria[29] as very close to Winch's actual position, even though I understand Bloor's criticisms of Winch as being in the spirit of those I developed in other chapters.)

Given the adherence to finitism, how plausible is it to suggest that we can specify the necessary social conditions to which one is conditioned in learning to play a particular language game? Are the prospects for specifying the conditions for a social epistemology any brighter than they proved to be for that of epistemology naturalized? Bloor believes that one finds in Wittgenstein just the desired sociologically significant account of language learning. On Bloor's reading of the later Wittgenstein, all learning is understood as guided by conventionally established criteria of use. These criteria, in turn, are reflected in social institutions: "The best way to understand criteria is to see them as social institutions." Although all determinations of how terms are to be applied are, then, conventionally determined, nonetheless the conditioning is such that, in some cases anyway, the connections are habitual, that is, noninferential (and so seemingly "natural"). Thus the connection of pain behavior and pain, oracles and witchhood (in the ubiquitous case of the Azande), are all taken to be cases of institutionalized criteria of meaning.[30] The philosophical rub comes when the status of these criteria is examined against the background of a general commitment to finitism. Bloor stresses (and he is not alone in this) that the criteria are *not* inductive generalizations. Their social status is quite different. "The link between a cue and the meaning attached to it is certainly something other than an

[26]Ibid., p. 39.
[27]See Bloor, *Wittgenstein*, pp. 168–171, 180–181.
[28]See Bloor, "Wittgenstein and Mannheim," p. 191 n. 46.
[29]Bloor, *Wittgenstein*, pp. 41–46.
[30]Ibid., pp. 41–43.

inductively supported generalisation. This is because criteria are taken, for all practical purposes, to convey certainty. They are authoritative."[31] Criteria are determinative; they may be faked, but they are not themselves subjects for justification. "Pain behaviour provides a criterion for imputing pain, but learning to operate with this criterion also means learning when to say that someone isn't really in pain."[32] But, recall, the finitist doctrine maintains that previous occurrences of a term cannot be determinative of how it is extended; this is an ineluctable consequence of the denial that there are natural kinds. Yet now Bloor is claiming that certain types of behavior do form a de facto natural kind.

The problem of resemblance is certainly not solved by invoking an appeal to institutionally sanctioned kinds, for the problem from the outset is how any *criteria* can be *determinative* and yet be learned according to the finitistic script. It does not matter, for the issues at hand, whether the criteria are termed "natural" or "institutional." What does matter is how they supposedly determine—establish fixed bounds—for the use of the term. Bloor's account of criteria repeats, indeed accentuates, the problem of understanding how social usage does manage to cohere given how, on his account, it is learned. Unless he sacrifices his finitism, Bloor's attempt to invoke the notion of criteria as an answer to the question of the *cause* of conformity begs the question. "Criteria" are what need explaining; they cannot be made part of the explanation.

At the root of the difficulty of specifying criteria is the strong programmers' abortive attempt to marry their doctrine of holism and a claim to be able to identify necessary and sufficient conditions. But what is it to give necessary and sufficient conditions except to say that a certain relation is analytic? Yet holism is developed, at least in Quine's writings, as an alternative to accepting the analytic-synthetic distinction. It is no accident that the causality principle, both here and elsewhere, constantly proves to be in conflict with the epistemological tenets of the strong programme discussed in the previous chapter.

Criteria, to repeat, are socially determined. Clarifying how these conventional determinations function is supposed to indicate, in turn, how social factors determine (cause) us to adopt the set of evaluative

[31]Ibid., p. 42.
[32]Ibid., p. 44.

standards that we do, in fact, have. But on examination the criteria are as indeterminate, and for the same finitistic reasons, as any other inductively established standard.

The problem of establishing the causal efficacy of social institutions, especially in light of the adherence to finitism, the criticisms of Winch, and the rejection of mental entities, is certainly not limited to Bloor. Barnes's writings manifest a variation on this problem. In his case, the problem is an appeal to a notion of rule following identical to Winch's rejected account. Barnes notes that there "simply is not, at the present time, any explicit, objective set of rules or procedures by which the influence of concealed interests upon thought and belief can be established."[33] This is, of course, a particular problem for an advocate of the strong programme, since the programme is just one of eliciting the concealed interests determining the selection and operation of the going standards of evaluation. What then is Barnes's solution to this problem? He proposes the use of thought-experiments: "However, it remains possible in many instances to identify the operation of concealed interests by a subjective, experimental approach. Where an actor gives a legitimating account of his adhesion to a belief or set of beliefs we can test that account in the laboratory of our own consciousness. Adopting the cultural orientation of the actor, programming ourselves with his programmes, we can assess what plausibility the beliefs possess for us."[34] The reference to "programming ourselves with his programmes" is, in light of finitist orthodoxy, remarkable enough. Moreover, in developing this line of thought, Barnes provides an account that is, all in all, quite Winchian: "Indeed, the essential difference between this kind of check and the check we would make before, say, accepting a mathematical proof is a remarkably minor one. In the former case we explore whether another actor programmed in a certain way would come to a certain belief or not, in the latter we explore whether we ourselves would do so!"[35] In short, despite his supposed rejection of the analytic-synthetic distinction (as finitism demands), Barnes makes illicit use of this distinction in the now familiar Winchian manner; that is, Barnes assumes a clear distinction of frameworks within which one or another culture pursues its form of life.

[33]Barnes, *Interests*, p. 35.
[34]Ibid., p. 35.
[35]Ibid., p. 94 n. 10.

Barnes attempts to cover the radically nonfinitistic nature of these remarks by blandly asserting that mathematical procedures, as interpreted by Bloor, are also "the product of the open-ended following of conventions."[36] But this is just mistaken. Even if one agrees that mathematical rules are conventionally determined (whatever that may mean), Bloor nowhere shows that the following of them is "open ended." Problems regarding definitions of polyhedra and his discussion of Lewis's notion of strict implication[37] do not establish that, in typical cases, logical and mathematical rules are indeterminate in their applications. Bloor seems confused by the well-known fact that different logical systems may define their connectives differently (or may introduce special, e.g., modal, operators). "Proofs" are internal to a system, and there is the freedom to choose among different systems. It is hard to see, however, why Bloor believes that this fact is evidence for his conclusions concerning logic. He has not shown that there is anything indeterminate once a formal system is chosen.

The point, then, is that Barnes treats rules as if they could be precisely captured (translated?) by others (or as precisely as need be for the purpose of scientific examination[38]). Yet the charge against Winch is just that he makes rules determinate, indeed makes them a condition for recognizing new exemplars of the relevant kind. Bloor insists that this is essentially antifinitistic, and so that the rules cannot have such a status. As I argue in Chapter 9, Bloor is quite correct on this point; a Winchian view of rules does lead to a positivist view of language and, indeed, to determinacy of translation. All these doctrines are anathema to the strong programmers. If they surrender on these epistemological doctrines, then the basis of their criticism of contemporary epistemology is lost. Yet if they adhere to the epistemological doctrines, the causality principle cannot be satisfied. Causality requires specifying necessary or sufficient conditions of social conditioning. If Winchian rules are employed, finitism is denied. Given finitism, however, the requisite causal antecedents cannot be made determinate. And without the causality principle, they have no claim to replace the philosophy of science.

The extent to which socially identified interests actually are necessary conditions is a further complication raised by Barnes's remarks.

[36]Ibid., p. 94 n. 11.

[37]Bloor, *Wittgenstein*, pp. 126–132.

[38]Barnes, *Interests*, p. 35.

Barnes, in fact, seems to explicitly deny that interests are necessary (understanding the term in the usual logical sense): "Unlike ethical codes, such as the medieval rules of chivalry, knowledge, with its directly instrumental dimension, does not necessarily decline when the particular interests bearing upon it are eliminated; instead it is generally modified into a more straightforwardly instrumental form. Biometry and Mendelism could continue (and did continue) as intellectual traditions, in the absence of the particular interests which sustained the controversy between them."[39] If some knowledge persists in the absence of a supposedly determining interest, then clearly this interest is not necessary, in the usual sense of the term, for the social acceptance of those knowledge claims in question. And it was noted above that the strong programmers admit that interests alone are not sufficient to maintain such claims (they acknowledge that experience plays a part, too). But if specific social interests are neither necessary nor sufficient, then what is all the fuss about?

Note that nothing said above implies that it is inappropriate for sociologists to study scientific activity. The issue, rather, is just what is plausibly to be expected as the result of such studies. In particular, I am concerned with the contention that "if sociology could not be applied in a thorough-going way to scientific knowledge it would mean that science could not scientifically know itself. . . . This would make it a special case, a standing exception to the generality of its own procedures."[40] But this is clearly false, since it just ignores *other*, non-sociological, approaches that advocate the use of science self-applied to account for scientific knowledge itself. The question is of the form scientific self-knowledge will take. We have reason to doubt that this form will be sociological.[41]

Are these social concerns relevant, in any case, to the final evaluation of the knowledge claims involved? It appears that the strong programme goes wrong because it commits the genetic fallacy, the fallacy of believing that the source of a claim is determinative of its truth or falsity. In particular, sociological procedure appears to confuse whatever idiosyncrasies might be involved in making a scientific discovery

[39]Ibid., p. 98 n. 18.

[40]Bloor, *Knowledge and Social Imagery*, p. 40.

[41]These remarks do not impugn the suggestion that scientific knowledge might be "multifunctional," that is, might serve both narrow instrumental and larger social concerns; see Shapin, "The History of Science," p. 187.

with the procedures used for formally validating those discoveries. Sociologist H. R. Collins, for example, notes that validation procedures do not explain scientific behavior in the laboratory and concludes that this is so much the worse for validation procedures.[42] On Collins's view, an analysis of scientific knowledge must reconstruct the process by which that knowledge is generated; otherwise it is historically unfaithful (indeed, downright misleading) and unrelated to any interesting cases of scientific inference.[43] In short, far from committing any fallacy by detailing the origins and development of accepted knowledge claims, Collins claims that only an account attending to the genetic factors is an appropriate account of how knowledge is actually created and accepted in such contexts.

Bloor is also quite aware that his approach is open to this charge of fallacious reasoning. I now turn to his vigorous rebuttal of this charge. Bloor's reply is to reemphasize two points: first, the conventional nature of standards, and, second, the fact that conventionally determined standards rationalize the interests of some group or other. With respect to the first point, his view of language and the standards governing its use as a social product, Bloor insists that it follows from this that the standards of evaluation in science (or in any other arena of cultural endeavor, for that matter) are neither ahistorical nor asocial:

> What makes the window-on-the-world model [the image of scientific inquiry as disinterestedly peering out at the world] a myth is the fact that knowledge still depends on social processes within the boundaries of the professional subgroup. . . . The point can also be made in a general way by going back to first principles and asking how any body of knowledge whatsoever is to be learned, transmitted and sustained. In other words, to see that this whole objection is a non-starter, all we need is the network model of knowledge. That was why I based my whole argument upon it and why I began my paper with it.[44]

Given the context dependence of standards (language use), in turn, the second point is held to follow: group interests determine which stan-

[42]H. R. Collins, "What Is TRASP? The Radical Programme as a Methodological Imperative," *Philosophy of the Social Sciences* 11 (1981):221–222.

[43]For a related critique of the justification-discovery distinction as a rationale for writing bad history, see Michael Mulkay, *Science and the Sociology of Knowledge* (London: George Allen & Unwin, 1979), p. 98.

[44]David Bloor, "A Reply to Gerd Buchdahl," *Studies in the History and Philosophy of Science* 13 (1982):311.

dards become prevalent. The strong programme position is that any of the standards encountered in a social setting reflect some general social interests in installing just these standards (for, ex hypothesi, there always could have been others to more or less the same effect): "Until the sequence of ideas is specifically checked for its social significance we are not in a position to pronounce on their full meaning or real relations to one another. The fact that one *can* construct a viewpoint, and that one *can* philosophically gloss them, in such a way that 'nothing particularly "social"' remains in view, proves nothing about the historical case."[45] Barnes echoes this position in the following striking passage: "The consistency of an existing set of beliefs is, in the last analysis, no more than a matter of style. Beliefs can appear perfectly consistent and still be held to be ideologically determined, and *vice versa*."[46] The logical or rational appeal of an explanation is no guard against its being used for purposes of ideological rationalization. (Sociological analysis is ideally a tool for providing a deeper understanding of the pervasive human interests that shape cultural life.)

Bloor's two points are taken to blunt the charge of fallacy as follows. On the one hand, he simply dodges the bullet by challenging someone to show what is wrong, in effect, with indicating how the scientific standards of a particular period reflect and are shaped by larger social concerns: "An advocate of Kuhn's approach could rightly say that highlighting the already obvious social metaphors on which it [his account of science] is based is no criticism of that account. Taking a leaf from a conventional philosophy book he might argue that the origin of a theory does not matter, provided that the theory is under the control of fact and observation. . . . So its origins, whatever they are, are not of over-riding importance when assessing its truth."[47] On the other hand, he also takes a more aggressive tack, insisting that only those with some vested interest in protecting the status quo could possibly object to a sociological analysis of the standards. If the analysis reveals that epistemology is a form of rationalization, then those who object are just agents of darkness:

The variable of perceived threat operating upon underlying social metaphors explains the differential tendency to treat knowledge as sacred and beyond the

[45]Ibid., p. 310.

[46]Barnes, *Interests*, p. 93 n. 4.

[47]Bloor, *Knowledge and Social Imagery*, p. 70.

reach of scientific study. I now want to examine the consequences of adopting a mystifying strategy and ways to evade its influence.

The claim that I want to put forward is that unless we adopt a scientific approach to the nature of knowledge then our grasp of that nature will be no more than a projection of our ideological concerns. Our theories of knowledge will rise and fall as their corresponding ideology rises and declines; they will lack any autonomy or basis for development in their own right. Epistemology will be merely implicit propaganda.[48]

Despite the ad hominem flavor of Bloor's attack, the force of the reply is clear. Put in somewhat different terms, it invites us to look at our usual metalanguage—the usual formulation of rules of inference and so forth—as itself an object language. This language is itself governed by rules that, in turn, are specified at yet another level as a higher-level metalanguage. The twist is that this next metalanguage looks somewhat different from that to which we are accustomed, since it is cashed out in terms of the controlling interests governing the earlier-cited formulations.[49] In other words, once we are trained to think of whatever is called knowledge as some form—however difficult to discern—of covert ideological rationalization, we can hardly consider the approach fallacious. It is, rather, a contribution to one's understanding of the logic of discourse after the fashion of any metalinguistic analysis.

Steven Lukes confronts Bloor specifically with the charge of genetic fallacy. Rational people, he suggests, might just be responding to a concern for truth. "But it is one thing to explain the use of science by clerics and even the interpretation of scientific activity by religious scientists. It is another to account for scientific discovery and theory choice by scientific innovators." Moreover, Lukes queries, why must ideological concerns be assumed to have precedence over a concern for truth? "Why should these interests always trump the distinctive interests of scientists, such as Boyle and Newton, in getting their explanations right?"[50]

Bloor responds by questioning, first, what is meant by "getting it right," and, second, by asserting that an interest in truth is never denied; the problem, rather, is that a concern with truth is never

[48]Ibid., p. 70.

[49]See ibid., pp. 70–71, for additional comments on this point.

[50]Steven Lukes, "Comments on David Bloor," *Studies in the History and Philosophy of Science* 13 (1982):317.

sufficient. With regard to the first point, Bloor argues that, by assuming that a certain sort of explanation is the appropriate type of scientific explanation, Lukes rules out of court from the start the sort of explanation Bloor is concerned to construct. What is it that is wrong with a sociological explanation, provided that it is appropriately scientific? Indeed, if Bloor could produce the sort of causal explanation to which he is committed, it is difficult to imagine why it should not be accepted. As it stands, Lukes's complaint simply begs the questions against the strong programme.

The second line of response also seems convincing. Omitting many of the details of Bloor's response, the key point is the familiar one regarding underdetermination: "Only in retrospect can it be made out to look obviously right or 'forced' upon men by the 'evidence'. This was why I said in my paper that historians had turned to the social context to explain the special attractions of the corpuscular philosophy."[51] And the "special attraction," as the now familiar story goes, is a function of the social interests at work.

For all this, has the charge of fallacy been answered? Can we conclude from the procedure of ideological unmasking, of epistemology as ideology, "that the genesis of beliefs has much to tell us about the extent of their validity."[52] The issue, I suggest, turns on the notion of "natural rationality" and the attendant evaluative-descriptive distinction the strong programmers invoke. Bloor, for example, speaks above of epistemologies lacking "autonomy or basis for development in their own right." Much of the "unmasking" rhetoric, indeed, clearly assumes that the interests being exposed are those of the people being studied. But what assures us of this? The strong programme cannot escape being indicted by the very charge it brings against the unreflexive application of standards in the natural sciences. If all standards of evaluation are a form of covert ideological rationalization, then how do we even know whose interests are revealed by a sociological unmasking?

By virtue of their finitism and network model of language, their explicit denial of an Archimedean point by which to study knowledge, and their advocacy of the indeterminacy of translation, the foregoing

[51]See Bloor, "Reply to Steven Lukes," *Studies in the History and Philosophy of Science* 13 (1982):321.

[52]Barnes, *Interests*, p. 93 n. 4.

problem is unresolvable for the strong programmers. Any proof must identify the "real" interests of those involved, but such proof either assumes an Archimedean point from which to judge such matters (and so denies the holist thesis) or violates the endorsement of the indeterminacy of translation (by presuming that there is a fixed, unique characterization to be given of human concerns). Indeed, even if indeterminacy is not considered, there is still the problem posed by the strong programmers' own reading of the underdetermination thesis, which has it that once can always expect to find alternative models.[53] If one account can be given of the interests guiding a group, surely an incompatible account can be constructed for the same body of historical data.

The foregoing remarks give renewed, although somewhat different, point to the charge of genetic fallacy. Now the genetic problem appears under the guise of determining just whose interests are being revealed by the analysis. The problem is deepened, or so I have suggested, by the assumption that any theoretical account (scientific or sociological) is underdetermined; hence empirically equivalent but logically incompatible imputations of interests can be formulated. Whatever the interest of such an unmasking, it can promise no escape from the very problems of rationalization and underdetermination imputed to the more conventional explanations of knowledge. One is faced with the question of why a sociological researcher prefers one account over another. The strong programme offers no real prospect for generating an epistemology independent of potentially distorting interests. Note that the problem here is not just the charge that the reflexivity thesis applies to the strong programme. What is of interest is that the strong programme is liable to just the same shortcomings (rationalization and underdetermination) and for just the same reasons as the philosophy of science of which it was alleged to represent an improvement.

The suggested unmasking function alluded to by Bloor in the remarks quoted above and the parallels with Winch's account of rules noted several pages back are both symptomatic of a deep tension in the strong programmers' claim for their program and their philosophical

[53]It is one matter to hold that, in principle, theories are underdetermined or that a given theory may always be adjusted to fit seemingly adverse evidence. And there seem to be well-documented historical instances of both types of case. But for a more cautious assessment of underdetermination, see Quine, "On Empirically Equivalent Systems of the World," *Erkenntnis* 9 (1975):316.

assumptions. The tension is this. On the one hand, what they call their finitistic view is basic to their critique of the notion that there is a "deep" or universal logic to cultural phenomena; on the other hand, their repeated suggestions that epistemology, once its sociological roots are laid bare, can become a disinterested account of knowledge is flatly at odds with this finitistic view. What, on their account, would qualify as an autonomous epistemology? How are we to know objectivity even if we look it in the face? If there is no Archimedean point from which to judge ongoing evaluative standards, then it seems pointless, given the strong programmers' starting point, to talk of "autonomous" or "disinterested" inquiry. The irony here is that they refuse to follow the logic of their own avowed relativism to the bitter end. There is no escaping from their naturalistic approach to the high ground of rationalism. Once at sea in Neurath's boat, there is no anchor to be had.

Barnes, however, asserts that "legitimate" interests, at least with regard to scientific inquiry, include a concern with prediction and control. But he offers no argument to indicate why this is so, and he also warns that an interest in prediction and control is by no means sufficient to assure us that the scientific inquiry in question is indeed disinterested.[54] The ambivalence of his view toward the possibility of disinterested knowledge comes out nicely in the following remarks:

> However, an institution wherein knowledge is generated and sustained entirely under the impetus of legitimate instrumental interests would seem a realistic and empirically realisable ideal. Knowledge does not have to be ideologically determined. . . .
>
> It remains the case that if we generate and sustain knowledge entirely in terms of authentic interests, we are still obliged to employ existing knowledge as a resource. And that knowledge will be the product of a historical development wherein concealed, illegitimate interests are bound to have been operative. In some ways, this is a very disturbing fact. . . . Hence present knowledge, sustained entirely as an instrumental resource, possesses, as it were, a suspect pedigree.[55]

Barnes's suggestion that knowledge can be sustained by interests other than those to which it owes its origins, that it can "shake free" of a

[54]Barnes, *Interests*, p. 41.
[55]Ibid., pp. 43–44.

suspect pedigree, is, it should be noted, contrary to the claim that certain sociological conditions are *necessary* to sustaining certain knowledge claims. Barnes is saying here that the governing interests can change completely but the knowledge claim be retained.

The problem is not just in discerning when we have knowledge for its own sake and not for the sake of some other interest; the problem is in understanding in exactly what respects the strong programme represents any advance from the problems imputed to conventional philosophy of science. My claim has been that the notion of knowledge guided by fixed social interests conflicts with the finitistic premise. This problem extends, as well, to the distinction between evaluative and naturalistic accounts of rationality. Strong programmers are apt to insist that "the major reason why such accounts [as theirs] are frequently described as 'naturalistic' is simply that they have no evaluative axe to grind."[56] Similarly, Bloor speaks of "natural rationality" as if it were, for all intents and purposes, a purely descriptive enterprise: "Natural rationality refers to typical human reasoning propensities; normative rationality refers to patterns of inference that are esteemed or sanctioned. The one has reference to matters of psychological fact; the other to shared standards or norms."[57] Yet this claim to be engaged in a putatively descriptive or factual enterprise must be measured against Bloor's repeated characterization of the network model as one in which "the organization of a classificatory system is not, and cannot be, determined by the way the world is. There is no such thing as a natural or uniquely objective classification."[58] One finds Barnes advocating the same position: "The problem of meaning variance occurs everywhere in science, as in culture generally. It is no less a problem where usage is routine and unthinking than where it is self-consciously developed and extended."[59] Clearly, then, what holds for schemes of the natural world must, and for the very same reasons, hold for those classificatory concepts by which one describes and explains the social world.

What is mystifying in Bloor's account is the regular transgression of the very philosophical limits that, he insists, constrain explanations in

[56]Shapin, "The History of Science," p. 187.

[57]David Bloor, "The Strengths of the Strong Programme," *Philosophy of the Social Sciences* 11 (1981):207.

[58]Bloor, "Durkheim and Mauss Revisited," p. 269.

[59]Barnes, *T. S. Kuhn and Social Science*, p. 87.

the natural sciences. If no set of physical "facts" or "experiences" determines the shape physical theory takes, why is it that we are to believe that some set of interests (and, by the way, just what are these?) does, in fact, determine the form *all* knowledge claims take?

Let us grant that constraints must be established by social convention. Let us even grant to Bloor that "public systems of knowledge possess laws and principles of organization that are binding and authoritative. These have the property of being 'an external norm, superior to the flow of our representations' and they function as rules or standards."[60] None of this answers the problem of how the sociological *epoché*, the bracketing of our own ideological blinders, is to take place. And if this cannot be explained, then what is the difference between writing sociology à la Bloor or history à la Lakatos? If the case against the latter is that he rewrites history according to his current favorite standard of rational inquiry, then how do we know that the former is not simply writing sociology according to his favorite list of interests? What assures us that any less imposing is taking place in one case than in the other? When Shapin titles an article the "History of Science and its Sociological Reconstruction" (see Chapter 7, n. 13), it is obviously meant to twit the historical nose of a Laudan or any erstwhile Lakatosians. But if we take such a title seriously, as I suggest we ought to in view of the claims being made on behalf of the strong programme, then we must ask just what distinguishes this reconstruction, with the interests it overlooks, from the historiography of science it purports to replace?

Barnes, in the process of making light of Laudan's appeal to our "pre-analytic" intuitions, asserts that "there seems to be nothing in the form of Laudan's argument which makes it preferable to a parallel argument based on strong intuitions of racial superiority. This raises again, in acute form, the query raised earlier. Should we really rest content to use strongly held intuitions as basic criteria, and thus exempt them from evaluation themselves?"[61] But are strongly held intuitions about interests any better? If epistemology is propaganda, as

[60]Bloor, "Durkheim and Mauss Revisited," p. 296. Notice, once again, how Bloor's own favored characterization of social rules is indistinguishable, for purposes of criticism, from the Winchian notion of rules and from the philosophical notion of rationality he elsewhere finds so problematic; see the Winch-style characterization of social rules Bloor provides in *Knowledge and Social Imagery*, p. 66.

[61]Barry Barnes, "Vicissitudes of Belief," *Social Studies of Science* 9 (1979):250.

Bloor suggests, then how is the regress broken? The problem, let me again emphasize, is *not* that we can constantly apply the reflexivity thesis; the problem is a question of the *causal* mechanism at work; it is a problem of knowing where and at what to look in order to discern the engine driving scientific and social changes. We have no reason to believe that the strong programme account is, even in principle, able to avoid any of those shortcomings with which it taxes the conventional philosophical accounts of scientific reasoning. If "getting it right" is, as Bloor insists, socially determined,[62] then this dissipates any alleged advantage, given the philosophical theses he advocates, that one form of scientific explanation might claim over another.

I have so far raised questions about the capacity of the strong programme to itself evade the criticisms with which it burdens philosophers of science. The answers to this point have been discouraging for the strong programme's prospects; the arguments indicate that its criticisms of philosophy of science apply to its own account as well. Moreover, there are grounds for a general concern about the direction of and the mechanism for causation. I have argued that there is no case made for the claim that the reduction must "run" in one direction rather than another. No argument yet made by advocates of the strong programme establishes that they have any monopoly on a general causal explanation of social beliefs; it is difficult to see, moreover, how they could so argue. A further concern is the fact that no clear *mechanism* of causal relations is established, although lip service is paid to behaviorism. (I return to this point below when analyzing some of the case studies with a view to understanding just what sort of causal relations are detailed in what the strong programmers take to be their most compelling studies.)

There is a final twist I want to consider to the questions surrounding the causal nexus of belief formation and change in the context of the network model of language. This concerns whether this model can, in fact, be exploited for purposes of the type of analysis the strong programmers propose to provide. I indicated in the previous chapter their tendency, most explicit in Barnes's writings, to conflate holism and underdetermination. These theses are distinct, although the tendency to conflate them is not Barnes's alone (see sources cited in Chapter 7, n. 31). In brief, holism is a thesis about the truth conditions

[62]Bloor, "Reply to Steven Lukes," p. 322.

for theoretical sentences; it asserts, in effect, that in order to assign these truth conditions, many other theoretical assumptions must simply be assumed true. A corollary is the claim that one may preserve a particular theoretical or observation claim by adjusting the truth values of other assumptions on which the statement in question depends. Underdetermination, however, claims that alternative, logically incompatible theories may yet be empirically equivalent. Quine puts the distinction rather neatly when he observes that, on the Duhemian account, statements imply their supporting evidence only when taken in conjunction; in the case of underdetermination, what is being claimed is that some disjunction of theories, all of whose disjuncts cannot be true, is supported by the available evidence. The philosophically important point is that the Duhemian view obtains for theories considered singly; underdetermination involves a comparative claim with respect to what may be formulated relative to a given body of data. Holism does not entail underdetermination, for nothing about the existence of alternative theoretical solutions follows from a thesis concerning the truth conditions of individual theoretical sentences.

Despite the fact that it is a mistake to identify the two, Barnes does so. He misconstrues the import of finitism as follows. On his reading of the finitistic account, a wide variety of interpretations will always be compatible with the available data;[63] hence all theories are underdetermined. In addition, since by virtue of the inductive procedures by which language is learned we are always in a position to "adjust" the application of concepts as need be, holism obtains. We only know the application conditions for terms when we know the whole language. "In the last analysis Duhem's position is simply a variant of the finitist account of concept application. . . . A hypothesis can never be conclusively tested because of our discretion in the application of concepts."[64] Barnes is apt, however, to speak in the same breath of "the range of possibilities both for imposing pattern and adapting pattern, simultaneously if need be, which the form of the language of essences makes available to the using community."[65] The "imposing pattern" hints at underdetermination, the "adapting pattern" at holism. Yet, as Quine has observed, the extent to which theories are genuinely under-

[63]See, for example, Barnes, *T. S. Kuhn and Social Science*, pp. 29–35.
[64]Ibid., p. 75.
[65]Ibid., p. 82.

determined, that is, empirically equivalent, logically incompatible, and not open to mutual interpretation by some reconstrual of their predicates, is an empirical question. In short, one cannot assume that underdetermination holds as a general epistemological thesis based just on those reasons supporting the Duhem thesis; the evidence in favor of the latter does not entail the former claim.

The conflation is critical since the primary philosophical point made by finitism is clearly just the holistic one.[66] Finitism denies that there are natural kinds or essences; therefore, classificatory concepts are conventionally determined. But in order to know how the bounds of the classificatory model are drawn, one needs to know the workings of the whole network. Hence, starting with finitism, one gets holism—or so their story goes.

If one does not distinguish underdetermination and holism, then the conventional nature of knowledge (holism) stands in need of strong and ongoing sociological reinforcement, since (given underdetermination) other, logically incompatible alternatives are readily available. The prevalence of alternatives to our conventional usages extends even to the use of individual terms: "In section 2.3 [a discussion of finitism] . . . it was emphasized that present proper usage is always underdetermined by previous usage."[67] This radical underdetermination, in turn, is what emphasizes the pressing need for all judgments to be subject to social control:

> Accordingly, everything in science, every act of concept application, every inference, every judgment, is of sociological interest. In normal science, even the most routine steps are interesting, not simply as symbols of conformity to authoritatively prescribed procedures or assumptions, but as displays of what such conformity consists in, and even as contributions to establishing what such conformity should consist in. The presentation of routine findings, as routine findings, helps to sustain the general sense of what is routine: as much as an act of social conformity, it is a form of social control.[68]

The conflation, in short, strongly abets the sociological interpretation of conventional standards as having a constant need for reinforcement and control.

[66]Ibid., p. 30; see also "Durkheim and Mauss Revisited," p. 269.
[67]Barnes, *T. S. Kuhn and Social Science*, p. 98.
[68]Ibid., p. 87.

Bloor urges precisely the same line: "Such stability as there is in a system of knowledge comes entirely from the collective decisions of its creators and users. That is to say: from the requirement that certain laws and classifications be kept intact, and all adjustments and alterations carried out elsewhere." In the context of his essay defending the thesis that "the classification of things [reproduces] the classification of men," Bloor claims that this idea "performs the vital function of giving the sociologist a workable account of knowledge that orients him to all its main social features, showing not merely how society influences knowledge, but how it is constitutive of it."[69] The constitutive notion appealed to here is not the bland claim that standards of evaluation, like all standards, are products of some social convention; the assertion is that particular social interests are being rationalized by, and were the cause for adopting, the standards of scientific evaluation we find employed at a given time in a particular society. The image of any network, then, is one in which, at every given moment, everything is up for grabs.

This fluid view of the linguistic situation is made plausible by the assumed ready presence of underdetermined alternatives to current social practices. Linguistic anarchy is avoided because societies provide institutional criteria. As I have already indicated, however, this appeal to institutional criteria does not explain social conformity. The invocation of criteria, at least as done by the strong programmers, involves the very notion of resemblances it is intended to resolve. If there are no natural kinds, how do the institutionally established authorities "create resemblances"? A further problem arises: as the account of criteria or rules is explicated, it becomes more and more idealized and "Winchian," and so simply a variant of the abhorred rationalist philosophy. The supposedly pressing need for determinative criteria arises only on the assumption that alternative practices must be constantly held at bay. But this assumption on the part of the strong programmers is just the result of their confused inference from the conventionality of knowledge to its underdetermination.

The strong programmers try to have things both ways. Against their avowed philosophical enemies (the rationalists), they want to exploit the underdetermined, hence radically open-textured, aspect of the network model. In order, however, to ensure that the type of analysis

[69]Bloor, "Durkheim and Mauss Revisited," pp. 280, 297.

they propose is possible, they insist on the presence of stable structures of rules and norms. The effects of this tension between both affirming and denying the determinacy of structure becomes particularly acute for the strong programmers' discussion of the relations between goals and interests. The core of their methodological proposal is to replace rationalistic explanations of scientific activity by causal ones, and their notion of cause is one of, at best, concomitant coincidence. As it turns out, they are unable to determine, on their own principles, if the coincidences noted are a function of the interests of those under study or of those doing the studying. They could do this only at the price of having a neutral vantage point from which to assess and untangle the various social interests allegedly at work; but the existence of such a vantage point is what their holism commits them to denying.

It is instructive, as a final pass at the problem of sorting out the causality principle at issue here, to examine closely Barnes's promise to unpack just this relation: "We must turn to the goals and interests which inform judgment when concepts are applied and usage is developed. It is by reference to goals and interests that particular modes of concept application, selected from and preferred to innumerable alternative options, can be made intelligible." Moreover, he suggests, "the fact of the relationship and a certain amount concerning its form can be asserted with confidence." Barnes goes further and argues that this relationship will be instrumental in nature.[70]

When it comes to actually fulfilling his promise by specifying the relationship as claimed, the tension between the need for an open-textured holist view and the need for a stable structure manifests itself. In the extended quote below, I analyze the interconnections between goals and interests which Barnes believes can be said "with confidence" to obtain. (For ease of reference, I have inserted bracketed numbers next to most sentences in the quote below.)

> [1] When esoteric, technical knowledge is encountered, like that of the physical sciences, then its use and development is intelligible in relation to specific, context-dependent technical, predictive goals and interests, rather than to abstract criteria, or 'correspondence rules', or any other verbal formulations.
>
> . . . [2] There is a crucial relationship between goals and interests on the one hand, and hence existing knowledge, on the other. [3] Goals and interests bear

[70] Barnes, *T. S. Kuhn and Social Science*, pp. 102–103.

upon the judgment involved in any act of concept application. [4] But such a judgment can only be made if *other* concepts are assumed to have a routine usage which others will continue to follow, and which can accordingly be taken for granted as a stable feature when the judgment is made. . . . [5] Hence goals and interests, considered in the context of an over-all, coherent, verbal culture, must, for the most part, act upon judgments so that concepts are applied in the expected way, the predicted way, the way that is called 'routine'. [6] There is a limit to the possible incongruity between habits and interests, between what is routinised and institutionalised and what is immediately indicated by reference to shared goals and objectives. [7] Interests cannot press too hard upon routine usage without counterproductive effects. [8] The role of interests can be no more than to develop and modify an existing basis and routine. [9] At the level of the over-all culture, goals and interests account for the relationship between old knowledge and new. [10] Old knowledge, old routines, are necessary conditions in the understanding of the new.[71]

Sentence [1] asserts what is to be established, namely, a determinate relation between, on the one hand, goals and interests, and, on the other, specific developments in what is taken to be knowledge. But this is all that sentence [2] states; sentence [3] expands the assertion to cover all cases of concept application. Collectively, the sentences assert some determinable interrelationship between, on the one hand, routines, knowledge, and concept application, and, on the other hand, goals and interests. Sentence [4] notes that, even in a holistic context, not everything can be questioned at once. Sentence [5] contains a conclusion indicator word; the apparent conclusion is that interests must act on concepts so that routines are sustained. But is this not what was asserted above? The point was to establish this relation, to say how it worked. Simply citing holist doctrine does nothing to clinch the point. Sentences [6]–[8] are equally vacuous, more oracular than informative. We know what the strong programmers need to prove; the question is, how do they prove this? The answer is nowhere forthcoming. Sentence [9], if taken at its word, would mean that we literally had to know the whole of history to understand, in their sense, any of it. As for sentence [10], if old knowledge is a *necessary* condition of understanding, but all knowledge is contextually defined and historically conditioned, then it seems that any strong programme analysis is committed to an infinite regress.

[71]Ibid., p. 104.

Not only is Barnes of no help in showing how causal explanations are to be constructed in accord with strong programme, his additional remarks on this topic appear to preclude the existence of the sort of regularities on which a causal account depends: "There is no way of asserting a correspondence between a concept or a belief, and a specific kind of objective or interest, once the character of this historical sequence is recognized."[72] Nor is this a recent wrinkle in his account; similar remarks may be gleaned from earlier writings: "Since there is nothing in the intrinsic character of a belief to reveal its provenance or the interests which were operative in its production, there is a technical difficulty in establishing an account of that provenance, invoking concealed interests, as superior to a legitimating account, citing legitimate interests only." Barnes's proposed answer, both early and late, is that in the absence of objective rules for determining the influence of interests on beliefs one should employ the experiment of rethinking the other person's thoughts for him or her.[73] I have already shown how this violates restrictions on the status of social rules, indeterminacy, and, now, considerations of the open versus closed natures of concept application. Institutional kinds do no better than natural kinds if the question is one of how perceptual similarity is propagated across society (see Chapter 2).

It might be objected that, while complaining, as I have, of the notion of causality, I have overlooked just the area in which all (or, at least, the most vexing) questions regarding this issue would be resolved—the many case studies produced by the strong programmers. It is here, it might be suggested, that any doubts regarding the efficacy of the program are to be answered. Judge them by what they do, not by what they say they will do. So be it. It is to an examination of whether, or to what extent, selected case studies answer my questions about causality that I now turn.

## II

I have been assuming from the outset that the claim of the strong programme to philosophical interest is as a replacement for epistemol-

[72]Ibid., p. 112.

[73]Barnes, *Interests*, pp. 34–35, 94 n. 10; see also *T. S. Kuhn and Social Science*, p. 112.

ogy by virtue of the fact that it offers an analysis of belief legitimation according to which standard epistemology is misguided and misinformed. Standard epistemology is misguided because it seeks the logic of justification in factors internal and unique to scientific method; it is misinformed because epistemologists imagine that they somehow stand aloof from the temptation to rationalize their social interests. The strong programme seeks to make good its claim to provide a "social epistemology" by demonstrating that it provides a better (i.e., more accurate) account of how knowledge claims are warranted in a natural scientific context. It does this by subjecting the accepted standards of evaluation to sociological scrutiny. It is by analyzing how standards come to be set in place that a perspicuous account of theory selection, theory change, and belief legitimation is to be obtained.

The suggestion of the strong programmers, in other words, is that as "as a typical form of culture, science should be amenable to whatever methods advance our understanding of culture generally."[74] In order to see just how this is done, I examine a collection of essays edited by Barnes and Shapin, a collection dedicated to the analysis of scientific knowledge in the style of the strong programme: "We have sought to compile a collection of original essays *explicitly* concerned with natural knowledge as culture, and *explicitly* exploring the possibilities of anthropological and sociological methods in understanding it."[75] In what follows, I analyze the claims of three particular articles. Two are found in the volume *Natural Order*; the other is Paul Forman's "Wiemar Culture, Causality, and Quantum Theory, 1918–1927: Adaptation by German Physicists and Mathematicians to a Hostile Intellectual Environment."[76] The editors claim that the two essays from *Natural Order* exemplify, if any do, the social determination of scientific knowledge:

> If the arguments of these two essays are accepted, then they establish two important general points of continuing relevance throughout the book. First, both essays point out that conceptions of the natural order may be multifunctional. Both identify social interests bearing upon the production of represen-

[74]B. Barnes and S. Shapin, "Introduction," in *Natural Order*, ed. Barnes and Shapin, p. 10.

[75]Ibid., p. 12.

[76]In *Historical Studies in the Physical Sciences*, vol. 3, ed. R. McCormmach (Philadelphia: University of Pennsylvania Press, 1971).

> tations of the body, but both also emphasize that the "technical" value of those representation should not be thought of as thereby diminished. . . . Secondly, it is a mistake to imagine representation of natural order being, as it were, *constructed* by an examination and direct rendition of reality, and then being *used* in a social context. . . . Accordingly, they [scientific representations of the natural order] cannot be studied by methods which assign them independent, inherent characteristics (of meaning, or implication, or truth) prior to their use.[77]

Forman's essay is given similar status in the writings of all the strong programmers; if any case study demonstrates the social determination of scientific knowledge, this one does.[78] Based on an examination of these key case studies, I offer an assessment of their important claim that "the 'interest model' has been shown to work convincingly and in detail in a large number of cases."[79]

It is interesting to note that Forman, at the outset of his essay, proposes to provide a *causal* analysis of why a "large number of German physicists, for reasons only incidentally related to developments in their own discipline, distanced themselves from, or explicitly repudiated, causality in physics."[80] The causal connection to be established is precisely an explanation of scientific theory—in this case, quantum mechanics—in terms of social determinants: "I am convinced . . . that the movement to dispense with causality in physics, which sprang up so suddenly and blossomed so luxuriantly in Germany after 1918, was primarily an effort by German physicists to adapt the content of their science to the values of their intellectual environment."[81] It is not within the scope of my knowledge to challenge the facts of the case as Forman marshals them.[82] I am more

[77]Barnes and Shapin, "Introduction," p. 16.

[78]See, for example, Bloor, "The Strengths of the Strong Programme," pp. 201–202.

[79]Ibid., p. 210. One important question to be kept in mind in discussing the case studies is the extent to which the strong programmers (or those of whose work they approve) are faithful to their much-talked-of model of "natural rationality." Problems raised in prior chapters, and those discussed in particular in the final chapter, should make us wary of the claims of those who purport to identify the canons of rationality employed by others. I do not, in the context of this chapter, press this particular point. It has been pressed to telling effect, however, by Stephen Turner; see his "Interpretive Charity, Durkheim, and the 'Strong Programme' in the Sociology of Knowledge," *Philosophy of the Social Sciences* 11 (1981):231–243.

[80]Forman, "Weimar Culture," p. 3.

[81]Ibid., p. 7.

[82]But John Hendry does; see his excellent "Weimar Culture and Quantum Causality," *History of Science* 18 (1980):155–180.

concerned with the particular form his "causal" explanation of events takes. Specifically, I suggest that what makes Forman's case appear plausible, to the extent that it does, is the very point about which I have earlier criticized the strong programme—the complete lack of specification of a mechanism for belief formation and change, especially on a social scale. For it is just our *ignorance* of such a mechanism on which Forman's argument depends. Since we do not know what either the necessary or the sufficient conditions of such formation and change are, we cannot possibly verify Forman's claim that internal factors (to then current theory in physics) are not sufficient to explain the changes that took place. How can one reasonably judge what is, indeed, "incidental" to theoretical concerns if no account is presented to specify what sort of concerns are tangential and what are not?

> And while it is undoubtedly true that the internal developments in atomic physics were important in precipitating this widespread sense of crisis among German-speaking Central European physicists, and that these internal developments were necessary to give the crisis a sharp focus, nonetheless it now seems evident to me that these internal developments were not in themselves sufficient conditions. The *possibility* of the crisis of the old quantum theory was, I think, dependent upon the physicists own craving for crises, arising from participation in, and adaptation to, the Weimar intellectual milieu.[83]

Barnes ridicules Laudan's appeal to our "pre-analytic" intuitions. But one's appeal to "pre-systemic" intuitions regarding causal relations ought to be at least as suspect. The use of terms such as "necessary," "sufficient,' "dependent upon," and "possibility" is merely rhetorical ruse. In context, the terms have no meaning; indeed, in the absence of the requisite theory of belief formation and change, they can have none. Forman's rhetoric aside, he explains nothing in terms of a "causal" account of theory change.[84]

Christopher Lawrence's "The Nervous System and Society in the Scottish Enlightenment" is the first of the two essays that Shapin and Barnes regard as exemplifying the sort of determination the strong

[83]Forman, "Weimar Culture," p. 62.

[84]John Hendry makes the point, moreover, that the notion of causality is doubly clouded in Forman's work. It is unclear, first, in the sense I have indicated above, that is, with regard to the specification of how social factors function causally. But the account is unclear, in addition, Hendry complains, because it fails to be sufficiently precise with regard to the issue of what notion of causality was actually being debated and, ultimately, rejected; Hendry, "Weimar Culture," pp. 168–169.

programme seeks to establish between social and scientific modes of thought. And what Lawrence initially promises to prove certainly has the appropriate form: "This *uniqueness* of Scottish medical theory is, I suggest, only explicable by invoking the particular context of the upheaval in Scottish economic and social life in the 18th century, and, in particular, by referring to the social interests and self-perceptions of the improving landed class that came to dominate Scottish culture."[85] Notice, once again, that essential to evaluating the truth value of the claim is a completely unverifiable condition, the claim that the upheaval in Scottish society is a necessary condition for explaining the particular medical theory developed in Scottish medical schools (that, anyway, is how I understand Lawrence's remark that the medical theory is "only explicable" by reference to the social conditions).

When we turn to causal details, the account is not just obscure but obscure in precisely the way one would expect in light of previous criticisms. As earlier observed, there is tension between the strong programme views on the open-ended character of beliefs, on the one hand, and on the desire to define a causal structure on the other. Barnes's theoretical analysis gives no account of the interaction of interests, routines, and concept application. The sort of regular connections needed for even a minimal imputation of a causal relation are not only not in evidence but also said not to obtain by Barnes. It is not surprising that Lawrence establishes that certain intellectual movements were *concurrent*; nothing he says, however, establishes even a *temporal* precedence of one or the other elements of social and scientific thought. The best Lawrence can do is to assert what he is to prove, that the various intellectual elements causally interacted one another:

> Rather than look, then, as is so often done, for the 'influences' of philosophy on medicine or the reverse, both must be interpreted by referring them to the common social context. To do this is not to suggest the model of the body was a *mere* celebration of the social order. It arose concurrently with that social order and, as part of the whole ideology of improvement, served to give the social leaders their strong sense of identity and to sanction their natural governing role. But this is not all; instrumentally it was at the same time a brilliantly innovative exploration and interpretation of physiological evidence.[86]

[85] Christopher Lawrence, "The Nervous System and Society in the Scottish Enlightenment," in *Natural Order*, ed. Barnes and Shapin, p. 20.

[86] Ibid., pp. 33–34.

But the problem is worse than the preceding remarks suggest. All that is acknowledged in the foregoing quote is that no regularities, from interests to beliefs, have been documented. The strain the thesis is under becomes explicit when Lawrence turns to recapitulating what he takes his essay to have established. He begins by straightforwardly asserting to have established his thesis, but this time without acknowledging the limitation noted above:

> In my attempt to elucidate the contextual significance of Edinburgh physiology I have discerned certain formal similarities between conceptions of nature (in this case, the body) and conceptions of society. . . . I have sought, however, to say more about this similarity in physiological and social theory than that both deployed common material. I have tried to identify the specific social groups which elaborated social and natural thought, to ascertain their historical situation and social interests, and have attempted in turn to show that the model of the body was developed, evaluated, and deployed in a context of legitimation. Thus I would claim that physiological conceptions were sustained by social interests, and that the present account is broadly compatible with anthropological orientations to natural knowledge.[87]

The key phrase here is the suggestion that the medical model was developed and evaluated "in the context of" a concern for legitimating certain social interests. This appears to be a much stronger statement than Lawrence ventures just two pages earlier in his essay, where he suggests mere temporal concurrence. But it has this appearance because "in the context of" is ambiguous. It may mean no more than concurrence; or, Lawrence can be read as claiming that the social concerns were a significant factor (a necessary condition for the way the theory developed, as he claims at the outset) in evaluating the scientific acceptability of the physiological claims. The last sentence of the quote clearly invites the stronger reading. Yet in a footnote appended to the penultimate sentence quoted above, Lawrence writes: "In practice, physiology was not often resorted to as a legitimation of social interests. Improvers were after all a powerful group and had only occasional need to buttress their arguments with naturalistic sanctions."[88] It now appears that, if ever there were an unfalsifiable thesis, it is the "strong" reading of Lawrence's. For his attribution of social

[87]Ibid., p. 35.
[88]Ibid., p. 36 n. 9.

interests to science is patently ad hoc. If interest groups use scientific arguments, it shows the mutual interdependence of science and social interests, and if scientific arguments are not used, or are only occasionally so used, this still shows the interdependence. This is what establishes a causal connection between the scientific and the social? This is a proof that the social interests are what sustained the scientific endeavor? If this is a model of the sort of causal explanations the strong programme proposes to produce, so much the worse for the strong programme.

The second of the two model essays is Shapin's "Homo Phrenologicus: Anthropological Perspectives on an Historical Problem."[89] Shapin claims that, although "the growth and credibility of phrenological knowledge cannot be understood independently of judgments informed by an interest in prediction and control," nonetheless, "whatever its scientific merit, the anatomical was designed to *legitimate* a theory sustained by other factors. This, however, leads us to consideration of phrenology as the product of *social* interests." Shapin's account appeals explicitly to class categories.[90] This is strange enough in the context of a work that claims to be purely descriptive; it is even stranger if one considers the difficulty of specifying such categories. Nonetheless, having cast the account in terms of how anatomical theory, at least with regard to phrenological research, is a piece in the play of economic forces, a weapon of the rising bourgeois, Shapin goes on to argue that the data fits this class-struggle account. But was not one of the promises of the strong programme to clarify interests? Shapin's account is clearly an exploitation of a specific mode of historiography, that is, Marxist. But what argument do we have that this is the correct metastructure of interests to assume?

Again, when we look into the essay for proof that the social interests are what legitimated the scientific work, we find nothing approaching a proof. A concurrence of events is noted; but, once again, we do not even have note of bare temporal, much less causal, priority of the social over the scientific concerns. Moreover, by Shapin's own account, the leading advocate for the phrenological movement was a lawyer,

[89]For problems with Shapin's work on this general topic other than those I discuss, see Hesse, "The Strong Thesis of Sociology of Knowledge," pp. 33–34, 59 n. 11.

[90]Steven Shapin, "Homo Phrenologicus: Anthropological Perspectives on an Historical Problem," in *Natural Order*, ed. Barnes and Shapin, pp. 54–55.

George Combe.[91] But how are Combe's remarks evidence that the *anatomists* evaluated their scientific data to serve the bourgeois ideology? Reading the local newspapers in Missouri is enough to teach one that advocates of creationism are quick to exploit any criticism of evolutionary theory they happen to come accross. Is one to conclude that the scientists, too, are motivated by an interest in creationism—or by whatever are the larger economic or social interests moving creationists—because creationists cite their research? I am prepared to believe that Combe exploited the scientific data to a social end, but the causal link we are concerned to find runs, supposedly, in the other direction. And while Shapin provides a great deal of information on the social flux of the time, the requisite causal links are never detailed. The talk of class struggle certainly hints at how Shapin thinks the story ought to unfold, but one finds no such unfolding in his essay.

None of the foregoing is to deny that knowledge is or might be "multifunctional," that it might serve more than one purpose. The point to be borne in mind is whether what is provided by the strong programme is a better explanation of scientific knowledge than the account provided by certain philosophers of science. To repeat my central claim, the explanations promoted by the strong programmers not only fall short of their announced goals but also exhibit just the same faults imputed to traditional philosophy of science. The "causal" explanations of the strong programme prove to have critical gaps and threaten to simply license a rewriting of history in terms of one's favorite interests. This makes the proposed account simply a causal version of epistemological rationalizations.

What I have urged to this point is that insofar as the strong programme aspires to provide a replacement for the account of scientific rationality promoted by traditional epistemology, it both runs afoul of its own philosophical assumptions and is susceptible to the very criticisms entered against philosophical explanations. The adherence to a causal principle, in particular, has been incriminated as engendering these difficulties. There is, however, another problem with the strong programme that does not involve any of the difficulties so far cited. It involves, rather, the use made of Kuhn's account of the history of science. We saw in Chapter 7 how this account is understood to provide the raison d'être for the strong programme approach; it is

[91] Ibid., p. 50.

Kuhn's history of science that first "revealed" how many crucial episodes in the history of science cannot be explained by simple appeal to rational procedures. Yet despite the unquestioned importance of Kuhn's work for the strong programmers, their interpretation of Kuhn is, I argue below, inconsistent.

The inconsistency arises, I show, because the strong programmers want to deny, on the one hand, Kuhn's account of scientific revolutions, but, on the other hand, they want to take Kuhn's work to have established that the history of science is not "Whiggish," that is, not a history of progress or a march toward truth. The denial of scientific revolutions is important to the advocates of the strong programme for two reasons. First, their conflation of the Duhem thesis and underdetermination leads them to assert that no anomaly can "force" a crisis; adverse evidence can always be incorporated into the theory at hand. Second, Kuhn's account of normal science stresses the authoritarian nature of scientific subgroups, and this account fits best with their sociological reading. In other words, denying revolutionary science and stressing normal science minimizes the importance of the *internal* dynamics of a theory and maximizes the significance of sociological considerations.

There is irony in this revision of Kuhn. By denying that there are scientific revolutions in Kuhn's sense, the strong programmers remove the linchpin of Kuhn's argument against the view of the history of science as cumulative.[92] On Kuhn's account, the paradigmatic nature of normal science does not alone argue against Whiggish historicizing; rather, the fact that the history of science is a history of successive paradigms, each incommensurable with the other, precludes the sort of cumulative history of science positivistically inclined historians are apt to write. Thus, if the strong programmers deny that there are scientific revolutions, they undercut the very argument against the historical reconstruction of science on which they extensively presume. But if the strong programmers accept Kuhn's account of the history of science with crises and revolutions, they allow more to the internal dynamics of scientific theories than they want. In the face of this difficulty, the most reasonable tactic would seem to be to bite the bullet and acknowl-

[92]See, for example, Kuhn's own remarks in *The Structure of Scientific Revolutions*, 2d ed., enlarged (Chicago: University of Chicago Press, 1970), chap. 9. See also Frederick Suppe's exposition of Kuhn on this point in F. Suppe, ed., *The Structure of Scientific Theories*, 2d ed. (Urbana: University of Illinois Press, 1977), pp. 135–151.

edge that there may, after all, be something to the internal (nonsociological) logic of science. Unfortunately, the strong programmers have instead chosen to deny revolutions and to affirm a noncumulative history of science. As shown, it is just that conjunction that is inconsistent.

Barnes's rejection of the distinction between normal and revolutionary science is not part of his early writings on Kuhn.[93] (Bloor's expositions of Kuhn exhibit from the outset a deemphasis of Kuhn's account of revolutionary science. Greater significance is attached to Kuhn's notion of normal science.) When Barnes turns, however, to a full discussion of Kuhn's views, he dismisses this distinction as having no theoretical significance:

> Any particular change which occurs in a revolutionary period can occur equally in a period of normal science, whether it be meaning change, technical change, the invention of new problem-solutions, or the emergence of new standards of judgment. If there is anything worth calling a revolutionary episode, it is a period when a large number of cultural changes all occur at once, or when scientists find themselves obliged to opt for one or other alternative cluster of practices and beliefs. The concept of scientific revolution is suited to historical narrative. For the narrow sociological end of identifying basic processes of cultural change it is irrelevant.[94]

The reason for the alleged irrelevance of the concept of a scientific revolution is that the notion of normal science can carry the necessary theoretical freight:

> Once more we are led to the conclusion that Kuhn's insistence upon the 'necessity' of scientific revolutions is misplaced. . . . There is nothing in normal science to prohibit any particular kind of development. . . . Hence there is nothing to compel a leap out of the system: nothing makes it necessary to replace, rather than to develop, existing practice. Perhaps Kuhn's own conviction of the necessity of revolutions arises from an incorrect appraisal of what is possible under the rubric of normal science. [p. 86]

Kuhn, the charge goes, incorrectly appraises the malleability of normal science.

[93]Barnes, *Interests*, p. 23.

[94]Barnes, *T. S. Kuhn and Social Science*, p. 86; see also p. 57. Parenthetical page references in the remainder of this discussion are to this volume.

Bloor enthusiastically endorses Kuhn and yet reads his significance in a Barnesian light: "The fact remains, though, that Kuhn's book is the single most fruitful account of science that we possess. Its real achievement, however, lies in the description of what Kuhn calls 'normal science' rather than in the ideal of 'revolution'."[95] (Bloor cites Barnes's book by way of justification of his characterization.) What is of significance in these comments of Bloor's is that they make explicit the reason for denying Kuhn's notion of revolution—to minimize the role of the internal logic of science:

Kuhn treats the eventual downfall of a paradigm as a quasi-inevitable consequence of the accumulation of anomalies. His critics don't see why, if commitment and dogmatism are present, they shouldn't in the end prove triumphant. The point is a good one, but the correct answer will not be welcome to them. They have put their finger on a point where Kuhn is not being sufficiently sociological. A potential anomaly can only create a crisis and precipitate a revolution if somebody makes it do so, hence the whole process depends on the balance of power in the relevant group.[96]

By stressing Kuhn's account of normal science to the virtual exclusion of his account of scientific revolutions, the strong programmers are able to emphasize the sociological and exclude the rational elements of Kuhn's account. By invoking once again the doctrine of finitism, they have reason to insist on the need for institutional guides to concept application in the sciences.

Normal scientists are not rational automata, using words according to their inherent meanings or extensions. Existing usage always leaves future usage to be developed by users themselves. It is precisely because of this that the *continuing* role of authority and social control is of ineradicable significance in normal science. . . . This is the profound sense in which normal science is a social activity. And this is why Kuhn's matter-of-fact account of routine scientific activity threatens epistemological orthodoxy more radically even than his explicitly philosophical discussion of revolutionary states of affairs. [p. 84; see also p. 12]

The strong programmers clearly adhere to the first half of the inconsistency just identified. They deny that scientific revolutions are signifi-

[95] Bloor, *Wittgenstein*, p. 200 n. 9.
[96] Ibid., p. 142.

cant, and they do so in order to make the strongest possible case against the internal logic of science having anything interesting to do with the reasons for scientific change. The embrace of normal science is linked to the license for sociological analysis it provides: "Kuhn's approach not only exemplifies good historical method, it is also exactly what is needed for sociological study" (p. 5). The question now facing us, however, is how the strong programmers, in denying Kuhnian revolutions, also manage to explain that Whiggish history is inappropriate. It is to their answer to this question, and the second part of the inconsistency, that we must now turn.

Barnes's analysis of Kuhn sometimes reads as if the significant difference between Kuhn and the Whiggish historians is only that Kuhn refused to "read back" our current standards of truth and falsity into earlier historical episodes in the history of science (pp. 4–7). In this respect, he reads the historical significance of *The Structure of Scientific Revolutions* in light of the strong programme account of natural rationality. Kuhn's significance to the history and philosophy of science is, on Barnes's telling, due to Kuhn's being the first great practitioner of the method of natural rationality:

> These sources [Wittgenstein and Piaget] reflect Kuhn's recognition that to understand the way a tradition develops one has to address the basis of human behaviour; moreover, what is involved is social behaviour, as much a sociological as a psychological problem. It is this insight, combined with his historical sensibility, which gives Kuhn's work its originality and significance. The continuation of a form of culture implies a mechanism of socialisation and knowledge transmission. . . . When there is a continuing form of culture there must be sources of cognitive authority and control. Kuhn was initially almost alone among historians in giving serious attention to these features of science. [p. 9]

It is quite startling to anyone familiar with Kuhn's actual role in the development of the history and philosophy of science to discover Barnes's revisions of this history. His retelling of the story appears as a violation of his own repeated exhortations against reading present standards back into the past.

Also puzzling is Barnes's move from praising Kuhn for doing non-Whiggish history to claiming that Kuhn has shown that "all procedures of research—manipulative, cognitive, and evaluative—[possess] a conventional, culturally specific aspect" (p. 10). Nothing has been said so far in Barnes's account to show that Whiggish history is mistaken. Yet Barnes asserts, seemingly on Kuhn's authority, that

> culture is far more than the setting for scientific research; it is the research itself. It is not just problems, techniques and existing finds which are culturally specific; so, too, are the modes of perceiving and conceptualising reality, the forms of inference and analogy, and the standards and precedents for judgment and evaluation which are actually employed in the course of research. Science is not a set of universal standards. . . . Scientific standards themselves are part of a specific form of culture; authority and control are essential to maintain a sense of the reasonableness of that specific form. Thus, if Kuhn is correct, science should be amenable to sociological study in fundamentally the same way as any other form of knowledge or culture. [p. 10]

But *none* of this follows from the simple preference for doing historical case studies instead of grand Whiggish histories. Without some attack on the cumulative view, none of what is attributed to Kuhn is implied by what Barnes claims to be his major contribution to the history of science. Just why are we to understand Kuhn as showing why the old historiography is wrongheaded? Barnes's revisionist history omits the key premise that, on his account, the story requires.

Later in his account of Kuhn, Barnes offers a more conventional explication of Kuhn's views, although without emphasizing how it is required to fill the aforementioned gap in what he takes Kuhn to have established. When writing of Kuhn's concept of a scientific revolution, Barnes now acknowledges that "Kuhn goes out of his way to emphasise that revolutions constitute discontinuities in research and the growth of knowledge. By reconstructing it around a new achievement scientists effect a truly radical transformation of their culture, at the verbal and symbolic level as well as at the level of procedure and perception" (pp. 54–55). Moreover, Barnes admits that "it was this account of scientific revolutions, with its explicit relativistic implications, which ensured that Kuhn's work became widely known" (p. 55). But then he expresses sympathy with those who criticize Kuhn's account of revolutionary breaks. So the question remains as to how Barnes is entitled to lay claim to Kuhn's conclusions if he has stripped Kuhn's argument of its central premise?

The argument, if I understand Barnes correctly, may be paraphrased as follows: Since scientists could, if they chose to do so, *always* maintain the theory at hand (p. 75), any significant change actually occurring must be a response to considerations apart from the theory (p. 76). Put another way, pressures due to the "logic" of the theory can never be sufficient to "sink" the theory; there are no crucial experiments (p. 75). Since the experimental results, that is, what experience shows, do not explain why views change, sociological factors must. Therefore Kuhn's account of scientific revolutions, which supposedly rely on the pressures arising from *within* the theory due to anomalies, must be mistaken (pp. 83–87).

This argument assumes that "any particular change which occurs in a revolutionary episode can occur equally in a period of normal science" (p. 86). But this, in turn, rests on the assumption that "scientists, if they so desire, can always maintain their verbal culture as an unfalsifiable system" (p. 76). If scientists could not always do this, some experiences anyway would "coerce" theory change; but if this were the case, then we would be back to talking about "crises" and "revolutions" in the Kuhnian sense. And so it would be false that normal science could accommodate whatever is characteristic of revolutionary episodes.

The only argument Barnes provides for this accommodation view is that, since adjustment can in principle be made anywhere in the system, it is always possible to impose the pattern the community wants: "A whole conceptual fabric can always be *made out* as in perfect accord with experience, if the community sustaining it is of a mind to do so" (p. 75; see also p. 82). It is one thing, though, to maintain holism for the purpose of denying the existence of an Archimedean point; in that case, the argument simply points out that making a judgment with regard to one hypothesis requires accepting in an unquestioned way many others. It is quite another point to assert that any experience can be adapted to something like the present scheme; that view posits that it is a matter of logical indifference whether to tamper with an existing scheme or to adopt some other. The strong programmers are clearly committed to such an "indifference" view. Only social pressures, they maintain, are sufficient to motivate a theoretical change. Yet what evidence is offered to show that it is a matter of logical indifference to tamper indefinitely with one scheme as opposed to change? The mere fact that it might be *possible* to do so does not imply that it is a matter of intellectual neutrality whether one does or not, or even that one is justified in doing so in all cases. In practice, moreover, as Kuhn's own case studies indicate, crises are generated insofar as adaptations of an existing account do become more and more of an intellectual burden. Nothing Barnes offers indicates that the theoretical possibility of perpetual adaptation negates explanation by appeal to the internal logic of theories. Indeed, what the case studies appear to establish is just that crises are generated as the intellectual tinkering becomes too much of a burden to bear.

If Barnes is unable to replace Kuhn's account of revolutionary changes with a more plausible account (and I have argued above that he does not do so), however, Whiggish history remains unscathed by his version of Kuhn. And if Whiggish history prevails, then the strong programmers' emphasis on normal science does not suffice to establish the noncumulative nature of scientific history on which their project presumes. But if they do accept Kuhn's account of scientific revolutions, then there appears to be more to the internal logic of science than they want to allow. In addition, as the foregoing argument indicates, the accommodationist view is less plausible than the revolutionary account it is intended to replace. This reading of Kuhn, in any case, is either committed to views that are not ultimately consistent (that the history of science is nonrevolutionary and noncumulative) or does not support the radically sociological account of scientific activity. In either case, the strong programme must revise the account of scientific activity to which it is committed.

The problem posed by the strong programme is reminiscent of the problem faced by Socrates as dramatized in the *Apology*—how to distinguish rhetoric and logic. The problem, in the context of that dialogue,[97] is how to convince an audience not to be swayed by rhetoric without becoming an instance of the practice you are seeking to condemn. Socrates' admirable, albeit unsuccessful, resolution of this dilemma is to adopt a harshly antirhetorical and austerely logical approach in his own defense. His conviction is not just a vote against Socrates; it signals the fact that the Athenians are unable to distinguish rhetoric from logic. Worse, actually, the vote to convict shows a marked preference for rhetoric. What counts is not what is said but the way it is presented. The logical weight of arguments given in the dialogue is clear; the tragic irony is that the jury has not yet learned how to weigh arguments.

[97]See Chapter 3.

It is tempting to read the strong programmers as urging us to believe that the Athenian jury had it right; rhetoric is all. In Chapter 7 I indicated that, on a number of philosophical points, I am in sympathy with the strong programmers. The issue dividing us concerns just what holism and indeterminacy imply for our understanding of the process of warranting beliefs. And despite their claims of allegiance to the methods of science, it is clear, in the context of their social reductionism, that what the strong programmers take the premises to imply is that there is no interesting distinction between logic and rhetoric. What separated Socrates and his accusers is, in effect, dismissed as a matter of no more than rhetorical style. Socrates, on this account, was just a stylist ahead of his time. And yet, while I too have denied that we have knowledge of autonomous standards of reason, I have also argued that this does not reduce reasoning to rhetoric and so make sophists of us all.

CHAPTER 9

# Resolving the *Rationalitätstreit*

The last four chapters have been devoted to examining various arguments for methodological exclusivism. Chapter 5 discussed arguments for the claim that the social sciences must be sciences; these arguments were rejected because they relied on conceptions of science not relevant to the social science case. Chapter 6 took up a longstanding dispute arising from the claim that it is conceptually impossible for the social sciences to be sciences. Both those championing this conceptual impossibility and those protesting it rely on a metaphysical assumption I dubbed meaning realism. By rejecting meaning realism, I undercut claims by all parties in the debate that proper social science can only be done their way. Chapters 7 and 8 analyzed and rejected the claim that the sole proper epistemological procedure, given the philosophical framework articulated in the first four chapters, is to replace epistemology with the sociology of knowledge. None of these exclusivist positions is consistent with or a satisfactory alternative to methodological pluralism.

In this chapter, I address another persistent methodological dispute in the philosophy of the social sciences: The alleged existence of alternative standards of rationality and consequent questions about how an investigation of another culture ought to proceed in order to discern and properly interpret these standards. Methodological pluralism might be thought to condone or legitimate a belief in alternative standards of rationality. It does not. As I argue in this chapter, the methodological disputes generated by debates on how to study alternative standards of rationality are predicated on philosophical confusions. By exposing and dispelling these confusions, I spike the remaining reason responsible for perpetuating the *Rationalitätstreit*.

The *Rationalitätstreit* turns on the questions of whether and to what extent different standards of rational evaluation are themselves rationally comparable. But the debate, as it develops, reveals some surprising and odd philosophical twists. One surprising aspect of this discussion, as it has been played out in the literature, is that, although conceptions of rationality are assumed to be varied, (Western) scientific rationality is spoken of as if it connoted some univocal account of standards of rational inquiry. Indeed, much of the "our standards or theirs" debate proceeds as if *we* clearly knew what is meant by the phrase "the logic of science." Winch, for example, is prone to remark on the (socially determined) criteria that, he claims, speakers of a language *must* share in order to share a social world.[1] Since the criteria are necessary conditions for socially meaningful behavior, different cultures must have, in this regard, different criteria.

This way of talking is, prima facie, at odds with the way epistemology, philosophy of science, and the history of science have developed in the last twenty to thirty years. Indeed, one has reason enough, following Richard Bernstein, to puzzle over just what all the fuss is about. As Bernstein notes, Winch, for example, seems insensitive to the sort of Wittgensteinian revolution wrought in the natural sciences by Kuhn's work.[2] Kuhn has made it difficult to speak confidently of *the* logic of science. And even before *The Structure of Scientific Revolutions* appeared on the intellectual scene, Quine and others had already cast strong doubt that the positivists' dream of explicating the logic of science could be carried out in anything like the fashion Rudolf Carnap and the others had envisioned. Criticisms of the analytic-synthetic distinction, together with aspersions cast on the notion of an empirical given, proved to be telling criticisms of the sort of canons of rational inquiry Carnap et al. had sought to develop. When Kuhn entered the

[1]Peter Winch, *The Ideal of a Social Science* (London: Routledge & Kegan Paul, 1958); "Understanding a Primitive Society," *American Philosophical Quarterly* (1964):307–324; reprinted in *Understanding and Social Inquiry*, ed. F. Dallmayr and T. McCarthy (Notre Dame, Ind.: University of Notre Dame Press, 1977); page references are to the Dallmayr and McCarthy volume.

[2]Richard Bernstein, *Beyond Objectivity and Relativism* (Philadelphia: University of Pennsylvania Press, 1983), p. 28.

scene, the sort of skepticism that had been raised concerning the viability of efforts to specify the logic of contemporary science were extended to include the history of Western science. (What seems to have gone largely unappreciated in the context of the *Rationalitätstreit* is the impact Quine's holistic view of theories had on the notion of rationality; see Chapter 6.) Thus, whether one took a long view or a short view, there was no univocal logic of science to be located. But if the message from historians and philosophers of science is so grim, how then are the feuding philosophers and social scientists to locate the crux of the debate when opposing "our standards" to "theirs"?

In what follows, I indicate why much of the debate surrounding the *Rationalitätstreit* has been confused and unfruitful. The debate is confused, in the first instance, because the putative points of contention—"our standards" versus "theirs"—are never specified. The debate is unfruitful, in the second instance, because none of the contending parties has any argument by which to establish that there is or is not a method for comparative judgments concerning rationality. It is no surprise, in other words, that the point of the debate remains vague and so resistant to resolution.

Once these oversights and presumptions are made plain, moreover, any point to talk of *evaluating* alternative standards dissipates, at least with respect to the question of which is more rational. I hope to establish that the controversy, as presently cast, is a pseudoproblem, a controversy that, once its assumptions are stated, ceases to appear plausible. Having suggested why the debate, as presently conceived, is misconceived, I then outline a method of recasting the points at issue, one that indicates an empirical method for settling at least some of the claims. The method I propose is to view differing accounts as alternative *translations*. Put another way, I reconstrue the *Rationalitätstreit* as an empirically testable dispute concerning how best to translate the actions and utterances of others.

I proceed, in Section I, by reviewing what is at issue in this debate (at least if its principals are to be believed). I discuss why the issue as described by the participants is a pseudoproblem. In Section II I examine certain epistemological disputes concerning what is required for translation. Section III develops my account of translation. I argue there that this account provides a more perspicuous construal of the issues at hand.

## I

How is the *Rationalitätstreit* understood by its principals? Although it focuses on Winch's position in "Understanding a Primitive Society," the key philosophical presumptions were already explicit in Winch's earlier book. Winch there emphasizes, in the context of his discussion of Pareto's brand of positivism, a distinction between "illogical" and "non-logical" inferences or actions: "An *il*logical act presumably involves a *mistake* in logic; but to call something *non*-logical should be to deny that criteria of logic apply to it at all."[3] Where Pareto went astray, Winch goes on to charge, is in confusing these terms. What is important is that Winch takes Pareto's confusion here to be a representative one of positivists and positivistically inclined thinkers.

Pareto, to continue Winch's example, condemns religion as nonlogical. But he is only justified in doing this, Winch observes, if there is only a single standard of logic by which to judge the reasonableness of all human actions in all spheres of social life. But there is obviously no such single standard:

> A large part of the trouble here arises from the fact that he has not seen the point around which the main argument of this monograph revolves: that criteria of logic are not a direct gift of God, but arise out of, and are only intelligible in the context of, ways of living or modes of social life. . . . For instance, science is one such mode and religion is another; and each has criteria of intelligibility peculiar to itself. So within science or religion actions can be logical or illogical. . . . But we cannot sensibly say that either the practice of science itself or that of religion is either illogical or logical; both are non-logical.[4]

Winch's philosophical guide here seems to be less Wittgenstein than Carnap, or, at least, the Carnap of "Empiricism, Semantics, and Ontology." What Winch is proposing, and as he maintains against Evans-Pritchard, is a version of Carnap's distinction between internal and external questions. Carnap insists, in drawing this distinction, that questions regarding existence and validity are *internal* questions—questions answerable only within the context provided by a particular

[3]Winch, *Idea of a Social Science*, p. 100.
[4]Ibid., p. 101.

framework. If one is asking, however, which framework to choose, they are asking an external question. The considerations in this case are primarily pragmatic and not logical: "The acceptance or rejection of abstract linguistic forms, just as the acceptance or rejection of any other linguistic form in any branch of science, will finally be decided by their efficiency as instruments, the ratio of the results achieved to the amount and complexity of the efforts required."[5] Similarly, Winch insists that what is logical or illogical, real or unreal, is a framework question: "For connected with the realization that intelligibility takes many and varied forms is the realization that reality has no key. But Pareto is committing just this mistake: his way of discussing the distinction between logical and non-logical conduct involves setting up scientific intelligibility . . . as the norm for intelligibility in general; he is claiming that science possesses the key to reality."[6] Notice that Winch conflates ontological and logical issues in this remark; he shifts between talk concerning criteria of intelligibility—logical issues—and "keys" to reality—ontological issues. As becomes clear, Winch too maintains that *both* are determined by matters internal to a given framework (or, to put matters in the Wittgensteinian jargon Winch prefers, a given language game).

Indeed, Winch's whole discussion is curiously positivistic under the guise of rejecting positivism in the social sciences. He writes as if, once one is "playing" a particular language game, the ontological and logical criteria are determinate and determinative:

> When the 'things' in question are purely physical the criteria appealed to will of course be those of the observer. But when one is dealing with intellectual (or, indeed, any kind of social) 'things', that is not so. For their *being* intellectual or social, as opposed to physical, in character depends entirely on their belonging in a certain way to a system of ideas or mode of life. It is only by reference to the criteria governing that system of ideas or mode of life that they have any existence as intellectual or social events. It follows that if the sociological investigator wants to regard them *as* social events (as, *ex hypothesi*, he must), he has to take seriously the criteria which are applied for distinguishing 'different' kinds of actions and identifying the 'same' kinds of actions within the way of life he is studying. It is not open to him arbitrarily to impose his own

[5]Rudolf Carnap, *Meaning and Necessity*, 2d ed. (Chicago: University of Chicago Press, 1956), p. 221.

[6]Winch, *Idea of a Social Science*, p. 102.

standards from without. In so far as he does so, the events he is studying lose altogether their character as *social* events.[7]

Winch's avowed purpose is, of course, to *separate* the logic of social inquiry from the unity-of-method approach that is part of traditional positivist doctrine. Yet what he retains is the analytic-synthetic distinction (by virtue of insisting on the strong epistemological distinction between internal and external questions) and a general type of verificationism (for disputes about what is real can, on his account, be settled internally). And these are epistemological theses belonging to the very core of the philosophical movement from which he imagines (rightly, in some respects) he is distancing himself. The problem, as we have seen, is that his remarks on criteria carry much more philosophical freight than Winch realizes.[8]

With the foregoing points in mind, we can put the dispute between Winch and Evans-Pritchard, in particular, and some of the issues surrounding the *Rationalitätstreit* in general, in sharper focus. Winch's point is that Evans-Pritchard, and those who share Evans-Pritchard's methodological assumptions, have confused internal questions and external questions concerning criteria of reality and rationality: "To describe what is observed by the sociologist in terms of notions like 'proposition' and 'theory' is already to have taken the decision to apply a set of concepts incompatible with the 'external', 'experimental' point of view."[9] Evans-Pritchard's error, it is claimed, is of a piece with Pareto's; actions are logical or illogical by reference to the norms determined by a framework. Choices between frameworks are, both Winch and Carnap would insist, nonlogical matters.

I think that Evans-Pritchard is right in a great deal of what he says . . . but wrong, and crucially wrong, in his attempt to characterize the scientific in terms of that which is "in accord with objective reality." Despite differences of emphasis and phraseology, Evans-Pritchard is in fact hereby put into the same metaphysical camp as Pareto; for both of them the conception of "reality" must be regarded as intelligible and applicable *outside* the context of scientific

7Ibid., p. 108.

8For details, see Chapter 6. For more on the criticisms of Carnap sketched here, see W. V. Quine, "On Carnap's Views on Ontology," in Quine's *The Ways of Paradox* (New York: Random House, 1966).

9Winch, *Idea of a Social Science*, p. 110.

reasoning itself, since it is that to which scientific notions do, and unscientific do not, have a relation.

. . . . .

Reality is not what gives language sense. What is real and what is unreal shows itself *in* the sense that language has. Further, both the distinction between the real and the unreal and the concept of agreement with reality themselves belong to our language. . . . We could not in fact distinguish the real from the unreal without understanding the way this distinction operates in the language. If then we wish to understand the significance of these concepts, we must examine the use they actually do have—*in* the language.

Evans-Pritchard, on the contrary, is trying to work with a conception of reality which is *not* determined by its actual use in language. He wants something against which that use can itself be appraised.[10]

Actually, Evans-Pritchard is being charged with a twofold error. On the one hand, he confuses internal questions and external ones, and so makes accusations of irrationality (i.e., illogical thought) where, properly speaking, the charge has no point. On the other hand, Evans-Pritchard is accused by Winch of compounding his philosophical error by insisting upon, in Davidson's terms, an illicit scheme-content dichotomy.[11] Any account of scientific rationality relying as straightforwardly and unproblematically as Evans-Pritchard's on a correspondence account of truth is to be rejected out of hand. Indeed, without his invidious distinction between scheme and content, the sort of contrast Evans-Pritchard wants to draw between "our" standards and "theirs" cannot get off the ground; without the distinction, there is no neutral test of disputed statements.

Equally, however, without an appeal to the analytic-synthetic distinction and the rest of the conceptual baggage Winch unwittingly imports into his account, there is no making sense of his insistent appeals to internal and external questions. If Evans-Pritchard errs by falsely assuming that we can neatly distinguish reality and conceptual scheme, Winch is remiss in believing that we can distinguish between "our criteria" and "theirs." More specifically, he errs insofar as he speaks as if the social criteria for communication were intersubjectively

[10]Winch, "Understanding a Primitive Society," pp. 161–162.

[11]Donald Davidson, "The Very Idea of a Conceptual Scheme," *Proceedings and Addresses of the American Philosophical Association* 47 (1973–1974).

determinate, as if, in other words, these criteria have a univocal sense for those who are said to share in a particular form of life.

Both Evans-Pritchard and Winch, I am charging, are wedded to outmoded conceptions of philosophy of science and positivist doctrines, albeit not to the same aspects of each. Given what is assumed in endorsing either side of this controversy, then, the *Rationalitätstreit* is best adjudged a pseudoproblem. Once the underlying philosophical assumptions are made explicit, both sides are seen to be philosophically untenable.

But this analysis may seem too quick. One might insist that the issue has a point even if separated from the way Evans-Pritchard or Winch have chosen to put it. Surely it is correct to say that there are subgroups within societies and whole other cultures whose views are very different from the logic of our science (however that notion is to be clarified). The problems attending how to explain the inferential connections in such beliefs systems, and the question of how to evaluate their efficacy, do not disappear or become less pressing on the analysis offered above.

What the foregoing analysis suggests, or so I urge, is that the terms of this discussion need to be changed. Lest it be thought, however, that a change in terminology represents a difference that makes no difference, I sketch how the terminological change I propose involves a reconception of the methodology to be used in arbitrating disputes concerning judgments of the rationality of other groups and cultures.

## II

Just how should one approach the problem of understanding and evaluating different belief systems? My claim is that the problem should not be posed as a problem of standards of rationality at all, but, rather, as a problem of translation. My primary reason for this is, as I show below, that translation schemes are readily construable as empirical theories (although not in the style of, say, physics). Disputes about the rationality of practices, at least those disputes that concern me here, are best understood as questions about who has the most adequate translation, once translation schemes are construed on the model of Kuhn's account of normal science. My proposal builds on some points sketched by Steven Lukes[12] and, especially, by Stephen Turner.[13]

As I have argued earlier,[14] Lukes (and Martin Hollis) misconceive the necessary conditions of translation. The debate can be characterized, on this point, as a dispute between what I call the "impositionists," on the one hand, and the "a priorists," on the other. The impositionists would say, following Quine, that there is no separating the cases where we just impose our logic and ontology on the available evidence of another's behavior and where we claim to discover that, lo and behold, these individuals too share in mankind's epistemic homogeneity. Quine's argument here, in brief, is that there is no behavioral fact of the matter to separate the two cases; moreover, at least on my construal of Quine's argument for the indeterminacy of translation, there are no introspective facts of the matter to settle the question either.[15] An a priorist, however, holds that translation is made possible only because people share a similar epistemological "profile." I return to this issue below.

Hollis and Lukes are a priorists. This view, or so I argue, cannot be sustained. Yet, like Hollis and Lukes, I am swayed by the argument that if some group's beliefs about the world, or their construal of logical connectives, were radically different from ours, then translation would be impossible.[16] Davidson speaks for (and has been a powerful voice in forming) a consensus on this issue when he asks, "Can we then say that two people have different conceptual schemes if they speak languages that fail of intertranslatability?" and responds that no, we cannot both

[12]Steven Lukes, "Relativism in Its Place," in *Rationality and Relativism*, ed. M. Hollis and S. Lukes (Cambridge, Mass.: M.I.T. Press, 1982), and "Some Problems about Rationality," in *Rationality*, ed. B. Wilson (New York: Harper Torchbooks, 1970).

[13]Stephen Turner, *Sociological Explanation as Translation* (Cambridge: Cambridge University Press, 1980). My serious differences with Turner are few and not sharply defined. It is unclear from Turner's writings (here and elsewhere) whether he conceives of the pattern of explanation he identifies as the sole legitimate pattern of sociological explanation. Other articles by Turner suggest that he thinks that a true social *science* is not possible; see, in particular, D. Huff and S. Turner, "Rationalizations and the Application of Causal Explanations of Human Action," *American Philosophical Quarterly* 18 (July 1981). This view is no part of my position (see Chapter 5).

[14]See Chapter 6.

[15]See Chapter 1.

[16]See Lukes, "Relativism in Its Place," pp. 262, 272, for allusions to this argument and further references.

reasonably impute a language to others and yet deny that it is translatable.[17] Talk of sameness or difference of beliefs or of conceptual schemes makes sense only in light of some ability to make statements intelligible. Controversy concerning translation does not arise here.

The rub enters in one of Davidson's concluding remarks. In it, Davidson appears to be offering a brief for impositionism. The remark, however, is one on which Davidson does not much elaborate. In his penultimate paragraph, he writes as follows:

> It would be wrong to summarize by saying we have shown how communication is possible between people who have different schemes, a way that works without need of what there cannot be, namely a neutral ground, or a common coordinate system. For we have found no intelligible basis on which it can be said that schemes are different. It would be equally wrong to announce the glorious news that all mankind—all speakers of a language, at least—share a common scheme and ontology. For if we cannot intelligibly say that schemes are different, neither can we intelligibly say that they are one.[18]

The point of contention is this. On Davidson's view (and Quine's) there is no basis for positing, to use a phrase favored by Hollis, the "epistemological unity of mankind." Even if one agrees that we understand anyone only because we can translate, and even if translation states what they believe in a form we find intelligible, it does not follow that there is a basis for positing the "epistemological unity of mankind." And although Hollis insists that "any field-work" is bound to confirm this unity, he concedes that he has nothing specific to offer on the nature of this epistemological core. He draws comfort, however, from the observation "that the anthropologist can tackle other cultures armed with truths which he knows in advance that he will find embodied in the scheme he seeks to understand."[19] But, or so Davidson

[17]Davidson, "The Very Idea of a Conceptual Scheme," p. 7. I am not concerned to defend Davidson's claim that, in order for translation to go through, "we must count them right in most matters" (p. 19). To what extent the principle of charity must extend in translation is, I suggest, an empirical question, and I do not have at hand the ethnographic data to decide the issue. Be that as it may, the general point made by Davidson holds good.

[18]Ibid., p. 20.

[19]Martin Hollis, "The Epistemological Unity of Mankind," in *Philosophical Disputes in the Social Sciences*, ed. S. C. Brown (Atlantic Highlands, N.J.: Humanities Press, 1979), p. 230.

suggests, this embodiment is not evidence for Hollis's conclusion. Why not?

Is the translation imposed or does it reflect the uncovering of deep-seated a priori principles? Consider Quine's much discussed example of a field linguist who is undecided as to whether to translate "Gavagai" as "rabbit," or "undetached rabbit part," or yet some other alternative.[20] Quine observes that it is all too easy to confuse what one is inclined to find "natural" in such cases with what is, in fact, "dictated" by the available evidence.

> An actual field linguist would of course be sensible enough to equate "gavagai" with "rabbit," dismissing such perverse alternatives . . . out of hand. . . . The implicit maxim guiding his choice of "rabbit," and similar choices for other native words, is that an enduring and relatively homogeneous object, moving as a whole against a contrasting background, is likely reference for a short expression. If he were to become conscious of this maxim, he might celebrate it as one of the linguistic universals, or traits of all languages, and he would have no trouble pointing out its psychological plausibility. But he would be wrong; the maxim is his own imposition, toward settling what is objectively indeterminate. It is a very sensible imposition, and I would recommend no other. But I am making a philosophical point.
>
> It is philosophically interesting, moreover, that what is indeterminate in this artificial example is not just meaning, but extension; reference . . . The indeterminacy of translation now confronting us, however, cuts across extension and intension alike. The terms "rabbit," "undetached rabbit part," and "rabbit stage" differ not only in meaning; they are true of different things. Reference itself proves behaviorally inscrutable.[21]

Providing a translation that works, in other words, does not resolve the question of whether the scheme that works is imposed on the evidence by the translator or is his or her discovery. Quine's thesis of the underdetermination of theories, which states that it is always possible to formulate empirically equivalent but logically incompatible theories, suggests that to show that the scheme is *not* imposed requires something much stronger. In particular, it requires showing that *only* such a scheme will do. Yet the very suggestion that object- and in-

[20]Quine uses this example in many of his writings; see especially "Ontological Relativity," in *Ontological Relativity and Other Essays* (New York: Columbia University Press, 1969).

[21]Ibid., pp. 34–35.

ference-positing patterns are our own imposition is anathema to at least one philosophically sophisticated anthropologist, Robin Horton. Horton insists that in the course of fieldwork "it is the experience of learning various languages, patterns of thought and ways of life from scratch . . . that we take as ground for our conviction as to the universality of a basic material object discourse." Quine appears as the villain, in this case, for, as Horton reads Quine, Quine is claiming that translation is just "a set of arbitrarily-established equivalences which beg the very question of translational correctness that are at issue. Worse still, he can have no other basis for such operations."[22]

There are at least two issues here. First, there is the question of whether the purpose of translation is reasonably thought of as the "capturing" of some underlying reality, the perspicuous expression via translation of what lies hidden in another's mind.[23] Second, Horton cites Jaakko Hintikka's contribution to *Words and Objections* in support of his view against Quine.[24] Unfortunately, Horton is not more specific. Hintikka does raise questions throughout his article about the available evidence for radical translation. Much of what he says, however, does not challenge Quine on the point of indeterminacy. Quine is not concerned to argue that we cannot find evidence for translation; rather, his concern is with what the available evidence is taken to be evidence of: "I am concerned only to show what goes into [translation], and to what degree our behavioral data should be viewed as guides to a creative decision rather than to an awaiting reality."[25] There is no restriction on using whatever empirical data a translator has at hand; rather, there is simply a warning against confusing what seems intuitively plausible as a translation with what *must* be the "meaning" intended: "Above all, in such a codification of available behavioral aids, every care would need to be taken not to relax behavioristic standards and inadvertently admit any intuitive semantics."[26]

The central point of the argument against a priorists such as Hollis

[22]Robin Horton, "Material-Object Language and Theoretical Language," in *Philosophical Disputes in the Social Sciences*, ed. Brown, p. 203.

[23]See Chapter 1.

[24]D. Davidson and J. Hintikka, eds. *Words and Objections* (Dordrecht: Reidel, 1969).

[25]Ibid., pp. 312–313.

[26]Ibid., p. 314.

and Horton, then, is that, barring a transcendental deduction, there is no showing that the translation is *not* an imposition on the data. Davidson's point—that we have equally no basis for asserting plurality or unity—is thus given support. (Of course one cannot validly argue that, if there is no support for a belief in the unity of translation schemes, then it is reasonable to believe in their plurality or vice versa. Quine's thesis of the indeterminacy of translation, however, at least as I interpret it, does provide a positive argument for the essential plurality of possible translations.) The ability to translate, in other words, and the need to assume a common basis in order to do so, cuts two ways. First, and this is to repeat the consensus view, it suggests a limit to just how different points of view can be and still remain intelligible. But, second, translation, or the ability to translate, indicates only that our account proves satisfactory, not that another could not. No conclusion concerning exclusivity of translation follows from the production of an actual translation.[27]

## III

How is it that viewing the *Rationalitätstreit* as a question of who has the better translation facilitates its resolution? In answering this, I rely on the analysis of the Spiro-Leach controversy in anthropology developed by Turner and expanded on by Lukes. The ethnographic data is as follows. A certain tribe, the Tully River Blacks, is reported to believe that there are just three possible causes of pregnancy, none of which has anything to do with intercourse (p. 48).[28] They hold these beliefs despite knowing full well about "the birds and the bees"; that is, the tribe apparently sees human reproduction as different in kind from any other animal reproduction with which they are familiar. The problem, then, is how to explain this imputation of difference in kind to human reproduction. Why has the tribe failed to make what seems to be the

[27]Hollis, in his reply to Horton noted above, recognizes this point and chastises Horton for, in effect, thinking that the epistemological issue could be settled empirically. Unfortunately, Hollis does not have in hand the requisite transcendental deduction to sustain his own belief in epistemological unity.

[28]Turner, *Sociological Explanation as Translation*, pp. 48–60. Page references to Turner in the following discussion are to this work.

obvious connection between, on the one hand, the breeding of all nonhuman animals and, on the other, pregnancy in human females?

The controversy in anthropological circles arose when one of their number, Melford P. Spiro, insisted on an "intellectualist" interpretation of the ethnographic data, that is, on interpreting it as indicating plain ignorance of the biological facts. Edmund Leach entered the fray and argued that the statements ought to be interpreted symbolically, as statements of religious dogma. On Leach's account, the Tully River Blacks who offer nonbiological explanations of pregnancy are no more ignorant of the facts than, say, an educated Christian who nonetheless affirms a belief in the Virgin Birth. The explanation of why the belief is held, in each case, is not by reference to an ignorance of biology; because the belief in question belongs to a different system of evaluating information, it is not to be accounted for in the way an outsider might assume it to be.

What interests me is not the details of this controversy (although they are interesting enough), but the account of the development of the debate Turner and Lukes provide. I suggest that the competing translations proposed by Spiro and Leach are fundamentally akin to two different scientific theories (I hesitate to say paradigms). This kinship is manifested insofar as, first, each translation dictates its own specific set of questions and, second, each generates its own anomalies, which, in the course of pursuing this anthropological version of "normal science," its practitioners must ignore.

> Viewed in another way, the issue between Spiro and Leach is a sociological matter. Spiro's translation commits him to asking certain kinds of questions, namely, questions designed to yield an explanation of the Tully River natives' adherence to a wrong explanation of a natural phenomenon. . . . Sometimes this sort of explanation suffices [i.e., explanations that cite ignorance of certain facts], but it often leaves other issues unsettled, like questions about the relation of this belief to other beliefs and practices.
>
> . . . . .
>
> Leach's translation commits him to a different question: not "Why this mistaken belief?" but "Why this dogma?" Such a question may be answered using essentially the same means available in the case of mistaken beliefs. However, because of the different characters of religious ideology and bodies of practical knowledge . . . these same means lead the explanations in other directions. A question like "Why the religious ideology?" is likely to lead us straight to the

portrayal of world views or to the description of the customs and practices of social organization that the ideology may be used to defend or rationalize. For explanations of this sort, the going, needless to say, will typically be difficult. [pp. 54–55]

It is important to appreciate, given Turner's account of the controversy, what my comparison with Kuhn's problem-solving model of normal science yields. The parallel I am urging suggests that the process of "checking" the empirical adequacy of translations follows basically the same pattern found when examining just how well a scientific model is capable of providing solutions to the questions it generates. The test of a translation is not static but involves hypothesis formation and testing: "Checking, then, turns out to be a much broader activity than the looking and seeing that Hollis takes to be definitive of checking a translation, and look-and-see checks can be seen to be one kind of check on sameness of use among many kinds, appropriate to one kind of issue among many" (p. 60). (My account, it should be noted, suggests a *closer* parallel between translation and science than Turner himself seems interested in countenancing; see pp. 2–3.)

Lukes is also anxious to insist that translation provides a pattern of explanation for issues surrounding rationality of beliefs:

After all any attempt to provide an explanation of the holding of some bizarre and apparently irrational belief or set of beliefs has to be set *forth* and set *against* other such attempts and the criteria against which they are finally judged are not all themselves internal to each explanatory scheme. Such criteria include simplicity, comprehensiveness, and, as I have argued, predictiveness, but also plausibility in the face of all available evidence. Consider Evans-Pritchard's explanation of how the Nuer's statement that 'twins are birds' 'appears quite sensible and even true to one who presents the idea to himself in the Nuer language and within their system of religious thought'. Or Christopher Crocker's account of why the Bororo suppose that they are red macaws. . . . In short, implicit theories of translation, like other explanatory theories, are parties to a game that can be, and constantly is, won and lost. [p. 275][29]

Moreover, Lukes effectively endorses, again without making the parallel explicit, Turner's implicit parallel between competing translations

[29]Lukes, "Relativism in Its Place," discusses the Spiro-Leach controversy on 283–292. Page references to Lukes in the following discussion are to this work.

and different paradigms, between different ways of doing normal science (pp. 285, 288–289).

Despite my respect for the suggestiveness of Lukes's remarks, I have serious problems with what he actually says. In particular, I cannot reconcile the stance Lukes takes toward translation (as outlined above) and his seeming desire to incorporate key philosophical weaknesses from the *Rationalitätstreit* into this otherwise new and more promising account of translation. Specifically, certain remarks by Lukes indicate that he holds to determinacy of translation. As he notes, there is no reason to insist that we have to make some single selection from among different strategies of anthropological interpretation—the intellectual, the symbolic, or the fideist. But he then goes on to suggest that, as in the Peircian account of truth, translational method practiced unceasingly on experience will bring us even closer to the *right* translation: "But, more deeply, how is the appropriate interpretation to be discovered? Here I wish to claim that it is, indeed, *discovered*, by confronting, and eliciting, crucial evidence" (p. 282). And, again, "if no given piece of evidence is decisive between alternative interpretations, some crucial mass of it will not fail to be so" (p. 292). Apart from my strong doubts, noted above, that any such appeal to determinacy of translation can be sustained by argument, Lukes's views on translation quickly become ensnared in the same assumptions that appear so implausible in the case of discussions of rationality. The standards for determining what a person or group means are no better defined, to say the least, than the operant standards of reasoning. And if philosophers have despaired of completing the latter project, what hope is there that the former and vaguer notions are to be determined? In addition, the claim that the "right" translation is "discovered" runs afoul of the impositionist objections reviewed in our discussion of the "discovery" of alleged linguistic universals.

But Lukes's position is yet more complicated; he apparently endorses what he terms a "soft version of strong perspectivism" (p. 303). This view holds "that some areas of social enquiry yield interpretive and explanatory accounts that are always accounts from different interpreters' perspectives, that no account that is neutral between such perspectives is available" (p. 303). Lukes also insists that this multi-perspectival account is subject to certain (very vaguely specified) evidential and methodological constraints (pp. 304–305), but my question is whether this Rashomon-like view, for all the talk of truth as correspondence and unwavering principles of rationality, is any different from the position in which an inquirer is left granting Quine's indeterminacy thesis. Lukes, early on in his essay, faults Quine (and Davidson) for their belief that more than one "translation manual" might be empirically adequate (p. 274). But his own multiperspectival view implies just that—incompatible accounts between which there is no (rational) grounds for choosing. As he notes, there is "no account that is neutral between such perspectives." But, one might respond, this is only to concede the underdetermination of descriptions of *events*; Lukes earlier point concerned whether a manual for a whole language could be underdetermined. I fail to see why underdetermination is assumed plausible in one case and not the other. Moreover, although I have elsewhere argued that indeterminacy can be established without appeal to underdetermination, one must note that if there is no *empirical* basis for distinguishing among competing and incompatible accounts, Lukes's basis for insisting that translation is determinate is problematic. I do not see, in the end, how his various remarks on perspectivism are to be reconciled with his earlier confidence that sufficient evidence will allow one translation to prevail.

If we return to the locus classicus of the *Rationalitätstreit*, Winch's essay on Evans-Pritchard, we can see that, despite Winch's use of the rhetoric of "our standards" versus "their standards," his complaint against Evans-Pritchard falls neatly into the translation mode I have suggested. When he responds to Evans-Pritchard's claim that the Azande seem unfazed by contradictions in their beliefs, for example, Winch's move is to suggest that the context, the way of translating the beliefs, is probably mistaken:

> The Azande, when the possibility of this contradiction about the inheritance of witchcraft is pointed out to them, do *not* then come to regard their old beliefs about witchcraft as obsolete. . . . This suggests strongly that the context from which the suggestion about the contradiction is made, the context of our scientific culture, is not on the same level as the context in which the beliefs about witchcraft operate. Zande notions of witchcraft do not constitute a theoretical system in terms of which Azande try to gain a quasi-scientific understanding of the world. This in turn suggests that it is the European . . . who is guilty of misunderstanding, not the Zande. The European is in fact committing a category-mistake.[30]

[30]Winch, "Understanding a Primitive Society," p. 172.

Similarly, when Winch responds, again in the context of "Understanding a Primitive Society," to criticism by Alasdair MacIntyre, the dispute is once more focused on the issue of whether *translating* Zande magic as a form of cryptotechnology is appropriate.[31] The argument, in short, is one of locating Zande beliefs and practices, and the task of ascertaining this "location" is just the task of providing the (most) plausible translation. (It is, perhaps, more philosophically exciting to speak of alternative standards of rationality; in some cases, it might even be appropriate. I do not take it that anything I have said would rule out some difference in licensed inference patterns, although global differences would presumably prove untranslatable.)

My claim has been that, with regard to what I have been calling the *Rationalitätstreit*, there is little to distinguish the charge that others are irrational from the claim that what one has is simply a bad translation. In addition, I have urged that it is potentially more fruitful, if only because it points to empirical strategies for testing disputed accounts, to take the question as one of the adequacy of one's translation scheme. Following the suggestions of Quine and Davidson, moreover, I have argued that, if we cannot make sense of there being many translations schemes, neither can we establish that there is just one. A characterization of the dispute as one regarding standards of rationality runs into numerous philosophical problems. Among those I have indicated is the fact that, in light of much of the debate in the last twenty-five years, it is problematic whether one can find a consensus on what represents the current standard of scientific rationality. More generally, those impressed by the host of problems attending attempts to specify necessary and sufficient conditions for knowledge claims will also be skeptical that "our" standard of rationality, to which so many writers on this topic make frequent reference, can readily be spelled out.

But the problem is not just with those who chauvinistically promote "our" standard of rationality, unspecifiable though it may be. We saw that Winch's own position, surprisingly, proves closer on this point to Carnap of "Empiricism, Semantics, and Ontology" than to the later Wittgenstein. Indeed, unless one is willing to resuscitate and defend Carnap's distinction between internal and external questions, and so the analytic-synthetic distinction, Winch's way of even *posing* the problem should appear quite unattractive.

[31]See, for example, ibid., pp. 79–80.

Finally, I have outlined how the issues that are of interest and that do compel intellectual attention can be perspiciously expressed in the idiom of competing translation. Following suggestions implicit in the writings of Turner and Lukes, I have indicated that competing translations share properties with competing scientific models or paradigms. Both dictate "ordinary" problem-solving lines of research; the success, or viability, of a given model can then be evaluated in terms of how its research project holds up over some period of time. This has the further benefit of suggesting how competing translation might be put to some type of scientific test. Again, given indeterminacy, the search here is not for *the* one right answer; the search, as always, is for the best—most empirically adequate, simplest—account we can give at the time.

If we are a bit more cautious about expressing ourselves than Winch is (in particular, if we avoid talking of translation manuals as if they represented reified world views), Winch's implicit use of the distinction between internal and external questions proves illuminating. It is enlightening, in the first instance, for the reason Winch suggests: it can be morally sensitizing. When our study leads us to unusual translations of what others are about, we are presented "with forms of life very different from our own which we can come to understand; and that thereby we can both come to see possibilities to which our involvement in the life of our own society blinds us and also see more clearly certain features of that life to which for one reason or another we have been insensitive."[32] In the second instance, it just might lay open an alternative some people would actually want to adopt. The success of modern science can be challenged, and has been, by calling into question whether and to what extent it has improved the prospects for human happiness. Predictive success cannot be taken to be some ultimate mark of the "rightness" of our cultural predispositions.[33] In short, external questions (in Carnap's sense) are, as Carnap insisted, not answerable on logical grounds; the grounds for choosing a "framework" are pragmatic, depending on one's needs.

I would say that Carnap is surely right here. The debate on choice of frameworks is not a matter of appealing to some higher standard of rationality, some algorithm for choosing the most rational from among

[32]P. Winch, "Comment," in *Understanding and Social Inquiry*, p. 210.

[33]See Lukes, "Relativism in Its Place," p. 297, for further discussion and references.

competing systems of beliefs; it is a choice of how one wants to live one's life. Indeed, to insist otherwise is perhaps the most dangerous of all the confusions engendered by the pseudoproblems in the social sciences.

# Index

Library of Congress Cataloging-in-Publication Data

Roth, Paul Andrew, 1948–
Meaning and method in the social sciences.

Includes index.
1. Social sciences—Methodology. I. Title.
H61.R683 1987 300'.1'8 87–47718
ISBN 0–8014–1941–7 (alk. paper)